More praise for *The Latehomecomer*

"Across jungles, refugee camps, and oceans, *The Latehomecomer* is a journey to the center of everything: one's fast-held understanding of home." **—CRIS BEAM**

"Yang turns her family's odyssey into a full adventure of survival in the face of adversity. It is a triumph of the human spirit that refuses to capitulate, to give up hope, that finds a way to start all over again from scratch, and, above all, inspires others to do the same." **—DR. GARY YIA LEE**

"In telling the story of her Hmong family's flight from genocide in the jungles of Laos and poverty in the refugee camps of Thailand to achieve a safe life in America, Yang has fashioned a bittersweet and engrossing epic that is mythic in its beauty, tenderness, and power." **—HONOR MOORE**

"This is a wise, important, and beautiful book—an evocation of extraordinary human courage and the inspiring strength of familial love." **—STEPHEN O'CONNOR**

"An impressive debut by a writer with an enchanting voice, *The Latehomecomer* reveals all that is worth knowing about endurance, the power of a family's love, and hope in the face of desperation." **—PATRICIA O'TOOLE**

"A moving saga, *The Latehomecomer* is both sweeping and intimate—an elegant, evocative story of a family, a way of life, a culture, a people." **—DR. PAUL HILLMER**, Director of the Hmong Oral History Project at Concordia University

"A powerful book documenting the refugee experience that I believe, one day, my children will read to their children."
—LEE PAO XIONG, Director of the Center for Hmong Studies at Concordia University

The Latehomecomer

The Latehomecomer

A HMONG FAMILY MEMOIR

Kao Kalia Yang

COFFEE HOUSE PRESS

MINNEAPOLIS

2017

First edition published by Coffee House Press in 2008

Coffee House Press books are available to the trade through our primary distributor, Consortium Book Sales & Distribution, cbsd.com or (800) 283-3572. For personal orders, catalogs, or other information, write to info@coffeehousepress.org.

Coffee House Press is a nonprofit literary publishing house. Support from private foundations, corporate giving programs, government programs, and generous individuals helps make the publication of our books possible. We gratefully acknowledge their support in detail in the back of this book.

LIBRARY OF CONGRESS CATALOGING-IN-PUBLICATION DATA

Names: Yang, Kao Kalia, 1980– author.
Title: The latehomecomer : a Hmong family memoir /
    Kao Kalia Yang.
Other titles: Late homecomer | Hmong family memoir
Description: Minneapolis : Coffee House Press, [2017]
Identifiers: LCCN 2016049403 | ISBN 9781566894784
Subjects: LCSH: Hmong Americans—Biography. |
    Immigrants—United States—Biography. | Yang, Kao Kalia,
    1980—Family. | Grandmothers—Biography. | Vietnam
    War, 1961–1975—Refugees. | Refugees—Laos—Biography. |
    Refugees—Thailand—Biography. | Saint Paul (Minn.)—
    Biography.
Classification: LCC E184.H55 Y36 2017 |
    DDC 305.892959/72073—dc23
LC record available at https://lccn.loc.gov/2016049403

PRINTED IN THE UNITED STATES OF AMERICA

24 23 22 21 20 19 18 17   2 3 4 5 6 7 8 9

For my grandmother, Youa Lee,
who never learned how to write.

To my baby brother, Maxwell Hwm Yang,
who will read the things she never wrote.

PROLOGUE

PEOPLE OF THE SKY

THE LITTLE GIRL WITH THE DIMPLES

THE AMERICAN YEARS

THE LATEHOMECOMER

EPILOGUE

LIST OF ILLUSTRATIONS

Before babies are born they live in the sky where they fly among the clouds. The sky is a happy place and calling babies down to earth is not an easy thing to do. From the sky, babies can see the course of human lives.

This is what the Hmong children of my generation are told by our mothers and fathers, by our grandmothers and grandfathers.

They teach us that we have chosen our lives. That the people who we would become we had inside of us from the beginning, and the people whose worlds we share, whose memories we hold strong inside of us, we have always known.

From the sky, I would come again.

Seeking Refuge

In Ban Vinai Refugee Camp, Loei Province, Thailand:
December 1980–January 1987

From the day that she was born, she was taught that she was Hmong by the adults around her. As a baby learning to talk, her mother and father often asked, "What are you?" and the right answer was always, "I am Hmong." It wasn't a name or a gender, it was a people. When she noticed that they lived in a place that felt like it had an invisible fence made of men with guns who spoke Thai and dressed in the colors of old, rotting leaves, she learned that *Hmong* meant *contained*. The first time she looked into the mirror and noticed her brown eyes, her dark hair, and the tinted yellow of her skin, she saw Hmong looking at her. Hmong that could fit in all of Asia, Hmong that was only skin deep.

In Phanat Nikhom Transition Camp to America,
Chonburi Province, Thailand: January 1987–July 1987

The feeling that she was Hmong did not happen until the preparations for America began as her family was being processed. Thailand wanted to close its refugee camps, send away the remnants from the war:

You are going to America on a one-way ticket.
You are going to America as refugees of the Vietnam War.
You are going to America as Hmong from the camps of Thailand.
You are going to America to find a new home.
We do not want you here anymore.

All this was said in the things that were happening: the classes that her mother and father attended that taught them new strings of words ("Hello. How are you? I am fine, thank you."); new kinds of food (pieces of chicken between bread with cilantro and green onion and a white, tasteless, fatty spread from a jar); the free set of clothing that each person was given: a dark blue sweater, walking shoes with laces, white socks, dark blue pants, a white collared shirt to go underneath the sweater. These were the Thai government's last gift to the Hmong for leaving their country, the American government's donation to a people who had passed exams stating they had fought under American leadership and influence during the Secret War in Laos from 1960 to 1975. All this was felt as she watched the preoccupied adults around her preparing for a new life, trying to end the yearning for an old one that she didn't know—she saw how their eyes searched the distance for the shadows of mountains or the wide, open sky for the monsoons, one last time before it was gone forever.

All these good-byes made her feel very Hmong inside.

She had heard stories of how Hmong people did not have a country, how we always had to leave places behind. First China because the Chinese didn't want us on their land—how they took away our written language, and how they tried to turn us into slaves, and so we spoke our fears to our ancestors and made our way to Laos. When the French came to Laos, they climbed the high mountains and they saw the cool of the land. They wanted opium for tax money. We fought them, but lost. When they left they had learned that we would keep fighting, and they told the Americans so. The American pilots dropped first from the sky, injured and scared, into the Hmong villages on Phou Bia Mountain, and we helped them get better again in the depths of the jungle. By the time their leaders came with guns, there were Hmong people who had seen enough Americans to trust in an idea of democracy: a place where we could live with others as if we belonged: a promise of home. Those who believed took up guns. Those who were still only struggling with their lives saw guns pointed at them. The explosion of flesh, the falling down of heavy bodies to the ground, wet blood soaking the dark of the earth. The North Vietnamese soldiers and the communist Pathet Lao soldiers could not and would not tell the difference: Hmong was only skin deep.

Skin is easy to penetrate.

When the Americans left Laos in 1975, they took the most influential, the biggest believers and fighters for democracy with them, and they left my family and thousands of others behind to wait for a fight that would end for so many in death. A third of the Hmong died in the war with the Americans. Another third were slaughtered in its aftermath.

From the clouds, the little girl's spirit watched her family escape into the Laotian jungle, run around in circles for four years, and then surface on the banks of the Mekong River in Thailand—starving survivors. Her spirit came to them in Ban Vinai Refugee Camp. Then her spirit and her body left Thailand—just as the Hmong had left so many other countries.

In St. Paul, Minnesota, the United States of America:
July 1987–today

What is Hmong?
Where is your country?
What are you doing here, in America?
Are you ever going home again?

In the beginning, she did not have the words to say anything. Later, she didn't know what to say. Eventually, she would learn to say, "Hmong is an ethnic minority. We don't have a country. We are here looking for a home."

For many years, the Hmong inside the little girl fell into silence.

And then one day, the little girl grew up into a young woman. Because she hadn't said very much in her first twenty years, all the words had been stored inside her. Because her people had only been reunited with a written language in the 1950s, in the break of a war without a name, they had not had the opportunity to write their stories down. In the books on the American shelves, the young woman noticed how Hmong was not a footnote in the history of the world. How Vietnam was only Vietnamese. How Laos belonged to the Laotians, and how the war was only American. She saw how the world only knew skin-deep the reaches of Hmong. She saw how they did not know that from the day she was born, she was Hmong. She saw how the children, born in America, lived life like Americans. She saw the diminishing memories of her mother and father on the hard road to remembering the strings of words and the new food in America. She said good-bye to her grandmother from Laos, from Thailand, from America, from the world of the living, and on sheets of white paper. The young woman slowly unleashed the flood of Hmong into language, seeking refuge not for a name or a gender, but a people.

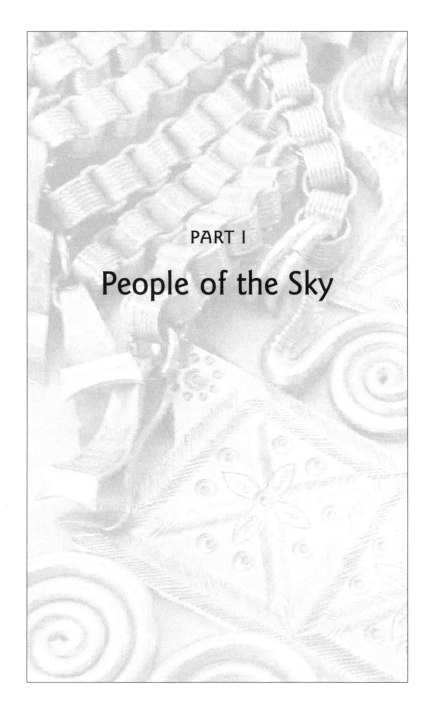

PART I

People of the Sky

CHAPTER I

A WALK IN THE JUNGLE

The world that they were living in could no longer hold them safe. It was 1975 and the Vietnam War, as the world knew it, was over. For the Hmong of Laos, for those who still lived in the mountains of Xieng Khuong, for my mother and my father, the American shield had been lifted.

The communist government that came to power in May of 1975, declared a death warrant against the Hmong who had helped the Americans in a war that would later be termed "The Secret War." On May 9, 1975 *Khaosan Pathet Lao*, the newspaper of the Lao People's Party, announced the agenda: "It is necessary to extirpate, down to the root, the Hmong minority."

The communist Pathet Lao soldiers and their North Vietnamese allies infiltrated Hmong villages and began a systematic campaign to kill off the Hmong who believed in the tenets of democracy and had fought against communist rule. While many of the 30,000 Hmong men and boys recruited by the CIA of the United States had been killed, the remnants of their fight remained, in the hearts and the homes of their wives and children, their mothers and fathers, their friends and neighbors. The Secret War, the biggest covert operation in CIA history, and its ramifications would tear into the history of a people, break into the pages of their lives, and let the winds of war and death blow them all over the world.

By 1975, the Hmong existed mainly as ragtag villages of mostly women and children. After most of the men had died, the CIA had gone to the boys, ten years old, eleven and twelve, and asked them to do the work that their fathers could not finish. In old photos, they hold guns in their small, dirty hands. Sometimes, with big smiles on their young faces. I know that their mothers waited by empty doorways for their return. By 1975, many of the Hmong were ready for peace.

The Hmong knew that the Americans had left: one day there were American pilots landing planes on the airstrip, tall men with fair skin walking around the village, laughing and buying local food items, giving candy to the small children. And then one day the planes flew away into the fog of the clouds, passed over the dark green mountain tops, and did not return. At first, they waited. When the murders started, and the last of the men and boys began disappearing, the Hmong knew that the only thing coming for them was death.

My mother was sixteen years old and my father was nineteen. She had dreamed of marrying an educated man and hoped to wear a white nurse's outfit. She imagined that one day she would be able to type with quick fingers on a typing machine, something she had once seen as a little girl in a provincial town. He yearned for a small farm with pens full of pigs and horses, a chicken coop of squawking, healthy chickens running around merrily about his feet. They were young. They did not know of each other. They each dreamt of a life that could not have included one another.

My Uncle Sai, my father's third eldest brother, was one of the first men to run into the jungle. He was only thirty years old. He had never been to school. He did not know how to write his name on paper. He could only vocalize in words. He had not fought as one of General Vang Pao's soldiers in the war. Still, it did not take long for the communist soldiers to come for him and his brothers.

It was noon. The soldiers were on a truck on the dirt road— men with guns in their hands. Uncle Sai saw that they were coming, and he looked at his family of starving children; because of the fighting, because Laos had been the most heavily bombed country in the war, and because of the bombs the Hmong could not stay in place and farm, and because the Americans had left and there were no more rice drops, because they were hungry and scared and they would die if he died, he looked at them, and he looked at the truck on the road, and he ran. He ran into the Laotian jungle. He was labeled a rebel. North Vietnamese and Pathet Lao soldiers were sent to hunt him and those who would follow him.

My mother's and father's families, like many others, fled into the jungle after Uncle Sai. For the families who surrendered to the soldiers, there were death and reeducation camps, syringes of hot liquid inserted into trembling veins, days in the blistering sun digging useless craters into the earth. For my mother's and father's families, the possibility of a new life, of foraging in fear, was a better choice than the separations of defeat, of death.

My mother and father met in 1978. By the time they met, both their families had been rebels in the jungle, scavenging for food and scrambling for shelter, for three years. They were hungry and dirty. They had gotten used to the scabs on their backs from the heavy packs, the gnawing hunger, the feeling that there was air in their stomachs all the time, and the bombs that fell from the sky destroying the green canopy and shattering the bodies of old men and women who could not run fast enough. They were used to the patterns of soldiers approaching, the bullets, the noise and the confusions of ambush, bullets that found home in hungry flesh. They saw this death all around them, but they were still young. They kept looking to live. Their first meeting was a small moment in passing.

I imagine sun-dappled jungle floors, a young man and a young woman, peeking at each other through lush vegetation, smiling shyly and then walking away slowly, lips bitten by clean, white teeth. Slow movements toward each other again, like in a dance. An orchestra of nature: leaves and wind and two shadows, a man and a woman, moving in smooth motions on even ground. How fanciful I am.

My mother does not talk about her past in terms of heartache. All the things that happened were things to live through. Her father had been a prosperous farmer; he left each son thirty heads of water buffalo. She was only six when he died. All she has of him are memories of an old thin man with a long braid who wore shoes all the time, whose feet were tender as a baby's. She was the only girl in her village to have the privilege of attending school with the boys. Her family could afford to do without her labor. She was an apt pupil who did her lessons carefully and recited them proudly, a rare trait in a Hmong girl of that period. If not for the Pathet Lao and North Vietnamese soldiers entering their village, my mother would have achieved her dream of becoming a nurse, learned to type with quick fingers, and attracted an educated man.

She was well loved. Her brothers told her stories late into the night about beautiful Hmong girls who ventured too deep into bodies of water, Hmong girls who were taken as dragon brides into worlds of shimmering liquid. Her mother bought her good-quality velvet to make the traditional Hmong clothes and cooked special meals for her because she had a light appetite. The people in my mother's life cherished her, and she carries warm memories of the times before her marriage. Even the years of eating cornmush and cassava, because there were no more rice harvests, are years full of people who cared for her. My mother holds on to the times when her mother would save the sweetest wild yam, the softest part of a roasted cassava for her, even in the jungle, even in a war that carried no name, even among the dead bodies; my mother felt loved.

Unlike my mother, my father had a difficult childhood, with only a mother to take care of him. He was the youngest of nine surviving children. His father had died when he was just two years old. My father carries an image of an old man twisting long pieces of dried grass into twine for him to tie around chickens. All his life he would love chickens because of this one memory alone. His childhood was spent wishing for a father; he watched his four older brothers with their children and he yearned for his. His mother was a shaman and a medicine woman. She was always busy trying to find food and money to support her younger children, to send them to school. She spent much of her time scurrying over the hillsides looking for healing plants and walking from one village to the next performing rituals for the sick and soul-weary, leaving her youngest child to look at the ways his older brothers loved their children. Whenever he was lonely or sad, my father climbed to the tops of tall trees and looked at the world, searching for the places where his father could be.

My father has never been to the place where his father is buried. All he knows is what his brothers told him, their fingers pointing to a mountain that looked like an uneven green box rising out of the ground. When his family ran out of their village, my father, with a chicken tucked underneath his shirt, his thick black hair sticking straight up from his head, kept looking back at the mountain where his father's body was buried. He says that if he closes his eyes, he can see the imprint of the mountain on his lids. He'll always know the way back.

The Hmong had been living in the mountains of Laos for nearly two hundred years—since they fled from the wars in China. The mountains were their home and they knew them well. When Edward Landsdale, an agent for the CIA, advised the use of the Hmong in Laos against the North Vietnamese and Pathet Lao soldiers, he could not have known what history would do to them. The Americans entered the country and recruited Hmong to serve, first as guides and then later as fighters, without thought to the price their recruits would pay with their lives and the lives of their children for generations to come. The old ones who survived would carry shrapnel in their bodies, broken lives in their souls. For the young, for people like my mother and father, seeing bodies on the jungle floor, pieces of cloth wilting in the humid heat, was a horrible sight but a fact of being alive.

The day my father met my mother was a normal day of scavenging for food in the jungle. My mother was with her mother— they were returning from a search for bamboo shoots—when they passed by my father and his two best friends, who were hunting. It was a small moment in passing. If the sun had hidden behind a cloud, if the sound of wild game had come from a different direction, then perhaps I would still be flying among the clouds. But it wasn't so: he noticed her. He saw that she had clear skin and long black hair. He saw that her complexion was lighter than the average

Hmong woman's. He noticed that there were beads in her hair. He thought her nose was too big. She pretended not to see him. She looked at him out of the corner of her eyes: a young man in rags with high cheekbones and spiky hair. She made note of his straight shoulders; her own were soft and curved. Discreetly, they passed one another; neither looked back.

After that fleeting moment, my father found out that the young woman with beads in her hair was named Chue Moua. Her family name was easy to trace; the Hmong families in the jungle had worked out a system of warnings and precautions against the soldiers hunting them. He found out that her family was camped not too far away from his, only a few hours of brisk walking. He admits with a smile that he was first attracted to her beauty, the way she carried herself with her chin parallel to the ground, and her fearlessness. She had developed a small reputation among the single men as being cold and haughty. Her smiles were reserved for those who knew her well, and she rarely spoke to strangers. When she did, it was efficient, straight talking. When the bullets started to fly and people were running in fear, my mother walked away. This to my father showed courage and calm, a rare maturity that he himself didn't have. She did not try to win his affections; she just accepted them.

My mother did not know very much about men. Her mother and brothers had always told her that when she wanted to marry anyone, she should let them know—they wouldn't stop her. She didn't find my father particularly attractive, although she thought he had a perfect smile (it would be years before she noticed that his two front teeth overlap a bit). He was different from my mother's other admirers because of the way he talked: he did not rush his words or slow them down. She had no patience for men who communicated, in their speech, the unsteadiness of hurried hearts, hungry bodies. She thought my father a serious young man; she had heard of his reputation for song poetry, although he never sang any for her because she was not the kind of young woman to seem interested. When they met, a handful of times under some jungle tree, he talked and she listened. There was a war being fought against them, and they were in the middle of a jungle, so she was not thinking about marriage. There were no moments of peeking through lush vegetation, no biting of lips, no even floors to dance upon.

My mother says she would not have married my father had she known that in doing so she would have to leave forever her mother and everyone else who loved her. For her, the future stretched only as far as the next step. It is hard to penetrate the density of a Southeast Asian jungle, with its heavy brush, its bamboo thickets, and its gnarled trees. The foliage, the paths, the terrain—it was all unmarked and unpredictable. There were no roads, no maps, only instincts. There had been news of a large regiment of North Vietnamese soldiers approaching the area. Many families had hidden for months trying to gather food, to wait out the harvest of wild plants, but it was no longer safe to stay in place. My mother's family wanted to go east, climb higher up the mountain slope; they hoped to find isolated peace and stay in Laos. My father's opted for the west, down the mountain; they had heard that there were refugee camps in Thailand across the Mekong River. It was dusk. They were supposed to say good-bye.

"I am not sure if I ever made a decision to marry your father," she says. "It was time for us to let go of each other's hands. I did not want to leave him. He did not want to leave me. So we thought we would walk together for a bit. I was thinking about how my mother would worry. The sun was setting, and the wind was rustling the leaves. At a tree where our paths would diverge, I realized that we were both standing still, not moving. The air came out of my chest, and I did not know where to look. If I had known that another sun would rise and I would see your father again, I would not have walked with him so far. I thought we were parting forever, and I wanted the walk to continue as far as it could go. Your father was not squeezing my hand, but his grip was firm. We kept holding hands. We chose a direction. I had no idea it would lead to marriage. Did I love him? Did he love me? It is the kind of decision that only young people can make in a war of no tomorrows. At that moment, I think neither of us saw the future."

Both families were unhappy with the match. My mother's family did not like the size and noise of my father's; they worried that my mother would not get enough to eat in a family with so many hungry children to feed. My father's family did not like my mother's size; she was small and they worried that she would not travel well amid the harshness of life. Worse yet, my father's older brother had married just a month earlier. There was no more money for a bride price, not even a modest one. My father's mother had nothing but a few cans of sweetened condensed milk and her shaman's tools, a bag of medicinal herbs, and a small collection of rags. My father begged and promised to pay back whatever each of his brothers could give. They looked at him, and they remembered that he had no father and that they were like his father, and so they worked hard to find a small bride price as a token of tradition. My mother heard about my father's family's objections. She asked if it mattered to him that she was small. He told her that small was cute. She believed him.

They were married in a clearing in her family's camp, which was little more than three or four banana-leaf-covered lean-tos around a small fire. There was no lavish wedding feast and only a few guests. Surrounded by the vast jungle, with the threat of soldiers approaching, a small group of people sat, at their center two young people concentrating hard on the ground. Whatever hopes my mother and father carried were suddenly caught in fear, in unknowing. They sneaked glances at the faces of the adults.

The attention to the formalities of the wedding, usually occasions for joy and laughter, was muted. My father's family presented the small bride price wrapped in a piece of cloth, torn from some remnant, maybe an old prized shirt. My mother's family told her to be a good wife to my father, a good daughter to his mother, a good relative to his family. They said she was leaving the family that had taken care of her for another. They had given her as much as they could: a small education, clothes to keep the cold away, and shoes to soften against the hard ground. They were sorry that the world was the way it was and that they could not have given her more to start a new life with. She was young. Would my father's family please be patient with her? Teach her as they would a daughter of their own?

Both families said that if times had been better, things could have been different. In the old days, before the war, surrounding villages would have collected, first at the bride's house and then later at the groom's, to wish them good health, many strong sons and daughters, and long years together. There would have been at least two great feasts with pots of steaming bamboo shoots and poached chicken, pig stews, barbecued beef, and tables laden with steaming white rice. But it was no longer like the old days. It had been a long time since anybody had eaten their fill. A collection of too many people would have brought noise and attention, and both were deadly. All the adults were full of worry for the two young people who had decided to marry in a time when the future stretched only in days.

They sat, two young people, with the jungle around them. They don't remember the songs of the birds or the bothersome hum of the insects. They listened carefully to the voices of the adults, and for the sounds of guns. Everyone had heard the whispers: a group of ten thousand North Vietnamese soldiers had entered from Vietnam to help the Pathet Lao soldiers capture the remaining Hmong. From the very beginning of their life together, my mother and father knew that time was ticking on their marriage.

Before my mother left the clearing for the walk to where my father's family was camped, her mother gave her gifts—fine embroidery she had spent hours in the hot sun making, little pieces of cloth carefully lined with flowery symbols and connected squares that told the history of the Hmong people, a lost story, a narrative sewn but no longer legible. The Hmong in Laos had fled from China. Legends told of war and murder, slavery and escape. The Hmong language had been outlawed. The written language was hidden in flowers. It was a women's rebellion; they devised a plan to hide their stories in their clothing, in the child-carrying clothes that bound their children to themselves. They did not know that in the passage of time the written language would become lost in the beautiful shapes and colors, no longer legible in words, holding on to meaning. My mother knew that the gifts her mother was handing her were pieces of the history. She also knew that a Hmong woman needed to have something of her mother's if she hoped to find her way back to her mother once life ended.

Many of their belongings, their wealth, and their keepsakes had been forsaken in the three years of flight and homelessness, but for my mother's wedding gift package, her mother gave her a heavy silver necklace. She would not have her daughter begin a new life with nothing. Such necklaces, a part of the formal Hmong clothing, weigh three to seven pounds. It drapes down a woman's chest, nearly to her waist. It is more than jewelry. It is a symbol of being a Hmong woman.

A month after they were married, my mother visited her mother with my father. The smoke of bombs had risen in the sky and sounds like dry thunder had resounded for many days, and she worried that the soldiers were getting closer. She wanted to see her family to make sure they were all right. By that time, their two families had traveled a full day's walk away from each other. It was no longer just talk: there were thousands of North Vietnamese and Pathet Lao soldiers encroaching from all sides. She insisted on going to visit her mother. My father unhappily relented.

They climbed the mountain together. He had on an old army coat from one of his brothers. He carried a gun, an AK-47 that they had found in an old American cargo box. He walked in front of her. She carried a woven bamboo basket on her back, with two pieces of roasted cassava inside for their lunch. She had to run to keep up with his steps. Her small feet ached. She was on her last pair of shoes and the thin soles could no longer soften the harshness of the mountainous jungle terrain, but she refused to tell him about the pain. They were silent. He felt that her family did not like him. She thought he was being mean to her. His family did not like her either. But she lived with them and worked like she had never before in her life, taking care of children she barely knew. She did everything his mother told her to do. Did he not see her sacrifice? He walked with his back to her, straight and fast, the gun in his right hand.

They were two young people, in the middle of a jungle, angry and silent, climbing only up, not really knowing where their footsteps would lead. But they were fortunate, because when they reached a dense banana grove, just as the sun was burnishing the late afternoon sky, they saw her family. It was a happy reunion for my mother. She went to her mother and her sister, her sisters-in-law and their children. How glad she was to be with the people who understood her, and how much she had missed them in the month away. She had never thought marriage could be lonely. My father sat with her brothers; he did not say much. For her the waning day passed much too quickly. He saw her joy and was content to wait.

When night arrived, she walked over to him and asked quietly if they could spend the night with her family and set out together early in the morning. He did not look at her when he responded. He felt it wasn't safe to stay with the soldiers coming. He felt uncomfortable. He wondered if she was still angry at him. Was she purposely asking in front of her brothers in an effort to embarrass him? He shook his head, said it wasn't a good idea. She wanted to argue, but didn't. She had her pride. He had his, too. In the month that they had been married, they had learned quickly about the formidability of each other's insistence upon respect. She felt like crying but she swallowed her tears and stood up with him. She could not fight with her new husband in front of her brothers. They made their good-byes.

Her mother had walked away from the clearing to get some water from a nearby mountain stream. She wanted to go say good-bye to her, but my father said the dark could not wait any longer. She thought that they would visit again, so she did not stamp her foot, shout for her mother to stop, run after her and hold her close. She just stood beside my father and watched as her mother, an old woman with a water pail on her back, her left hand on her hip, walked away, into the darkness of the Laotian jungle.

"That is the dream of my mother I carry with me," my mother says quietly. She never saw her mother again.

My father could not know that he was taking my mother away from her family forever. Nor could he have known of the hardships that would come their way, the separation that would occur when the soldiers arrived.

My mother and father tell us about the way the country was, the dreams they had before everything was destroyed: the educated man and the nurse's outfit; typing with quick fingers; the farm with the chickens and the pigs; the quiet life on the mountains. They tell us how it was that they ended up in the jungle, and they speak of the things that they could not control. They both insist that in a time when there was no room for choices, they had chosen each other. Together they had gone for a walk with no end in sight.

CHAPTER 2
ENEMY CAMP

My mother was three months pregnant when the group was ambushed by North Vietnamese and Pathet Lao soldiers. The women were preparing a meager breakfast of soft-boiled yams for the children. Many of the men were guarding the perimeter of the family groups. They were scattered throughout the jungle, men standing around little pockets of families, some with guns and some with knives, others with nothing more than bamboo poles.

The day had begun like many others. Children were sitting around their mothers, waiting for food, their small hands around their bellies. My mother was trying to keep the feeble fire of twigs alive so the yams would stay warm. The morning sun was in the sky when the first bombs fell. Women grabbed their children by their bony wrists and looked for places to run. Fingers sticky with yam tried to protect young eyes and ears from the guns and falling bombs, while Laotian and Vietnamese voices rang from the dark jungle around them. My mother remembers the moment of stillness before the smell of guns and the echo of artillery filled the air, when confusion struck amid the rising smoke. In an instant, families were separated. Little children ran after people they thought were their parents, mothers ran back and forth finding this child or that one. Smoke rose from the fallen trees. Jagged pieces of broken mountain rained on them. The men tried to protect the women and children with their arms. They knew that there would be no fighting back. The sun disappeared behind the smoke.

The cries of children accompanied the falling of bodies to the ground. The bombs scattered the people. The earth blew up in their faces. Everybody tried to run for high ground through the smoke. Caves had been designated for each family group in case of an attack.

The remnants of my family collected in a high cave and waited in silence. Two of my father's brothers and their families had disappeared. The sound of rain mingled with the sound of explosions. The group would have to separate: the women and children might survive if they surrendered to the soldiers—a helpless group led by an old woman would not be a threat. There were only five men left, but if they stayed with the group surely all would be killed. The women would surrender with the children, and the men would run into the jungle, try to find the missing families. They would return for the women and children if they could, and together they would run away to Thailand. That was the plan, but no one wanted to be the first to say good-bye. Did all the struggling and the poverty, the hunger and fear, come down to this? Would it all end here? The adults cried, wet streaks down their dirty faces like the children around them.

They were all torn and broken: shrapnel into skin, blood seeping from scratches, jagged cuts from rocks flying through the air.

My mother was three months pregnant. They had been married for only six months. Up to that moment, my mother had thought that she only liked my father as a young woman liked a young man. She had never said it was love. Neither had he. They were shy. They had been unsure. Now, there would be no time for love. It was in the moment of parting that she knew she loved him.

"'I love you' are three words that only Americans say," my mother says. "We were not embarrassed: the world had come to an end. Your father wiped his eyes with his forearm. I did not see tears fall. He told me that if we surrendered and made it through to the enemy camps, I should try and look for my mother. 'Your mother loves you best,' he said. I did not know what to think. I did not want to think about death because we had worked so hard to stay alive. I thought maybe there was a chance I would see my mother again. Your father said, 'If I do not return and two to three years have passed, go and find a new life for yourself.' I did not think I would ever marry again. I had married *him*. I wanted him to escape. I knew that if I had not loved your father in a real way when I married him, in the six months since I had been with him, I loved your father so much that I wanted him to be free from death, even if it meant freedom from me."

My father and his brothers walked their mother, their wives, and their children to the ridge of a hill. The rain had stopped; the ground was wet and slippery. They wore no shoes; they had no more to wear. They followed each other's footprints. The sounds of bombs had not waned. The gunshots were coming from downhill. The rain had settled the dust. There was no looking back. There were no more cries or good-byes. My mother remembers how the shade of my father's dark green jacket merged with the leaves, how the foliage swallowed him up, and only the moving of the leaves marked his disappearance into the shadows of the jungle.

My father's mother led the women and children down the hill. Her wide feet clung to the ground, her girth making her appear bigger than she really was. The lines on her face were frozen as she led the group away from her sons. From somewhere Grandma had found a scrap of white cloth. They all knew that white was the color of surrender. She tied it to a twig. The women surrendered, their children at their center, like mother elephants.

The soldiers saw the group of women and children approach. They wore camouflaged uniforms; some of them had tree branches tied onto their helmets. They were like little pieces of wilderness with guns. Grandmother shook; the little flag of surrender in her hands danced in the air. The children were hugged tight against the bodies of the women. They thought they were all going to get killed. My mother thought about her family, and hoped that her mother and her sister and brothers were far away. She thought about the children she had helped care for since she had been married to my father, and wondered what would happen to them. She pleaded silently to my grandfather, a man she had never met.

She asked him to keep my father and uncles safe. It was a litany in her head, a silent song caught in her throat, "Please help them escape. Do not let them hear any gunshots and return to us."

The soldiers saw no men, so they held their guns steady and waited silently for the group of women and children. There were six women, including Grandmother, and about twenty children, boys and girls, young babies born in the jungle. The group was slow. The thin women and children were hunched over themselves. The soldiers lost patience and began shouting orders in Vietnamese and Laotian.

They could not see that the women and children were walking slowly not only because of fear but because their bare feet were raw from running. When they reached the soldiers at last, a young soldier gestured to my mother. He poked his gun into the load on her back and gestured to the hills and mountains. Without words, my mother understood the expression on his face: he did not believe that they could not walk, since they had run for many months, many years. She pretended not to know what he meant. Her small feet had been bleeding for a long time.

The soldiers ordered them with guns to march. In a long line, they walked between groups of soldiers for many hours, until they came to an occupied village, where they were led into an empty hut. The place was silent except for a howling dog that the soldiers in the village had on a leash. The women did not know if the dog belonged to the soldiers or if he was a captive, something like themselves. In the empty hut, the soldiers gestured with their guns for the women to unload their packs and sleep. In the deepening dusk, the cigarette butts of the soldiers floated in the air like fireflies. The night thrummed with the sound of men's voices and the buzzing of insects.

The group of women slept with their arms around the littlest children. Despite their fear, exhaustion had taken hold of the group. It was a dark, silent sleep that was broken by gunshots in the early dawn. They woke to stiff joints and achy muscles, their feet were encrusted with dried blood, swollen and pale in the morning light. But the greatest pain did not come from their bodies; it came from a churning tightness in their chests. A few of the younger children cried meekly from hunger. The guns told them to get up and start walking.

They were told that it would be a long walk to captivity. Everybody was to be in a line, my mother behind my grandmother and in front of one of the aunts. A Vietnamese soldier, a young man, approached my mother. He had his helmet tilted up so that she could see his smiling face. He pointed to her pack. She held on to the tattered straps. He grabbed hold of it. She held on as tightly as she could. He pulled. She limped. In her effort for balance, she lost the battle. He laughed. She took hold of a little cousin, and looked at her bleeding feet. There was little she could do but limp on as bravely as she could. The young soldier carried the pack for the day's long journey, until they reached an enemy village. They would be kept as captives in the village for seven months.

As they approached the outskirts of the village, my mother started to worry. She wanted her pack back. What if there were

Hmong people inside the camp? What if people started thinking bad things about her character? She was a prisoner but also a married woman. She knew why he was carrying her bag. She did not know what to do. Her throat felt thick.

She remembers, "Your grandmother looked at me from the corner of her eyes. In the pack, I had my mother's silver traditional necklace, my dowry gift, and pictures of my brothers. I had whatever remained of my clothes, and some of the things that your aunts had told me to carry for them: a rice pot, a blanket, a child-carrying cloth, and a badly dented metal bowl. I did not want to lose these things. We needed the supplies. He must have guessed my thoughts. He laughed and on the edge of the clearing into the village, he placed the pack on my back. All I remember is a yellow face. He was very thin."

In the village were old men and women who had stayed behind when their sons and daughters had escaped; they had been too weak to run. The small collection of huts and the red dirt looked lifeless to the women.

My mother recalls, "It seemed slow motioned and the people were weighted in a way that caused their shoulders to fall low. I remember the slow rise and fall of the chests of the old men and women there."

The North Vietnamese and Pathet Lao soldiers walked the perimeter of the village with guns in their hands.

My mother remembers, "We saw them around us like shadows. Everything in that place happened like a slow dream. Every breath felt suspended in the air."

They were told to settle into an old hut near the edge of the forest. A Hmong man from Vietnam in a uniform acted as an interpreter between the women and the soldiers. He told them that if they stayed put and behaved, there would be no problems. They were nothing more than bait for the men. The soldiers believed that my father and my uncles would return for their wives and children, and at the very least, for their mother. The women were allowed to walk around the jungle to find firewood and food if there was any to be found. He told them that there were two rivers holding them captive. He knew that they were women from the mountains and that they couldn't swim; there was nowhere to run. To try would be futile, even dangerous.

The next day my mother and my aunts went out to gather firewood. My grandmother stayed behind with the children. The women were spread around, each working a small area. They would see a piece of dried wood that could burn easily, walk to it and pick it up, and then walk further on. My mother was busy. She was not thinking many thoughts. For my mother, the fear of immediate death had settled and there was the work of living to do. "When I cleared the top of the small rise, I expected more jungle. I was struck by what I saw: in the clearing, hundreds, maybe thousands of graves spread before me. The earth was freshly turned."

All the children had died of disease. The grass around the village looked like it had been scorched by boiling water. The old people talked about airplanes that sprinkled bad rain. People were kept in the village-camp for months and then the Laotian and Vietnamese airplanes would pass overhead and many of the people would die afterwards. There was no need for guns. My mother, grandmother, and aunts did not know it, but chemical warfare was being used in the killing of the Hmong. It would be years later before u.s. Secretary of State Alexander Haig would state that poisonous gas had been used in Southeast Asia and the State Department could identify Laos, Cambodia, and Afghanistan as three places where Soviet-supervised chemical warfare attacks had taken place. The women just became afraid of the water and the grass.

My grandmother refused to let anyone drink the water. She boiled special herb concoctions for the women and children. She took out her shaman's tool and performed rituals to protect them. She longed for her sons. She was strong for her daughters-in-law and her grandchildren. She kept them safe.

In that camp, my mother learned about loneliness. All her life, she had always had someone who attempted to understand her feelings, to make her feel good, to look to comfort her. She had been married to my father for six months and did not know anyone in his family well. She did not talk very much, and had made no friends. She simply did what was asked of her and responded to talk with careful words and shy smiles. But they were all women and bonded by the same set of circumstances; they worked and lived together. They found food and shared, but each had their own private thoughts and worries.

The days in the camp were long. My mother thought about going to look for her mother, but she couldn't think of where or how to begin. There were guards during the day. At night, trucks came to pick many of them up—where they went, no one knew. Only one or two soldiers remained behind to patrol the prisoners. Only one side of the village, the side where the graves of little children were, did not have water barring the way. There was nowhere my mother could go, so she put her arms around her stomach and wandered about the small camp aimlessly looking at the dirt (she noticed it was redder than the dirt from the village of her birth); she looked up at the sky (it was the most cloudless sky she would remember seeing); she looked at the foliage (thick enough so that if a person ran into it and stood still, the leaves and small branches would fall and no one would see her); and she felt the way the baby in her stomach started moving, giving her body sensations she had never had before.

My mother told my grandmother about what my father had said to her about finding her mother. My grandmother said that even if there were ways of leaving, she would not let her leave. She had lost her sons. She had only her daughters-in-law now. She would keep them together.

Away from the sons, my mother and my aunts saw my grandma's fortitude. They learned about her consistency and her care.

"It was during these months that I felt closest to your grandmother. She tried her best to keep us safe and together. But her trying to be strong for us did not make the days shorter. They only made them continue more predictably."

My mother's and my aunt's stomachs got round. After the third month in the camp, the North Vietnamese and Pathet Lao soldiers ordered the women to build themselves a new house. The women did not know how, but together they gathered brush and bamboo. They chopped down trees. My grandmother pleaded with the old men in the village to help them build a small hut. Together the village of captives put up a hut for the women and children, a square room with many bamboo platforms along the walls for beds and in the center of the room a place to make fire and cook. The soldiers were pleased that the women were "settling" into their new life.

The North Vietnamese soldiers showed them a movie, the first moving images many of them had ever seen. They could not escape the film. It was shown on a screen right outside their hut. It was a Vietnamese film with people dressed like Hmong. The movie had been translated into Laotian. My mother had been to school so she knew the language; she whispered to my aunts what was being said on the screen.

She still remembers what the movie was about: "There was a hero and a heroine who loved each other a lot. Their village was ambushed. He promised her that he would not leave her. He told her that if they should be divided by fire and death, he would still come back for her. They were chased by soldiers in the night. At first, he waited for her to catch up, holding her hand and trying to pull her along. But dawn broke and the pursuing soldiers got closer. When her strength was gone, and her face was all cut and broken, he stopped looking back to check on her. They were on the edge of a high mountain. He had climbed to the top. He was supposed to pull her up. A bullet came whizzing by. He looked at her dirty face, and he looked into the green jungle on his side."

In the movie, the man left the woman. My mother knew what he would do before he did it. So did my aunts. There was no interpretation needed. In the end, love was not enough. That was the point of the movie. The Hmong interpreter for the soldiers urged my mother and my aunts to marry communist men. Their husbands had abandoned them, he said. After the fifth month in the camp, and no news, the women could not know any longer, which tortured them. Those with children spent many nighttime hours crying quietly. My mother thought about the baby growing bigger inside her stomach.

She was young, only seventeen, and shy about the idea of being a mother, but she was lonely and she wanted the baby badly. "I was stupid. I thought that when I had the baby, I would no longer be alone. I thought that if every woman could do it, then why couldn't I? I did not know the pain of labor, the reality of your body being torn, of bones moving and muscles twitching, of blood seeping, and pushing against yourself all the while. I wanted the baby so much just so that I would not be alone. I thought of the baby as a friend. I could not see then that I would be a mother and that the weight of her body and her life would be in my hands."

My aunt had her baby first. She gave birth to a healthy little boy with soft black hair and chubby fists. A month later, my mother started labor. She told my grandmother when the child pains grew bad and she grew scared.

My grandmother said words my mother would never forget, "*Me Naib*, whatever are we going to do?"

Me Naib is the only endearment my grandmother used. She used it sparingly.

On March 5, 1979, in the early morning hours, my mother gave birth to my sister Dawb, the Hmong word for white. To have pale skin in a life lived outside was a valuable quality then, a sign of beauty in a culture dominated by sun-tarnished skin. An aunt said that Dawb would be a good name for a little girl who was born beautiful in an enemy camp. It did not cross any of their minds that *dawb* was also the color of surrender. If anyone had remembered that white was the color of the flag that had danced in my grandmother's hands, maybe my sister would have received a name that she would have liked better. When Dawb was born, my mother did not receive the friend she had wanted, but some-one who needed her love desperately.

She felt the energy of Dawb's small limbs and started to focus on the world around her again. Dawb, with her small eyes that looked like a little mouse's, was a healthy baby. She did not cry often. Each day my mother held Dawb against her chest and wondered what my father would say when he saw the baby for the first time. There was life in her hands, so thoughts of leaving and death became faraway things.

And then the Hmong interpreter reported that my father had been killed. How did they know it was him? Where did the news come from? He shrugged the questions away. All he knew was that my mother's husband, my grandmother's youngest son, had been found dead in the jungle.

At first there was disbelief, but in the days after, the women began to believe. In the beginning, when the missing had hope, my mother promised herself that if she had another chance to be with my father again, she would be less prideful and more patient and say kinder things to him. When she came to believe that he had died, she could only feel how much she loved him and how empty the world was without him. She did not know whom to cry to; Dawb was too young to understand. She did not want to burden Grandma's pain with her own, and so when the baby started to cry, my mother would cry. Together, they cried for my father.

Dawb was a month old when two fishermen entered their camp at night and whispered through the bamboo walls: Grandma's sons were nearby. Everyone should get ready to leave by midnight. The women did not know whether or not to believe, but they were desperate. They were scared that more deaths would be reported. My mother wanted to ask the men how many sons there were but there was no opportunity. Grandma told her to prepare the baby to leave. For her baby, my mother would do anything, leave anywhere, go any place at all.

At midnight the two men returned. The women packed up the children. My mother tied Dawb tightly to her chest. She carried her pack high on her back. She had a blanket for the baby, the heavy silver necklace, the pictures of her brothers, and the embroidery her mother had given her. It was a full moon. They followed the two men into the night. A dog barked. The men ran toward one of the two rivers. The women ran after the men with their children in tow. The soldiers began shouting. The women could see that there were two bamboo rafts waiting in the shallow water.

In the dark, my mother made out a shape that she believed was my father's. He stood by the shore. In the moonlight, she made out the span of wide shoulders and the hollow of a familiar body. She ran to him and she held on blindly. To my mother, "it was a reunion in a dream. You hold on and do not think about waking up."

There was no room for talk. Only whispered commands to move faster. The soldiers came in pursuit, not just the two who

usually guarded the camp; the arrival of the men had been antic-
ipated. It was a plot to capture them all.

There were gunshots, and they heard voices hurrying from
behind, dogs barking urgently. Their own breath was loud in their
ears; pounding of frantic hearts. The men shoved off the edge
before the first dogs reached them. Along the edge, one of my
uncles had planted grenades they had found in the jungle—wooden
boxes halfway covered by the canvas of parachutes and jungle
foliage that the u.s. government had left behind—unretrieved from
drops made when the Americans were in the fight. The men had
carried what they found, mostly grenades and bullets. When the
grenades were triggered, fire exploded into the jungle night. From
the water, my family heard screams of familiar pain.

When they reached the other side of the river, they could hear
motorboats chasing after them. The men told the women and children to run toward high ground. They would plant the last of the
grenades and then catch up. The men went to work in the soft
mud of the river's edge, digging with their hands. They planted the
grenades and did not bother to cover them up. They yelled for each
other to run. They did not wait around for the explosions. In their
flight, they heard the cries of pain in Vietnamese and Laotian. The
trees were so thick that the men could not see their hands or feet.
They used their hands to measure the slope of the terrain, stumbling over their feet. When they reached the group of trembling
women and children, they told everyone to start walking.

Together they walked until the light of dawn allowed them to
see their way. They would go higher, up to the mountains, the
landscape they knew best. For a week, the group walked back-
wards, with sticks in their hands, covering up each step as they
treaded higher and higher toward safety.

High up in a mountain cave, on another dawn, my father, for
the first time, held Dawb in his arms and looked at her small face.

He was twenty years old, gaunt, his cheekbones rose high on his thin face, his hands trembling with the baby in his arms.

He would remember the moment of their meeting forever: "She was my child. I knew that. When you hold on to something and you know it is your flesh and your blood, you cannot feel nothing. The feelings were heavy. I could not let her die now that I had seen her. I felt shy before the baby. Everything was too new and strong."

The men and women talked about what had happened to them, about how it was in the jungle for seven months searching for their brothers, how close they had come to death, how they were hungry and sick, and how when they had all given up, they had found each other again. The women told the men about the children, the times they got sick with diarrhea, and about the cries of hunger that never stopped but were only quieted from exhaustion. It eased their hearts that the family was together again.

In private, each couple promised the other a love that they had not yet known together. My mother told my father how she would become a better wife to him, say more of what was in her heart. She missed him more than even her own mother. He told her that she had lost weight and that she looked tired and that he was sorry for bringing her so far from her family. How he wished he could have been there to see Dawb's birth, and how he would not have chosen her name, but how happy he was to see his wife and his child. They looked at their baby and at each other and they both felt grown up, like real adults holding together a family.

They made a plan. They could no longer survive in Laos. All that the children knew was the jungle and the calls to run, to not look back. This could not continue. The family decided that the only option for survival was to get to the Mekong River, cross it, and head for the refugee camps of Thailand. The men had met two scouts while they were lost, and the two men had generously explained the way to the river. The men calculated that the journey would take ten days of walking at night, as fast as they could, if they encountered no soldiers along the way. They could not afford to look for food on the way to the river. They would need a few weeks to find as much cassava and taro roots as they could to dry in preparation for the journey.

It was the beginning of the monsoon season. The sky opened up in slates of cold rain every day, at unpredictable times. In the mud of the wet jungle floor, the group searched for wild roots. Under the protection of banana leaves, the women made small fires with twigs to dry thinly sliced cassava and taro roots.

In the rain, the fevers began. Chills racked my mother's body. Her breasts became infected and there was no milk for the baby. Grandma gave one of her last cans of sweetened condensed milk to feed Dawb. My father boiled water in a rice pot that had the residue of chili pepper; he fed her spicy condensed milk. The baby began to have diarrhea. In the enemy camp, my mother had fed Dawb on her milk and the baby had grown. In the week after their escape, the week of gathering for food, with the diarrhea, she became thin—wrinkled skin and small bones. Her cry lost its strength. The other children in the group became sick as well from the lack of food and the constant dampness. Fearing for their children's lives, the family decided they could wait no longer. Three weeks after their escape from the enemy camp, they began their journey to Thailand.

They traveled in the dark. During the daylight hours, they rested on their packs beneath jungle leaves on wet, slippery mud. My mother was weak with hunger and the infection on her breast. Dawb had stopped crying entirely. Her eyes no longer opened. One night they slept in a ravine, water gushing between my parents. My mother held Dawb tightly so that she would not fall into the small current. They had a small piece of tarp to put over the fevering little body.

That night, my mother learned how hard rain could fall. She understood how it was that such a sound and feeling could drive a person to madness. She talked to her baby all night long, crooning promises she could not know she would keep, "Shhhh. Go to sleep, everything will be all right. My little baby will get better. Tomorrow my breast will have milk again and the hunger will go away. Tomorrow the sun will rise and the rain will stop. Tomorrow, I will become a better mother to you and give you a better chance at this life."

She knew her baby could no longer cry. She shushed the silent body anyway.

Both my mother and father felt that the night would never end, that the rain would never stop, that they would never get up again. But in the early morning hours, the downpour ceased, and in the drizzle, they did get up again. The family got up and without talking, tied their babies close to their chest, held the hands of their bigger children, and started walking.

They reached the banks of the Mekong River on the dawn of May 20, 1979. It had taken them exactly ten days. They had to wait for nightfall before crossing the river. It was raging and wild and high. It was a block long, my mother remembers. It was forever, my grandmother had said. My father thought he would never be able to swim across; it was like the Mississippi River; it was like the Hudson River. It was a river that had fed much of Southeast Asia for hundreds of years. The twelfth longest river in the world, the Mekong is known in both Laos and Thailand as the mother river. Along the border between Laos and Thailand it stretched three-fourths of a mile wide. The Mekong River saw the deaths of more Hmong people than any other river.

The Hmong had been people from the mountains. They were not good swimmers. Only the men, when they were boys, had gone fishing and learned a little bit about the push and pull of water. They knew how to keep afloat. They knew a little about how to move in water. Few of the women or children could swim at all. My mother and my grandmother both did not.

There was no moon the night of their crossing. There were soldiers stationed along the stretch of the river. Hmong refugees had made the crossing, or died trying to ford the river, since 1975. That night, there were a few Laotian men near the water's edge selling rafts, trying to make a living in an economy devastated by war. A few of my uncles, with their big families, traded their remaining possessions for rafts. My father did not have any money. The most expensive thing they owned was my mother's silver necklace, but even that had no value for the men with the rafts; what was a symbol of Hmong womanhood when life and death were on the line?

My mother and father stood near the banks, hovering in the bamboo brush. My grandmother stood near the river looking as each of her sons set off into the currents. My father had an idea: he would cut the bamboo, tie it around himself, tie it to my mother and the baby, tie it to his mother, and he would drag them across. They had gotten this far. He would not give up. If they died, it would be together. If they survived, it would be together.

Why did my grandmother cross the Mekong River with my father? Couldn't she have crossed with the other uncles?

She explained to me why she crossed with her youngest son, "The river was so wide. I could not swim. Neither could your mother. Some of your uncles had traded things for rafts. Your father did not have one. He was the youngest, you see. And he was poor and I was his mother but I was poor, too. So we got to the river and I could see it glitter and I could not see how to cross it. Your uncles took their wives and their children on the rafts with them; they all would have made room for me. I could not go with them. Your father had no raft. I was his mother. I chose to die with him."

In a rough whisper, my father told my mother to hurry. Did she not know the soldiers were coming? Everybody was running into the water. Couldn't she see? She tried to hurry. With her fingers she dug into the moist ground of a bamboo patch. In the shallow hole, she placed all the pictures of her brothers, her mother, herself. She felt the bamboo trunk with her hands in the dark. If she ever touched that bamboo again, she told herself, forming the words on her lips, she would remember. One day, she would find the pictures again. One day, she would tell her brothers and her mother that she still had the photos of them from before the war. She would tell them that she would never forget them because the way they were was burned into her heart. Her baby shivered against her body, calling her back to the night. She ran to my father's side.

He tied her to himself. On her neck she wore the heavy silver necklace her mother had given her. The pieces of embroidery, gifts from her mother so that when she died she would find her way home, she put in between her child and herself; she tied Dawb to her front. My grandmother was already tied to my father. He took off everything but his underwear, and then he dragged everyone into the cold water. It was after midnight. Behind them there was the crack of more guns, the sounds of more yelling in the madness of pursuit.

The currents were strong. Somehow my mother hung onto the baby. Somewhere in the undertow, when her head was beneath water, the heavy silver necklace slipped from her neck. My grandmother had her shaman's tools, her iron gong and her ring of copper coins, the sacred water buffalo horns, all tied to her. They gasped for air and tried to breathe. They thought they heard voices in the water. My father tried to swim. His muscles hurt. He thought he would never make it. He saw the lights of Thailand across the expanse of night.

When dawn streamed in on folds of soft pink, layers of white, a rising blue, they knew they had passed the midway point between the two countries, the old one they loved, where so many had died, and a new one they did not know, where so many would be born. It was very still. The water was very cold. Their hopes had gone numb in the night. The baby was white against the black of the water.

When my father's feet touched the river bottom, he did not know if they were far underwater or close to shore. He walked on the shifting pebbles, and he pulled, for all the years of running through the jungle, the weight of his wife, his mother, and his child. He fell to his knees on the shore. He looked behind him. There were men on the other side with guns, firing. He could not hear sounds; there was silence in his ears. In the river, he saw a family being dragged into a Laotian gunboat. He shivered. He knew the fate that awaited them on the shores of Laos. My grandmother and mother had crawled to their feet and were hovering over the baby, silent and pale and unmoving. Her little arms dangled limply at her side. My mother started to cry. She rocked the baby in her arms, and she gulped the air as if she were underwater. Had it all been for nothing? The sun rose higher, a cool breeze blew, and in the layers of pink and orange, in the leaving of the gray dawn, my mother saw the lids of the baby flutter.

CHAPTER 3
REFUGEES

On May 20, 1979, my family found themselves wet and shivering along the banks of the Mekong River, my father in his underwear, my mother with Dawb strapped to her chest and her long hair undone, and my grandmother with her shaman's tools clasped in her hands. The Thai air smelled different to them: instead of moist jungle air, there was the scent of smoke and people nearby. In the night, they had seen the lights beckoning across the river. In the light of a rising sun, they saw the line of trees that stood away from the muddy bank waving in the wind of a new day. They looked back across the expanse of the river, and they felt they were safe. My father said that they should walk upriver to look for the rest of the family. He led the way, shivering. The curve of my father's spine was a vulnerable descent of bone on a body that had long been deprived of food; the blades of his shoulders rose high, an instinctive gesture to protect his body. My mother and my grandmother trailed behind him, their wet clothes dripping drops of water onto the soil of a foreign land. My mother cradled Dawb in her arms carefully. Her baby was alive.

If my family had crossed the river two months later, they would have been massacred. Thailand was no longer taking Hmong refugees from Laos; there were too many coming in because of the continued influx of North Vietnamese soldiers to help the Pathet Lao kill the remaining Hmong. Jane Hamilton-Merritt, a journalist from America, recorded the deaths of two hundred Hmong people, families with small children, on the Mekong on July 27, 1979. The group was on a sandbar gathering vines to weave a bridge to Thailand. They built fires and boiled water in old u.s. Army canteens. The women took off their shirts to put over sticks to shelter their babies and the old women. They fed their hungry children. Many of them were little more than skeletons. The adults didn't eat. They saved their rice for the children. Thai soldiers appeared on the Thai bank in jeeps with a machine gun bolted to the front hood. In two Thai patrol boats, the soldiers traveled to the island. The Thai soldiers slashed the vines that tried to connect the people to Thailand. Thailand had had enough Hmong refugees. On August 2, 1979, Hamilton-Merritt learned that a group of thirty to forty Pathet Lao soldiers had landed on the river island and the Hmong were massacred.*

My family was fortunate. As they walked along the bank of the Mekong River that May morning, the sun shining over their heads, slowly drying their clothes, they felt the relief of danger dissipating. They were weak from a journey that had taken four years, but in their bellies, alongside the hunger for food, they carried a yearning for the land on the other side of the river—the foundations of centuries of myth, of legend, the soil of so many Hmong dreams. They looked to the land of Laos as they walked on the soil of Thailand, their feet making soft prints on the wet earth. They walked for nearly a half mile before they found the rest of the family hovering underneath the overhang of a bamboo grove. Each family had been swept to a different place on the riverbank, but they had all walked, looking for one another.

* Jane Hamilton-Merritt, *Tragic Mountains: The Hmong, the Americans, and the Secret Wars for Laos, 1942-1992*. (Bloomington, IN: University of Indiana Press, 1993).

There was a hungry weight in the air. The children were alive, although many of them had swallowed much water in the crossing. Uncle Chue, my father's second eldest brother, and his family had been picked up by a Pathet Lao gunboat at the halfway point in the river. Uncle Eng had seen how the soldiers had grabbed little Nhia and Pakou, tied together to a small float, and dropped them into the boat. A soldier had held a gun to the little girls until Uncle Chue swam to the boat, dragging the rest of his family with him. The boat had zoomed back to Laos. As Uncle Eng spoke, my grandmother started to cry, great heaving sobs that made her legs unsteady.

Grandma sank to the wet ground, holding her hands in fists up to her chest. There were few words of comfort. Grandma shook her head at the world around her, the men and women, the children with hollowed eyes, and called my grandfather's name.

She said, "Do not let my child die. I have done all I can. It is your turn. Bring him back to me. We gave birth to him together. He is where I cannot go. Bring him across this wide river, to this shore, to me. You are his father. Bring him back to his mother."

The group sat under the rustling bamboo leaves for a few hours in silence; everybody's hearts were tired. The eyelids of children were closing with exhaustion. They did not sleep but they rested against each other, very still. When the smaller ones began whimpering, the women said the children needed food, so the men got up, saying there was little they could do sitting along the banks of the river. The family would walk into Thailand a little and see if there was food to be found, and later, when they could, they would find a way to help Uncle Chue's family escape. Uncle Eng had to lift my grandma off the ground. She leaned on him as they walked away from the expanse of the Mekong River, and Laos, a land that they loved, the land holding their brother, the land holding the grave of their father.

The tattered group, six brothers, no longer seven because Uncle Chue was gone, and their wives and children and their mother did not make it far into Thailand before they were spotted by farmers. Refugees had been streaming into Thailand for the past four years, since the Americans had left and the Laotian government had started killing Hmong people. The village chief had been notified that a new group had entered into the country, and he had sent word to the Thai soldiers. Men with guns waited for the group at the end of a dirt road. The farmers stood in place to watch the shivering group make their way toward the men in uniforms.

A farmer on the road threw an old black T-shirt and a pair of tattered shorts at my father. The shirt hit him on the arm. The shorts fell to the ground in front of him. My father picked up the clothes and did not know whether to say thank you or not to the silent man who looked at him with unblinking eyes. My mother stopped her slow walking and waited for my father to put on the shirt and shorts. She loved him very much in that moment; she wanted to protect him from the life around them, but her baby held her back.

"I never thought I would see clothes thrown at my husband," she says, looking at the floor, as if all the years had not erased the memory. "When he picked the clothes off the ground and tried to wipe the dirt away, I could not look."

My mother could only wrap her arms more securely around Dawb. Her long hair fell about her shoulders; there was nothing to tie it back with. The wind blew the long strands into her face. Her hair had dried since the crossing. She was a proud young woman. I wonder if she hid behind the curtain of her hair and sought comfort in the small, unmoving baby with fluttering lids.

The Thai soldiers spoke to them in Laotian. They were informed that there was a place for incoming refugees to register with a group called the United Nations. After their registration, they would be sent to a fenced compound where they would stay until further arrangements could be made. They were told that they were in Nong Khai, a Thai province, but that the refugee camp there was full. The soldiers told them that they were refugees now, *opoyop:* people fleeing for a home. Like times before, they were told to follow the men with the guns.

It was not such a long walk, but the farmers on the road stared at them, and every step felt stiff and hard. Maybe it was an hour. Maybe it was less than that. They had no watches, and they were too tired to count the ticking of time, too embarrassed in their rags, with their hunger and their children with bones jutting from thin shoulders. An expression on one man's face is the memory my mother and father both carry, even twenty-five years after the fact: it was only a look, but it said that we were not human, too poor to walk on the earth. It was in that image of that Thai man with his red-and-white turban wrapped around his head, looking at them making their way into his country, that my mother and father learned what it meant to be poor, to be without a home or clothing to hide in.

The soldiers led them to a house my mother remembers as beautiful. "It was wooden and it was on stilts and the roof rose to the sky, and there were stairs that led from the ground to its patio. I wished, even then, to see the inside, but we could not go in."

The Thai soldiers told them to wait outside. The group sat admiring the house, not saying very much, wondering what was going to happen. They were surprised when the soldiers returned with plates of rice and dried fish. It was only a little food and the adults could not eat away the hunger, but they nibbled a little as the children ate. They watched as the children with their small, hurried, dirty hands put pieces of rice and fish into their open mouths. Like little birds, many of them just swallowed the food. After the plates were empty, they noticed a bus waiting for them.

The soldiers told them to get in. They would go to the UN compound to register as refugees of war.

When they reached the compound, they noticed the wire fence, as tall as two men standing on each other's shoulders. They were told to get out of the bus and enter the gates. My family hesitated before the entrance; they had escaped from one country and had not expected to be captives in the next. My father's feet stilled. A Thai soldier punched him and he fell to the ground. The man kicked him. My father got up as fast as he could. Not to hit the man back, but because he did not want my mother and grandmother to see him on the ground. My father looked at the man and did nothing.

He would tell me, years later, "My heart hurt more than my body—the flesh can take blows, the heart suffers them. It was the first time I felt that there would be no other place like Phu Khao, the village where I was born. The soldier who hit me was an older man. I was like a prisoner. I stood still, and then I walked into the place they would keep me. And I kept thinking: I was a man, too. I had a wife and a child. But it didn't matter because we had no home anymore."

They walked into a place that felt like an enemy station, only they were told it was for the refugees of war fleeing into Thailand. It was late afternoon and the UN workers had left. The soldiers said that they would be locked into the compound for their safety at night. They asked about food for the children but the soldiers said they had none. My mother wanted to ask for a piece of dry cloth for the baby, but my father told her that it would be futile. The UN building was covered in corrugated aluminum. There was a small roof overhang. They sat along the walls of the building.

Night came slowly, with drizzle that turned into heavy rain. They could not see the sky, only hear and feel the rain falling in fat drops. The humid air was thick with mosquitoes. Both my mother and father tried to protect Dawb from the hungry creatures: their hands did not rest the night through. They took turns waving the insects away from their barely breathing baby, who suckled weakly at my mother's breast.

"I drank rain water so that there would be a little milk for my baby," my mother recalls. "There was only a light liquid coming from my one uninfected breast, but she kept on trying to feed. I was hungry, and there was no food, so I drank a little rain water and then a little more."

When morning broke, they found themselves before a crowd. Thai villagers, on their way to the fields, had stopped by the compound to peek at them from outside the fence. Men and women, children, pointed fingers at my mother and her small baby, at my grandmother and her shaman's tools. They could hear the Mekong River and felt a kind of freedom that was in the jungle, despite the bullets, that they would not feel ever again: the rush of wind through the bamboo groves, the sounds of birds chattering comfortably in their busy skies, the echo of their voices against the towering mountains. Their stomachs numb from hunger and their bodies weary from their long journey, the family sat and said nothing to each other while the people outside peered and pointed at them.

With morning came the UN workers. They stood in a line, one family and then another, while the UN people, all Thai, wrote their names on paper, gave them numbers that would replace their names, and asked for their birthdays. Some of them had good estimates, like my mother and father. She had been born at the beginning of the monsoon rains so she said May 6, 1961, and he had been born during the harvest so he said January 10, 1958. My mother said that Dawb had been born on March 5, 1979, exactly one year from the day my mother and father had taken that walk that had led them to marriage. Nobody knew my grandmother's birthday, so Uncle Eng picked August 8, 1910, for her. Grandma said that she was older than that but it was not worth protesting and she did not have a better date so she accepted it. For many other people in the family, Uncle Eng chose different days in February, in different years, because he thought that was a good month to be born, a new month to start a new life. For many of the Hmong, their lives on paper began on the day the UN registered them as refugees of war.

After the registration, the UN people told the family they would be taken in a bus to So Kow Toe,* a place where refugees were temporarily placed until further arrangements could be made in the seventeen refugee camps in Thailand. Most Hmong people would go to Ban Vinai Refugee Camp, the largest. It would house over forty-five thousand Hmong people. They were told that it was in the hills, not quite like the mountains that they had called home, but not so flat that you could see forever.

A bus took them to So Kow Toe, a place that was also fenced in, this time not with barbed wires, but with high aluminum walls. The dominant feature of the camp was the stench of feces. There were toilets, but they were all flooded. There were no trees, and my mother remembers that there were little huts without walls, and that inside the huts there were badly made bamboo platforms for beds. Little children pooped underneath the beds. There were many Hmong people all around, strange faces and tattered clothes, everyone speaking different Hmong dialects.

In the mountains, the white Hmong and the green Hmong had lived in separate enclaves. They had each spoken their own dialects and eaten their own foods of choice. Though friendly, they had hardly intermingled. Out of the mountains and into Thailand, they would all live together, sleep together, be comforted and scared together. In this camp, they found themselves listening carefully so they could understand each other; they felt they were

* The official name was Sob Tuang, and it was located in Nan Province.

all just Hmong—people without a history, rooted in the same past. There was long-ago China and despairing Laos—and the tones of a tongue, one lyrically smooth, the other stark and simple, both born in an experience of being Hmong. The difference was their own. They had learned from their years in the jungle that when no other peoples would help, Hmong people could help Hmong people. They had found that it was not necessary to have a country to stand together as one people. They found that without a country, finding a place to sleep was difficult.

There were no places to sleep and nothing to sleep on. Once again, as in the jungle, Hmong people helped Hmong people. The Hmong families from the camp in Nong Khai gained permission to come by and offer the newcomers old woven mats, some plastic, some bamboo. They said that they did not have much, but they would not let their own people sleep on the hard ground of a foreign country.

My family slept in the open for a week, and the sky looked out for them—there was no rain that entire week. Everybody slept on the hard ground, together, on mats. For the adults, the stench and the humiliation of human waste were the worst part of that long week. There was no more fear, because they had escaped from Laos and there were Hmong people all around. Twice a day, they were brought food in huge trucks. They were fed soup, a watery concoction of bits of pork fat and cucumbers mixed with rice, seasoned with salt and black pepper. Each Hmong person could only get one ladle of soup, and people had to share cups and bowls and plates and various containers, anything they could find that might hold food.

"There were trucks that look like the kind that you see on highways carrying oil," my mother tells me. "They would come, and everyone would get in line. There was a big rubber hose. The soup did not gush out. The soybean drink did not run in a large stream. It trickled out, into the containers. It was not enough food because everything was watery. Sometimes the children would get in line twice because they were so hungry."

My family stayed in So Kow Toe for a week. The camp was filling up, and they needed to be temporarily moved into the refugee camp of Nong Khai. My mother and father and my aunts and uncles and my grandmother and cousins all stood together so that the UN people would know they were a family. The UN people saw them helping each other to stand straight, and told them to all walk together in a line out of the camp. They did not have to walk far, maybe only one or two hours before they came to another camp, this one better than So Kow Toe. They saw a relative's face in the crowd, a second cousin. He said that he would take all of them into his hut with his family until the UN people figured out where to send them.

My family stayed in his hut for a month. They slept on the dirt floor, and together they ate modestly of rice and the bits of green his wife purchased at the camp market or received from the rations truck. It was a long month of trying not to eat very much and holding onto semiempty stomachs before a relative with little to offer but kindness. At the end of the month, the UN people came back and told them they would be returning to So Kow Toe to sleep for two nights and then be bused to Ban Vinai Refugee Camp.

In So Kow Toe, they were reunited with Uncle Chue and his family. My grandmother cried and cried and she hugged him and each of his children. Grandpa had heard her by the Mekong River. His spirit had everybody together again. He had not forsaken her or the children.

Grandma asked, "What happened? What happened? How did you escape?"

Together Uncle Chue and his wife told the family what happened:

In the river they could only see each other's heads. They didn't see the Pathet Lao patrol boat come their way. Uncle Chue was the only one who could swim; he was too busy dragging my aunt and Sue, their baby boy, who was only a year and three months old, and then their two older children, Lei and Kong, who were thirteen and eleven, and then their middle girls, Pakou and Nhia, five and three year olds. He felt the pull of the rope at his back and he stopped to look behind. That was when he saw that his girls were out of the water and there were guns to their heads. The soldier said, "choose," so of course he swam toward them with the rest of his family in tow.

The family was taken to an enemy camp on the bank of the river on the Laotian side. The soldiers did not say much; they just pushed Uncle Chue ahead, and his family followed. They were taken to a house on stilts and told to sit. They took my uncle into the jungle. My aunt heard a gunshot ricochet from the direction they had taken him. "I thought they had killed him for sure."

Laotian villagers came to look at the children. Before her eyes, her children were split up. An old couple took Lei, another took Nhia, and another took Pakou. No one wanted Kong. He was too thin and he looked weak. Sue was only a baby, and the couples shook their heads at the prospect of taking a baby from his mother.

My aunt remembers, "The part that hurt me the most was when the couple that took Nhia threw away her dress before my eyes. It was only rags, but I had kept sewing it, even in the jungle with my needle and thread, to keep the garment on her. They took it off and just threw it away. I gave my daughter life, but I could not give her clothes to wear, and now this couple was throwing away the only thing I had left for her."

The couples took the girls to their homes. My aunt and her two boys were left sitting, waiting, not knowing for what, when

Uncle Chue walked back into the camp with the soldiers as night was falling. He had told the soldiers that he had been a teacher before the Americans left Laos. Perhaps they saw his air of lifelong obedience—he convinced the soldiers that he could be reformed as a good communist man. That night, they sat up all night. He told my aunt that they would escape. He had an idea. They were close to the river. There were Thai fishermen who came to the shore to pick up refugees for Thailand if they could promise them money after getting to Thailand. His brothers would not let him down. If the family did everything the soldiers said, maybe within a week, he could contact one of the Thai men sneaking in, and they could make an escape. My aunt wanted her girls back. She refused to leave the country without them.

In the morning, the soldiers brought them rice balls and dried fish. They ate with their fingers and drank water from a clay jar. The soldiers said that the three girls had cried all night long and that the couples didn't want them anymore. Did my aunt and uncle still want their girls? They nodded eagerly, and by noon the girls were returned. They cried and pulled the girls close. My uncle began thinking of a plan.

Uncle Chue told the soldiers that his family needed to bathe, and the men agreed, saying that since he was a good man he could take his family to the river and wash up. Uncle Chue figured that the soldiers would follow them so he took his family to the river, and they all bathed as best they could. They returned to the bottom of the stilted home and sat close together.

The soldiers did not know whether to kill them or not, because their leader was not in the local vicinity. Each morning they were given rice balls and dried fish. Each night, they went to bathe by the river. On the sixth night, they saw a Thai man, and my uncle took a risk and talked to him, saying he had six brothers who had escaped to Thailand; there would be money if they could get across the river. The Thai man said for them all to come on the seventh night. He was willing to take them across the river so long as they paid him once they were settled in Thailand. The actual escape was not very eventful: on the seventh night, they hurried into the Thai man's small boat, which had an engine. They kept looking behind them as they were taken across the Mekong River, away from Laos and to Thailand, where they knew the family would be waiting somewhere for them.

Finally, in So Kow Toe, all of Grandma's seven sons and their wives and children were together again. The adults talked late into the night. None of them knew what was coming ahead, in this place called Ban Vinai Refugee Camp, but they reassured each other that everything would be all right. If they were separated, they would find each other again. They had lived through the war. The final two days in So Kow Toe were spent comforting each other; the nights were spent looking up at the clean sky with the bright stars, a sky that could have been anywhere.

Three buses entered the camp on the third day, which would take them to Ban Vinai Refugee Camp, where they would live. My family got into a huge green bus. They had no time to get the morning food rations, so they were all hungry, but they went into the bus and they sat quietly, thinking ahead.

My mother sat by the window with Dawb, who was still very thin. But she had started crying, and there was more milk for her now. My mother looked out the window that whole day it took the bus to get to Ban Vinai. She saw green hills and green trees, and she felt everything would really be all right.

"I kept on looking out the window and feeling that I was not scared anymore. Your father was looking ahead of the bus, his hands clasped, with his thumbs moving one on top of the other.

Maybe the bus to Ban Vinai Refugee Camp had air conditioning. I don't remember the heat. I just remember the passing of the sun over the body of the bus as the day waned."

When my family reached the camp, it was dark, so they could not see what was before them, this place that would be my first home.

PART II

The Little Girl
with the Dimples

CHAPTER 4
BAN VINAI REFUGEE CAMP

 Ban Vinai Refugee Camp was a dirty place. Dust particles flew high in the hot wind. Young women held pieces
of cloth over their noses when they walked in the noon
sun to pick up rations for their families in a patch of designated
ground. The cotton prints of their tube skirts swooshed in the air.
Young men narrowed their eyes and breathed through their noses,
drawing the dirt in, eyeing the groups of women. The rough skin
of their feet were clad in blue-and-red flip-flops. Little boys and
girls ran around as they did in every other part of the world where
there is little to do and many people to look after them. The dust
went into my throat, got into my nostrils. When I blew my nose
on the inside corner of my shirt, when my mother was nowhere
around, I saw black dirt on the fabric. Somehow the dust turned
black inside my nose when in the air it looked orange. Small
pieces of the earth flew at me, small bits that matched the ground.
I couldn't ask an adult why and how the dust changed its color
inside my nose. Ban Vinai Refugee Camp was a place where kids
kept secrets and adults stayed inside themselves.

My mother and father speak of how little we had when I was
born. They had already been in the camp for a year and five months.
Each person had only a few pieces of donated clothing. This was

much more than they had when they crossed the Mekong River, but they still say that I was born when they were poor because they had stopped wishing for things other than their lives. I was their gift in a time when they could not dare to dream of presents.

There were a great many children born in 1980. The Hmong people in Ban Vinai Refugee Camp were all looking to make a life in the camp, to feel alive again after the war. So many had died, maybe they were all hoping to make up for the deaths of their loved ones with new lives to love. In my family alone, there were eight children born in 1980. One returned to the clouds, so there were seven of us.

Nobody said anything about being disappointed because I was a girl. Perhaps they all thought that my mother and father would have more children. They were young, my mother only nineteen and my father only twenty-two. Nobody knew then that after me there would be six miscarriages, all little boys, whose spirits could not make the journey to the earth, so in the blue sky they kept on waiting.

My father explained where babies came from to me. "Before babies are born they live in the sky where they race along with the clouds and can see everything—the beauty of the mountains, the courses of streams, the dirt of the paths that people take down on earth."

I loved the idea and power of a journey from the clouds. It gave babies power: we choose to be born to our lives; we give ourselves to people who make the earth look more inviting than the sky.

I came down to the world of my mother and father on a cool December dawn, during the New Year's festivities. Instead of the grand ceremony that the Hmong had celebrated for hundreds of years in Laos and China, the New Year in the camp was a sorry effort at courtship for the young men and women. There were no harvests, no abundance of food—only the memories of tradition and good times past to return to and smile about. I am a New Year baby, a symbol of hope that better things were coming.

My grandmother delivered me into the world. I fell from the clouds into her hands. When she first saw me, I was crying, my face suffused with color. My body was exhausted from my long journey, and overcome by the freedom of movement. I was small, but healthy. My eyes were wide open, my small feet kicked at the air, and my hands moved in fists against the bigger hands that tried to hold them still. Grandma named me Mai Kao; in Hmong it meant "the maiden." My mother was scared of me because I came into the world with a fear of the dark: every time she turned off the kerosene lamp beside the bamboo platform we used for a bed, an effort to save the oil, I would cry out in angry, frightened shrieks. The adults around me had a feeling that I would not be one to live life frugally.

In the only photograph that exists of me as a baby, I look as if I have a diaper on, but there were no diapers in the camp. It is only my pale pink cotton shirt tucked into baby underwear. In the picture, I have plump cheeks. I am maybe four months old; I can't stand yet; my mother holds me up for the photograph, her hands underneath my armpits. I am looking down, pouting; the corners of my eyes tilt up, and I have a small nose and the classic flat head that so many Hmong parents want for their babies, especially girls, so that our heads can be beautifully shaped in the deep turbans of the traditional head wrap.

Two months after I was born, I was sick. There was fever in my body, and bubbles came out of my mouth. My parents took me to the clinic. The nurses stuck a syringe in my spine. They gave me a shot and told my parents to take me home. At home I fed on my mother's milk, and I got better. I became round. I developed dimples in my cheeks. The sound of footsteps made me giggle. When I heard people talk, I extended my arms to them. My mother

bought beads and a small silver bell that she made into a bracelet for my right wrist. The bells jingled and I laughed. Along with the other members of my family, my grandmother responded to my cheerfulness. She changed my name to Mai Kao Kalia, the girl with the dimples (my name also refers to a rare, white insect found in the insides of bamboo trees that the Hmong consider a delicacy). Warm laps welcomed me. I felt the beat of many different hearts against my ear, the rhythm of life, steady and afraid.

My mother only had two girls. Other mothers had a lot more children. She felt it was her duty to keep us very clean, even if we lived in a refugee camp where many children were dirty. She washed Dawb and me two times a day, once in the morning and once at night. In the middle of the afternoon, when the sun was very hot, she would tell me to drag my aluminum tub to my father so that he could draw water for my afternoon bath. I was three or four, and the tub was tied to a string. The clanging of my bath against the hard ground would call my father, and by the time I reached the well, he would be there waiting. I would just sit in the bathtub and let the water take away the heat of the day, slapping the surface of the water with my hands. Dawb did not like to be clean as much as I did. She was the more difficult of us.

The doctor in the camp said that Dawb had polio as a baby. She almost died when she was just two and I was only a newborn. She had a horrible fever and my parents didn't know what to do, so they took her to the camp hospital. There, the people put her on a bed and watched as her body jerked until she sank into herself, and her body curled up like when she was inside my mother's stomach. She lay unmoving for three days and nights. My grandmother talked with the spirit world and offered the lives of chickens and pigs—she promised to find the animals if Dawb got better. They only knew that Dawb was alive on the third day because she blinked. She made an effort to point to the ceiling fan, and in a voice that had lost its intelligence, a tone that went nowhere, asked our father, "Why does it go around and never stop?"

My grandmother went to buy a small chicken for the spirits that had helped Dawb hold on to life.

The sickness took away the strength of one of Dawb's legs, as well as her obedience. I know that high on her thigh there is a scar, a curve on her skin like the face of a silent moon—a sad, hidden moon. She played outside after dark. She stopped listening to my parents. Whenever we passed the small noodle shop on the red dirt road that cut across the camp, she would ask for food. I never asked, because I knew that if my parents bought Dawb noodles, they would buy me a bowl, too.

Every night Dawb would need a reminder that it was bath time. When bath time came, my mother would hand me a small bamboo stick, a sign for Dawb that the call was serious and came from the authority of our mother. I never used the stick, except for one night, by accident, I let it fall on a cousin in the dark. I saw a shadow that was the same size as my sister's. I called. She did not respond. I tapped her on the shoulder. She turned around and jumped on me. The ground underneath the huge trees with their small pebbly fruits was hard against my back. When the shock went away, I decided: if my mother wanted us to be clean, she would have to do the job of calling Dawb herself.

The camp was a flat area of land, a huge valley, between sprawling hills of dried grass. It was two hours by car from where my family had crossed into Thailand. The soil was hot and dry and not good for crops, so few Thai people could make a living on the land. At four hundred acres, the camp became a place for people who had to leave their countries because to stay meant death; it became a place where we could wait in the dust. From 1980 to 1987 about thirty-five to forty-five thousand Hmong refugees lived in the camp. The money from the United

Nations was enough rent for the rickety collection of long, wooden rooms that housed many of the refugees.

The room where my family slept was connected to other rooms where other families slept, and the kitchen was a long hall where every family had its own iron fire ring and a wooden table with two wooden benches. We all lived together. Our lives were caught, entangled in waiting, hanging low on the dusty ground.

We ate from the same white enamel-covered bowls, with little cracks where the metal peeked through, used the same steel spoons, wore the same brands of cockatoo flip-flops, dreamed the same dreams: I want a pink doll with yellow hair that closes her eyes when I put her down to sleep beside me; I want a bicycle with three wheels so that I can show the other kids that we are not too poor and that I can ride a bike; I don't want to eat fish and rice again; I want to have a round boiled egg with a soft yellow center to eat with my rice today.

Rations came three times a week and consisted of dried fish, which caused little children to get stomach cramps, and old broken grains of rice that required no chewing to fall apart. Both smelled of mold and dark places. But ration days were good days because there was something; the other four days of the week each family had to find whatever they could to eat. There was no work, but some people had small gardens. My mother was always careful about what and when we ate. We craved the food that we couldn't have: like sticky durian, a smelly, sweet fruit with spiky outsides, or extra-spicy papaya salad. We wanted all the things that mothers did not want their children to eat. Sweet could cause a cough; spicy could cause a stomachache; both could kill.

Some of the bigger cousins climbed high up in the trees to eat the food they weren't supposed to. Among the leaves, they sat on the thick branches, little girls with their polyester skirts carefully clasped between bony knees, licking the juices off their fingers, wary of the adults (and younger children like me) on the ground below them. The rice noodle had fish in it, and the fish smelled a little. One of the girls had gotten a baht, a Thai quarter, from her mother to buy the dish; they were all sharing. But the fish could be rotten even if it tasted good. If a mother found out, if a grandma came by, it would surely be a big deal: Shhhhh. You are too loud. My hand smells. What am I going to do? Pee on it. That will get the smell out? It is the only way. I saw a Thai man wash his hands with dog pee after touching the dark liquid from the engine of his car. He smelled it before and he made a face. He smelled it after and he nodded. The girl who witnessed the cure shrugs nonchalantly. The girl with the smelly hands, her eyes grow big and somber, and she nods gravely. O.K., you pee and I wash my hands. Whispers: Later.

In the summers the land dried up. The grass on the hills turned yellow and began to die.

If I close my eyes hard, twenty years after living in Ban Vinai Refugee Camp, I see the way the camp was. I know that it no longer exists. Everything was left to ruin in 1995 when the camp closed. The shacks were taken apart, and the signs of people having lived there, wiped away by people, by nature, by time. The people that were buried in the place I was born: what has happened to their graves, unmarked even then, just little mounds across the hills?

I imagine bodies turning to dust. I imagine bodies, looking as they were in life, different people's faces and forms, walking about the place where they had lived, wondering where those they love have gone. Their spirits are like the wind blowing through the grass, grass that was green at the bottom but lighter up near the top, translucent grass tips that appeared pink in the late afternoon light. Sometimes, as I go through the motions of my life, I come across the smell of grass and water and I travel back to Ban Vinai Refugee Camp. It would be nice to find the scent in a bottle of shampoo or conditioner, in perfume—something that I could uncork and take inside of me, borrow forever. Ban Vinai Refugee Camp was the last place where my family was together, my mother and father and Dawb, my grandmother, my aunts and uncles, my cousins, and me.

In 1987, I turned six. I knew that the world I had been born into was not the entire world. Even as a child I understood that there were places I could not venture to despite the vast distances I believed my quick feet could travel. Even so, I did not know well the full life of the camp. It is easy for me to recall only the happy times: the tall grass waving on the hills; me riding on the back of a wide, brown buffalo, almost toppling into a rushing stream, saved by an older cousin; me standing on tiptoes to peek at a litter of puppies, their eyes still closed, their heads searching, disoriented by the light of my bright world.

A world that I would learn was seeped with the blood of the Hmong. A man I would come to respect would speak of memories he carried from this place I called home. Boys, women, and girls sneaked out of the camp to forage for food. The rations were insufficient. Thai men would come. The boys would run. The girls and the women, clutching their sarong skirts in their trembling hands, tried to escape. Futile efforts before the heavy tread of rubber boots. On a cliff, the boys waited for the lost ones, little girls and tired women, walking out of the groves of trees, blood seeping in between legs, some crawling along the ground. Threads torn, skin broken, eyes wild and empty. Hmong men were beaten. Hmong blood seeped into the Thai earth, drops and streams to be washed by the monsoon rains that fell each year.

I remember the routines of daily living within the arms of those who held me safe. I know the cement well that my family and our entire side of the camp bathed around, the cracks in the platform around the well. I had to stand carefully so that my feet would not touch the muddy, black dirt, which was always waiting to take the clean away. The clunk of the metal pail against the hard wall as it was pulled up from the dark bottom of the well. How I marveled and delighted at the cool shimmer of liquid from a place where dragons might dwell—I lived in a world where dragons waited in splendor for naughty little girls who reached too far into bodies of water.

I see my grandma's wide waist with various dangling keys. I never asked what the keys were for, which magic doors they could open, what secrets they held safe. I hear her walking into the compound, a patch of ground where bamboo houses with corrugated aluminum roofs stood surrounded by pieces of wood, pieces of metal, tied together to give us children a sense of having some area to play on. I hear the slap of Grandma's flip-flops on the beaten ground, the sound of keys jingling with her slightly lopsided steps, resonating always in some wind.

Ban Vinai Refugee Camp was located in what is said to be the poorest region in Thailand. In the old family pictures, there are hills in the background, and then the connected sleeping rooms and kitchens with their metallic roofs, baking in the sun. The dust covered everything: old bins, large and discarded metal cans, piles of rocks where children played. The lush green that I remember only happened after the monsoons, a month or two in a year of dry heat, weak grassland dying without water.

It was a place where death cried in familiar voices. I can still hear the wailing coming past our rickety gates, as mothers and fathers, brothers and sisters, lamented for the person they loved, lying heavy and stiff in the clothes of the dead, being carried someplace on the surrounding hillside, to be buried in graves unmarked, mounds of earth covered by a few toppled stones.

When I was a child my biggest fear was the cries for the dead. The echoes of despair would come and I would start running, my feet slipping in my plastic boots, to the nearest adult who I was sure loved me. I would bury my face in a warm lap, put my hands over my ears, and try to block out the sounds. But the weight of their voices resound in my memory sometimes—soundtracks that can't be erased. It begins with the beat of the human heart mirrored by the deepening *pom, pom, pom, pom* of the drums of the dead. Then enters the human voices, sounds that come from deep inside stomachs, hollow and windy, loud over the silence of covered bodies. The beating of my heart, the drums, the voices collide, and together we mourn, we fear, we miss in a way that won't disappear, the people who once were alive: "Why are you dying here? In this place where we cannot stay. Why are you dying here? This is not your home."

People were dying because of illness and disease. People were also dying because of suicide, especially during the New Year's celebrations, perhaps because that was a time for new beginnings; the Hmong had learned that death marked an opening to new lives. The Hmong were people who had just escaped death; we were fenced in and the thoughts of the adults could only run out to the past. There was no work to do in the present, no land to wander over, nowhere to run. We were stuck in a country that did not want us. There was dysentery from the bad food and water. There were nightmares that drove men and women mad. The adults around me woke up looking tired, sat on the shaky bamboo patio, and spoke to each other of long dreams where dead people came back to life and the schoolhouses and homes destroyed by the bombs looked as they did before. They spoke of dreams that tried to pull them back to Laos. There was so much grief for those who had died in the war, and for those dying in the camp. When the talk about death came, all the children grew quiet.

The adults and the older children who understood the context of our stay knew that Ban Vinai Refugee Camp was not home and so they could not settle into it like a home. There were Thai men in uniforms with guns that surrounded us. Hmong men and women were beaten, raped, and killed when they ventured too far from the safety of their families and friends. People stayed close together because they were scared. A child could not even trust food or water. I could only drink rainwater from the clay barrels after my mother, my father, my grandmother, or another person I knew had boiled it. Being sick was a horrible way to live because it meant that death was close by. There was the clinic, with its gray cement walls and bathrooms in a line, but more dead people came out of that door than any other building in the camp. I heard adults talking: this person is sick. And then the cries of death would come, rising and falling, as the stiff bodies were carried off into the hills.

In addition to the camp clinic, there were a few other important and serious buildings. One of them was a school. At six, I was not yet going to school. I could not reach my right hand over my head to touch my left ear, so I did not qualify. While Dawb and the rest of my older cousins went to school, the cousins my age and I sat around looking at the little babies sitting near their mothers. For me, the time moved slowly.

It felt like there was a magical wall that allowed us to see other people passing in and out of the camp, but we could not cross it ourselves. We could feel the air moving all around us, but we were heavier than air. We could only wish we had the freedom of air. If we did, the wind could blow us to our homes in the mountains of Laos—at least that is what the older people in my family yearned for. I was different from the adults. I believed I was as light as air.

One windy day, I held on to the end of an umbrella, the wind blew, and I was lifted off the ground. In that moment, with my feet on air, I was terrified: what if I flew far away from Ban Vinai Refugee Camp? The seconds stretched long. My fear did not come out of my mouth until the umbrella flew from my hands and

I fell back to earth. After that I learned how to miss the ground as if it were a person whose lap I had taken for granted.

"I love the ground," I would say.

"Why?" Dawb wanted to know.

"Because it loves me."

"It doesn't love me."

The ground didn't love Dawb. She could not walk straight, since her legs were not equal in strength. Everywhere she went, she limped her way there. Whenever there was a wall close to where she stood, she placed a small, dirty hand on it for support.

Mean children yelled things at her. They called her a cripple. But she refused to stop running for them. She always wanted to play. Even when kids were mean, she refused to tell our mother and father, and told me not to tell them either. What could they do? When Dawb ran, my parents were both stuck in place. Every time they saw her struggling after the other cousins on some adventure, they looked down at their feet, helpless but unwilling to stand still; they shuffled in place. I saw this and I knew that the ground did not love everyone.

Life in Ban Vinai Refugee Camp was hard for people who saw it clearly, those who remembered the freedom of place, and those who wanted to establish a life. But until I was six years old, it was my home. My grandmother was the only other person who shared fond memories of the camp with me. For us, in many ways, the life we had in the camp was ideal. We were surrounded by people who loved us.

My cousins ran around the compound, yelling and singing and arguing. My older cousins ran around playing Vietnamese and Hmong. Then we had believed that the enemies and killers were Vietnamese. We did not know of the Lao and Hmong communist soldiers. We played a simple game. When a Vietnamese found a Hmong and took a shot, the Hmong person would fall to the ground. Sometimes, a relative Hmong would run past a fallen Hmong and stop to lament, just like the adults: "Get up. Why have you fallen? Get up and we will run away together." Of course, like in the war, there was no running for fallen bodies. In the end, if you were fast and you left everyone else behind, if you stopped yelling to the other Hmong people: "Run, they are coming! Run, they are coming!"—if you just looked behind yourself and ran as fast as you could, if you were lucky, you escaped, and you got to live in a refugee camp. I knew the game by heart, but I have no memories of playing it until we came to America.

I do not remember jumping across plastic ropes or tossing rocks on the ground with the other girls. Did I? I see me, loved by the older cousins, the aunts and uncles, protected and approved. I see my grandmother busy with her little "shop," a stand where she sold yams and herbal medicines, and for a short time, rice noodles with stewed pork (only she would put in too much meat and never made any money, so she stopped). I used to ask her for money.

"Grandma, can I have a baht?" My eyes looked up at her from under the straight bangs that my father carefully trimmed. I extended my hands in front of me, in the fashion of begging. I had seen the passing monks in saffron robes do this when they passed through the camp.

"Go to your mother," she would say, looking down at me.

I shook my head, "My mother does not have any money."

Grandma would look at me sternly, but her hands would already be feeling around for the zipper to the cloth bag that she tied around her heavy waist to hold her important refugee papers and money. I would hear the jingle of coins. She would take out a Thai baht, the size of an American quarter. It felt heavy in my outstretched hands.

Grandma enjoyed the time in Thailand. Her sons were poor because there was no way for them to work. But she did not mind their poverty because her family was together and alive. The war was in the past, and for her that was enough to make the future a busy one, filled with living. Grandma's little stand was financed through the generosity of her two daughters, both of whom had escaped from Laos with their husbands much earlier than my family had. One had gone to California and the other to France. My family knew that if a family really wanted to, they could go and register to get out of Ban Vinai Refugee camp and go to new countries like France, Australia, and America. But she refused to let any of her sons register to get out of the camp. She said that she was old and that she wanted to see them together for as long as she could.

Although my grandma had always looked like an old person to me, in the camp, she never rested like one. She was always busy selling her herbal remedies because health care was bad in the camp and people were scared of Western medicine. Because Grandma was the type of woman who looked like she knew things, and did, people came to her for medicinal remedies frequently. Once they heard about her talent for healing, even the Thai men, the ones who wore guns and kept us in place, came to her, mostly for concoctions to nurse their sexually transmitted diseases. She was the only person whom I knew who could safely venture out of the camp under the supervision of armed guards. They allowed her trips to the hillsides to find herbs because they wanted her cures. My older cousins talked sometimes of accompanying her on these trips. I was too young to go along.

There were no paths beyond the roads. The Thai men would drop the old woman and her troop of excited teenagers off at the edge of a hill, wait for them to get out from the back of the dirty truck, and then light up cigarettes, talking and waiting. Grandma would lead them, her ragtag band of overly excited assistants, walking slowly first. Her grandchildren followed close by, mirroring her steps in the tall grass, each with a bag of some kind in hand: old distribution rice bags, random plastic bags—white, red, or black were common colors. It was a great adventure. Going beyond the camp lines was not something Hmong people did casually or easily.

Grandma made paths of pushed-aside brush and grass for them to walk on. She would see a green sprout and kneel down heavily to examine it. In her head there was an assortment of images: green plants, brown trees, little nuts, hard pebbles, and their various healing abilities. Her mother's sister had been a respected healer in Laos; Grandma had inherited her skills and as a little girl learned from her of the various properties of wild mountain plants. She would look at the plant, kneel down beside it, reach out to touch its texture with confidence, her fingers gentle. Yes, this is one, she would say. The various cousins would stoop beside her and ask questions: What is it good for? How should we pick it? Pull the thing out? But what if the hills run out? These are all questions that I would have asked if I could have gone along with her.

I have a memory of being sick and of my grandma curing me with a shaman's walk in the dawn of a misty morning. I felt like I had to pee all the time. I would go and I would want to go again and again. Even when there was nothing to pee, the motions of peeing would come to me, low in my belly. The toilets were holes in the ground; they smelled bad; they were dark; and they felt much too far for me to walk to during the emergencies. At night, with a flashlight pointed at the star-filled sky, my father would stand close by and allow me to pee at the base of the tall trees in the compound. I thought it was funny because it was where I saw the dogs pee during the day.

I had lost my baby chubbiness and become a skinny kid. I had small, small bones. Anybody could hold my wrist and I would not be able to struggle free no matter which way I pulled and tugged and jerked. My mother and father were worried about my constant need to pee. Grandma, too, was worried. She decided she would do a special ceremony for me.

She had carried her shaman's tools with her from Laos. She had her split cow horn in one hand, and in the other she held the big circle of special coins that jangled when she walked. On her face there was a piece of red cloth that covered her eyes and parts of her nose. I don't know how she knew where to walk or step around the bigger rocks in our way. She was looking into the spirit world, lost in spiritual chant. I walked closely in her wake. I couldn't go to the spirit world with her soul, but I did not want to lose sight of her body. I looked at her colorful shirt and the bump of her money bag underneath the fabric, the black Hmong pants, wide legged and short about her ankles. She wore her blue flip-flops. With a bowl of rice, an egg, and two sticks of incense in my hands, I walked carefully behind my grandmother.

Together, Grandma and I went to all the neighboring houses to ask for hospitality and care for my sick spirit. I was a little embarrassed because in my head the problem was not a real sickness. I was a shy girl to begin with, but I followed her, that dawn, before the sun was up, in my gold plastic boots that stuck to my feet when I walked, and the red shirt with white puffy sleeves, the matching red shorts that fell down to my knees. I was sleepy, but I remember feeling lucky to be in her presence. My grandma was in the spirit world fighting for my spirit to come back. My body was happy to be walking in the heavy fog, and my spirit was, too, because peeing became a normal occurrence again after our walk together in the white mist, from one side of the camp to the other, carefully walking from one stone to the next, crossing the stream of diluted feces and urine that divided the halves of the camp.

Like so many other children, in other parts of the world, in a time of nothing, we heard stories of what was before. There were always people to tell me stories in the camp. Through them, I could go places that I had never been, to worlds that were very different from the camp. I learned about lands and creatures that did not live in my world.

In Ban Vinai Refugee Camp, I discovered the shapes of stories, how to remember them, and how to tell them. It was there that I learned about the striped tiger. One of my favorite stories is the one about Yer, a beautiful Hmong girl. All the adults in my family could tell the story very well; I heard it so often, I learned to tell it too:

Long ago, in Laos, there lived a beautiful girl named Yer. She had long, flowing black hair. She wore formal Hmong dress, red and green sashes to narrow her waist, a glittering silver necklace that draped her chest, and a turban of deep, dark purple to twine around her thick hair and hold it in place, so that her beautiful face was easy to see. She could have had any of the eligible young men in the small village where she lived with her parents. In fact, the most sought-after man in the village longed desperately for her affections. Surrounding their village was the vast dark jungle. Inside it there lived a hunter—hungry and lean and feared—the striped tiger. One day Yer went to fetch water from a small mountain stream. She did not see the tiger lurking in the bamboo grove by the stream's edge. But the tiger saw her.

She heard a noise. She looked behind her—only the dense foliage of the jungle. She turned her attention back to the water. Hands grabbed her. (Tigers have hands in stories; they can walk like people and talk like people, and they can do anything that we can and many things we cannot; they can own real magic.) She was full of fear; she cried. She screamed for help, and then she started begging. But she was on the tiger's back, and he was flying through the jungle. He took her high up to a cave. There, his family of tigers waited for her hungrily. They did not know that their strongest one had fallen in love. Yer cried. They came close to sniff her flesh. She cringed in fear. He growled, "Leave her alone. If you are hungry, go eat outside." He looked at her from the corner, and he was as big as a small hut, and she could only shake her head in fear and denial. It was like a nightmare; his eyes glittered from the dark of his corner.

The days passed slowly. He brought her fresh meat. She refused to eat. He made a fire. She cooked. He never allowed her to see him take his meals. His family hungered for her, but he kept them away. He would allow her to go stand at the mouth of the cave and look down at the trees. She missed her home. She worried over her parents like a good daughter. But in time, her tears stopped falling, and without speaking, she came to understand that the tiger cared for her in a way that was fiercer than a human. She took up leaf blowing, holding up a folded leaf to her lips and blowing out sweet songs that questioned her loneliness and called for love.

In the village, the people knew Yer had been abducted; it could be no other than the tiger. Her admirers felt fear, and they looked at the other village girls for the first time. Only the most sought-after young man was brave enough and took his bow and a knife. He went to the house of Yer's mother and father and told them, "I will bring her back to be my wife." They cried tears of hope. They packed him a bamboo canister of rice and some dried beef and sent him on his way.

It took him many months to reach the lair of the tiger. He found it by following the sweet notes of a wind-blown song. He hid behind a big boulder and saw her, her clothes turned to rags, her hair falling wildly about her shoulders, gnawing on a piece of bone. He could not believe his eyes. Had this been the most beautiful Hmong girl in their village? And then she looked up and he saw that it was her and that her beauty had not diminished in the care of the tiger. In fact, a light seemed to shine from her; the cave was warmed by her radiance. He could not contain his hands. He threw a small rock at her, and Yer saw him. It seemed like the distance between them was very vast. For a moment, there was no recognition in her eyes, and then fear took root.

He did not know that her fear was not for him. He did not know that in the time since her capture, Yer had fallen in love. He could not know that in her stomach she carried three tiger children. All he saw was the beauty she had been and the beautiful woman that she was, and he felt himself to be a man, and the tiger only a tiger. He took out his arrow, filled with conviction, and shot it into the stones above the cave. Yer shrieked for the tiger. She jumped out of the way of the falling stones. The boulders tumbled, covering the entrance to the cave. The man quickly went to fetch Yer. She yelled for the tiger; in the cave, he growled for her. The earth rumbled like thunder was underneath the ground. The young man, in haste, took the screaming woman over his shoulder, and he ran. Her hands reached behind his back, trying to crawl through air, through boulders, to the one who loved her best, but it was no use.

When they got to the little village, the people crowded around her. Her mother and father cried; they were so happy that this brave young man had rescued their daughter. Her old admirers stood far away from her, looking at the long, tangled hair. Yer was embarrassed and could only look down at her feet. The brave young man looked at the woman, and he saw her as she had been, as she could be again: a good human wife. He said, "Don't be embarrassed and sad—you are saved now and you will become my wife."

Yer's tangled hair was combed, and she was dressed in new clothes for her marriage to the man who had saved her from being a tiger's wife. As the days passed, she got used to the life of being married to a man, the sound of human voices comforted her, and she learned to eat with a spoon. Her stomach got round. At first she did not know why so she tried to hide it beneath the red and green sashes at her waist. One day, while her human husband was out in the fields, Yer felt her stomach hurting. She ran to the grain shed, and there she gave birth to three little tigers. She was scared of them, so she moved to the corner and looked at them. They were only babies and they could not see the world yet. They waved their little paws out for their mother. For her. Slowly, she approached them. She touched them and they were soft. They mewed in hunger. She sat with them, and she gave them her breast, one at a time. She named them: Yellow, Black, and Stripe.

Each day Yer told her human husband that she would follow him to the garden. She had a few chores to do yet about the house. The days went by and he started getting suspicious. One day, he set out as he did every other day. She saw him walking the path to the garden, and she raced out to the grain shed to feed her babies. She was busy feeding them, holding each tiger baby to her chest. She did not notice the eyes peeking through the slits in the woven bamboo walls. "My babies, Yellow, Black, and Stripe, you must be hungry today," she crooned.

The next day, her human husband told Yer that he was not feeling well. He said for her to go to the garden by herself. He would stay home, and later, if he could get up, he would cook dinner for her. She did not know what to do, so she took her bamboo basket and started for the garden, worrying about her babies. He waited until her footfalls disappeared, then he got up, walked to the wall, and took down his sharpest knife. He walked quickly into the grain shed. Yellow, Black, and Stripe, thinking that it was their mother, started mewing for her. He slit their throats, one at a time.

He took their bodies back into the house. He boiled water and he put the little bodies in the water so that he could remove their furs. He used his knife to scrape them carefully. He chopped up the little bodies, and he steamed them with green onion and chili peppers. He tasted the broth and he found it delicious.

When Yer came home dinner was on the table. "Where did you get the meat?" she asked him. He said, "I felt better after you left so I went hunting." She did not ask any more questions, just set down her basket and joined him at their little table, low to the ground. Together, they feasted on her little tiger babies.

The next morning, he got up as usual and without her telling him, he said, "Come to the garden after you finish your chores." She thought how curious, but she said, "I will follow you as soon as my chores are done." After he had walked the path to the garden, she ran out to the grain shed. She did not hear the mewing of her babies so she hesitated at the door. She opened it slowly. He had not cleaned up the blood. When she saw the dried red stains, she knew. "My babies, Yellow, Black, and Stripe," she cried and cried and cried.

The end.

The story always made me quiet. I thought about the tiger, sorrowful and alone, and how he must have snarled and cried for Yer in a cave blocked by boulders. I thought Yer was a weak woman whose heart could be torn and then mended by the love of a man who ate her children. The story was sad to me—the part about how the tiger children cried out for their mother when the cold steel of her human husband sliced through their necks made me long for my own mother. Though I never told my grandma or anyone else, I felt bad for the tiger husband. Yes, he had kidnapped her, taken her far away and slowly made her need only him for food, for water, for talk, and had made her, because she was alone, fall in love with him. Still, to be a ferocious tiger with a raging heart caught in a cave blocked by boulders was too mean. Why had her human husband not killed the tiger to end his misery? I comforted myself by believing that the tiger could never die, even in a cave; he would stay alive because he was strong.

"Grandma, the tiger is a very strong animal, right?"

"Tigers are vicious animals."

"Are there any tigers here in Thailand?"

"Yes, but they are in the jungles. They cannot get into Ban Vinai Refugee Camp."

Not very many things could get to us in Ban Vinai Refugee Camp. Maybe this is why in my memories of the camp, it is just dust and flip-flops for people with rough feet and plastic boots for people with newer feet like my own. It is people I love living around me. The world of our lives then was contained in a way that life would never be again.

CHAPTER 5
THE SECOND LEAVING

Grandma was angry. My father wanted to leave for America.

It was clear that Thailand held no future for the refugees of Laos. Ban Vinai Refugee Camp did not even have designated burial grounds for the deaths of the camp, no set of provisions to mark of the ends of lives or to help the beginnings of them. In 1982, Uncle Nhia, my father's oldest brother, left for America with his family. He was the oldest and it was the proper thing to do. He would go and explore this new land first, discover its conditions, and try out a life. Grandma lamented his leaving. After he left, she worked even harder to hold her other sons together. She reminded them regularly of how much her children meant to her and how she had suffered their separation in the jungle. My father was her youngest, her baby, and she worried about him the most.

At first, she had tried to reason with him. She used his given name. She said, "Bee, you cannot leave the camp, because I am your mother and I do not want to go to a new land where they will cut into my body when I die. Bee, you cannot leave the camp, because when you are sick and away from me I will not be able to do anything. Bee, you cannot leave the camp, because in America you must work, and how will you work when you do not know the words they speak to you? Bee, you cannot leave the camp, because in America a woman controls a man, and I do not want to see my son be the slave of a woman. Bee, you cannot leave the camp, because I do not want to go to a new world so far away. I cannot start a new life. I would not know how. I would just wait to die. When I die, my spirit would not be able to find its way across the ocean, to Thailand, to Laos, to the place underneath the platform of the bed, in my old house, where the shirt that carried me into the world was buried."

My father, in an exasperated voice that grown men can use only with their mothers, responded to her pleas with rational arguments: "Mother, there is no life here for me or anyone else. The Thai people do not want us here. Mother, we have no country to go back to. Mother, you gave birth to me. You wanted to give me a chance at life. That life was ruined by the war. Now I have two girls. What would happen to me in America is not as important as what would happen to my girls here. You love me. I love my daughters as you love me, Mother."

Grandma told my father about the years in the war and the years after the Americans left, when they were in the jungle. She reminded him, like poor mothers the world over, of how she had raised him. She told him that my grandfather had died, leaving him when he was only two years old. She told him that all her life she had been an orphan, that all the people she had loved had left her, that she always thought someday, when she left the world of the living behind, her children would not be alone because they would have each other. She told him how much a mother loved her children; how she, a mere woman, had always worked hard to keep them together; how it had always been this thought of holding her children together that kept her alive. For my father or any of her sons to leave her, she said, was to tell her that her life had been useless. She said she would rather die.

Grandma's heart hurt. She could not watch him walk away from her, not because of death or illness, but because he yearned for a life that she could not help him make. She became tired and took long walks around the camp, caught between the leaving of her child and the meaning of her life. For my grandmother, his leaving the family unit would be her defeat—it was what she had spent so much of her life keeping intact. It occurred to her that safety in the camp was an illusion and that life in the camp froze the Hmong as prisoners of time. This realization made her desolate. My father and my uncles saw how she suffered, the silent walks that she took, and they promised her that they would not leave Ban Vinai Refugee Camp. They would rather live in captivity than live without her happiness.

By 1987 my father could wait no longer. There was talk that the Thai officials were closing the camp down. Those who remained would be sent back to Laos, a place that meant death. Even after all the years, there were reports from Hmong people that soldiers were still chasing helpless families in the jungles, seeking retribution for a war that had been declared over in 1973. In addition, there was the issue of children. My mother and father had been married for nearly a decade, but there were no boys yet. The pressure for him to marry another wife was mounting from all his brothers and his mother, too. They all said that my mother could not give him sons; he was still handsome; he could marry another and love my mother just the same. We were only girls, Dawb and I. What would happen to him when he died? What would happen to my mother? As girls, we could not perform the ceremonial rituals to carry my mother and father's spirits back to the land of the ancestors.

These things were said out of love for him. He was a Hmong man and he believed he would die a Hmong death; he did not know what would happen to his spirit after his death. He had

chosen to marry my mother, and he would not go back on his words by marrying another. He did not know what to do, so he would put me up on his shoulders, and we would walk around the camp. He told me stories about going to school in America. He wanted me to become an educated person.

"What is an educated person?"

"Someone who goes to school."

"Is Dawb an educated person?"

"Not yet. Maybe one day both Dawb and you will become such persons in America."

I held tightly to my father's hair and nodded as he spoke. I had never been to school. I did not know what he was talking about. He would continue talking, saying that maybe I would have brothers in America, too. He said that there were good doctors there. I had never had brothers. I could not see any good changes that a boy would bring to my life. Still, if my father wanted one so badly, fine.

I was too young to grasp the position that my mother was in. I knew only how hard she tried to give my father sons. There had been six miscarriages, babies who fell from the clouds too early to come to earth, babies who were formed enough for the adults to know that they were sons, but who were small and blue and dead. Some visited our lives when I was too young to remember. Two or three live in my memories:

Dark nights. Sleeping soundly. Waking up to adults talking loudly. Footsteps running. Getting picked up in the arms of aunts and uncles, firm hands trying to push my head toward their chests. Red on the blankets that we slept on. Where is my mother? Where is my father? I hold on to the person who is holding me. Hurried voices: Where is the water wagon? Too much blood. She is unconscious. She is dying. We heard Bee. We came here. Again? Yes, again. In the light of the kerosene lamp, I make out the limp figure of my mother in my father's arms. No one ever explained what was happening. I knew she was trying to give him sons.

My mother was a beautiful woman, although I do not remember when I came to know this. All the miscarriages made her thin and pale. She had smooth skin and black hair, brown eyes, and an infrequent smile that revealed slightly overlapped teeth. She liked to dress well—in the camp she did as best she could in the poverty that we lived in. Her long hair was usually pulled back cleanly from her face. Her colorful Thai sarongs were secured around her small waist with a metal belt bought from the camp market. She wore slip-on plastic shoes with small heels. She washed with green Parrot soap that smelled like Irish Spring with lots of flowers. But I have no memories of my mother smiling in Ban Vinai Refugee Camp—only of the gentle way she took care of Dawb and me.

While my mother took care of my father's daughters and tried to give him sons, he had nightmares about a life with only Dawb and me. One night, I woke up suddenly. In the dark, I felt for the warmth of my mother. The blanket was warm but she was not there. When my eyes adjusted, I made out the shapes of my mother and father at the foot of the platform we used for a bed. There was moonlight coming through the slits in the bamboo walls. I could hear sounds coming from my father, filling the room. His breathing was fast, as if he was gulping for air. Broken noises, deep like his voice, but without the same control. It is my first memory of knowing that fathers cry.

"Bee, what is wrong? A bad dream? Shhhhhh. The children will hear you. They will be scared."

Forced silence. A breath escaped and then another. He tried to whisper, but his voice was too rough. "It is many years from now. We are in America. The girls are grown and married. You and I— we are alone. First, you died. I did not live long without you. One day, I died in a silent house. There was nowhere to go. You were waiting for me. We wandered around, you and I. We walked in big American cities with loud cars and bright lights. Our spirits walked in lonely circles. How would we ever get back to the hills of Laos, the land of the ancestors?"

His voice, exhausted, tried to find steadiness in the night air. I have no memories of my mother's response. Perhaps she said nothing. What could she have said? Hmong tradition dictated that only a son could find the guides who would lead the spirits of his mother or father to the land of the ancestors. I blinked at the dark, and I made my body very still. I was too young to understand the idea of my mother and father dying. But I loved them enough to feel their fear. I liked being a girl. I could not become a boy.

I do not know who first told my father to marry another wife. Grandma had always felt bad that she was poor and did not have the money to pay my mother's bride price in the jungle of Laos during the war. She was sorry that her youngest son had had to borrow from his older brothers in order to marry. In Thailand, Grandma saved money from her noodle stand and her sale of herbs and medicines; she was determined to pay the second time— anything so that one day, when she was gone, and when he was an old man, my father would not cry because he had no sons. To her, the fact that my father had never known his father was already an incredible sadness that her love, no matter how much, could never make up for. Together, my grandma and my uncles pushed my father toward other women in the camp. It was not uncommon. No one would say he was a bad man. No one questioned the fact that he loved my mother or his girls. It was necessary, my father's family said. In Thailand, my father tried to fall in love again.

He never told my mother where he was taking me; it would have made her angry. My mother was not a woman to share the love of a man. My father told my mother not to try to have sons anymore. On the days that she knelt by the side of the dirt road, covered in dust, selling bunches of green onion and cilantro that she planted in a little plot of land behind the toilets, the rice cakes that she woke up at dawn to steam on the black iron of our fire ring—while she tried to find the money to keep her two daughters healthy, my father took me on a borrowed motorcycle to see the women on the other side of the camp.

My mother is not a stupid woman. She knew every article of his clothing, what he wore each day, the good shirt and the good pants, the clothes that were left in a neat pile for her to wash every day. Before setting out, he would wet his plastic comb in the jar of water by the side of the door, water that he carried from the well in two buckets tied on either end on a bamboo pole every evening, and brush my hair to the side of my face. He brushed my hair, let the fine plastic of the bamboo comb sift through my hair just as he had brushed his own. His hands were not gentle. Tears came to my eyes.

The women he visited always seemed to me to be too big and too loud. They laughed too hard. They gushed over me, and they said, "She is so beautiful. If we marry, will our children be as beautiful?" I hated that the most. They were not my mother. They could never have children like me. They could all marry my father, have hundreds of sons, and the sons would be too big and too loud and laugh too hard and gush too much, and they could never be like me. I sat in his lap and I looked at the women sitting around in groups with their embroidery in their laps. I would twist around in his arms, turn my head up and look at my father. He would smile at me and hold my hands in his, reassuring me that we would go home soon. I would blow air into my cheeks, make my eyes round, and pull at my ears with my hands. I made faces at my father. The women all laughed in chorus. The faces were not for them. If my mother had been there, she would not have smiled; she would have said: "Do not do that. You look like a naughty little monkey. Be a good girl." Her brows would have pushed together, and she would look like a headache was coming.

People knew that my father was a married man. They knew that I was his youngest daughter. Maybe they even knew that Dawb was in school and that that was why she did not go see the women with my father. Still, there were few men in the camp because two-thirds of the Hmong men had died in the war and the years after it. Some of the women were orphans looking for love and a sense of belonging. My father was a handsome man. He was not thin like many of the men in the camp; he had broad shoulders and strong bones in his face. He had high cheekbones, a set of fine, white teeth that he showed frequently, a prominent jaw, and dark, well-curved eyebrows. His eyes tilted a little at the corners. He had a head of coarse black hair that he parted to the side with water, but when the water dried, it sprung up, away from his face. His voice was admired by many for its evenness, its depth, and its strength. He sang the traditional song poetry well. He was young, and it didn't matter that he already had a wife and two girls—the lonely women in the camp were still willing to become his second wife.

Only he was not looking seriously. Each time he went to see the women, he took me along and I made monkey faces at him and he would laugh down at me, not at the women. He would come home to my mother and carry the water from the well and sit on the patio thinking. He never made up his heart to marry another woman or to fall in love again. Still, he was very worried about not having any sons. My mother was, too. She said she would leave him if he married another. She told him that during their separation in the jungle, she had learned how much she missed him, but she had also learned how to survive without him. She told him that if he took a second wife, she would not die, that while she understood his need for sons, she hoped he would understand her reason for leaving.

I knew that they loved each other. I knew that they loved us. And yet, I wondered if together, quietly, late at night, when everyone was sleeping, they dreamed together of having sons. I hoped that if they did, they would also look at Dawb and me sleeping and feel happy that they had us, too. We were good girls. I always tried to be.

I come from a family that believes profoundly in the strength of numbers. The adults talked about how they had survived the war in Laos only because there were so many of them; there were seven brothers who could help each other. They said that during the saddest times in a life, when the meaning of staying alive is all confused, the only way to survive is to hold on to each other. The only way to get through life is to have a big team on your side. The strongest thing that can hold people together is blood. They were all my grandma's children and they believed the same thing she did: the more of them there were, the stronger their hold on life— the more sons, the stronger their hold to the earth.

There were only four of us in Thailand, and that was sad for the adults. We have pictures from that time, a few with my sister and me standing in between my mother and father. Some with my father kneeling close to the ground, his arms around his girls, with my mother standing behind him, her hands on his shoulders. We do not smile in the photographs. The faces of my sister and I show serious regard for the camera. There is one photograph where I am standing in front of my parents with a stick in my hand, my head tilted to the side, and my tongue is sticking out between small lips. My favorite photos are the ones where we are in the trees, my father and Dawb or, best of all, my father and me. It was his idea. I don't remember how he got us up so high into the branches of the trees, especially with his slippery dress shoes on. I remember being in his arms, at the very tops of the trees, the leaves only to

my chest, looking down, my arms around his neck, a small knot of
nervousness in my stomach, a giant welling of happiness at the
great height from which I could look at the world. He always said:
"Your father is holding you up to see the world."

My mother stood below with the camera (always borrowed),
worried, calling for us to get down quickly. Maybe she was worried because there were only four of us, and so to lose even one
would be too much. To me, four was a fine number, enough to fill
up a whole photograph, a moment, a life.

The life we shared changed fundamentally in 1987. We were
leaving Thailand. It was something that my grandmother and I
did not understand then. Grandma only knew that she loved her
children and that her youngest son was going to leave for America
with her two granddaughters. All I knew was that I was leaving
my grandmother crying.

We were on the orange bus. Dawb looked around the bus and
her face did not smile or frown. She told me that she was trying

to remember everything. She said that we would be all right in America because we had my mother and father to take care of us. I nodded and tried to remember, too. My father worried his thumbs in his lap. My mother looked at the people, and she looked ahead at the road out of Ban Vinai Refugee Camp.

All my aunts and uncles knew that the Hmong people from Laos would have to leave Thailand eventually. They had all registered to leave the camp for America. My family was one of the first in our larger family. The adults knew that their hearts may miss Laos but their children had futures across the ocean. Grandma would come to America with Uncle Hue and his family. But on the day of our departure, she did not believe that she would ever see us again.

People were crying all around me. I sat very still on the sticky seat of the big orange bus. Grown-ups pushed themselves tight against the open windows, trying to reach down, to hold the hands of friends and family. Sounds of sniffling came from the men who tried to sit or stand tall.

Before my father lifted me onto the bus, my grandma had smoothed my hair away from my face with both hands; she had ruffled my bangs, and said, "Little one, you are going far away from Grandma."

She looked down at me and she swallowed a few times. Perhaps there were words that she wanted to say but could not.

She took a deep breath, "Be good and listen to your mother and father."

In a voice that tried to be strong, she said, "Grandma has asked all the spirits of the land to protect you. Do not be scared in the new land."

Tears streamed in wet lines down the wrinkled skin of her face before she turned away. I looked at her earlobes, the broken one, knowing I wouldn't remember which side it was on. I saw her bottom lip trembling. Her one tooth was visible. I bit my bottom lip so that it would hold strong.

On the bus, I sat looking at the people shifting around the seats and the aisles, jostling each other to get to the open windows. The voices rose in sing-song motion.

A woman cried out, "Mother, we part here. If we do not have the good fortune of meeting again in this life, I will be your daughter again in the next life."

A cacophony of words, of partings without the one word: good-bye.

Instead, they said: "We will meet again. We will meet again. We will meet again, if not in this life, then surely the next."

I could tell my father was agitated because his thumbs were moving on one another in his lap. My mother was calm. Her hair was clipped back from her face. She was looking ahead, ready for the trip to America to begin.

The engine of the bus gurgled into life. The cries of the men and women rose around me. My mother reached her hand out the window to an aunt.

My father said, "We will meet each other again, Mother."

I sat silently, my legs dangling off the ground. We were all wearing our best clothes. I had on my pale yellow pants with the creases down the center of each leg. My white shirt had puffy sleeves and small pink flowers on the front; there was a string that tied in the back. In my lap, I held my white and pink hat with yellow flowers. I felt the stiff lace around the brim of the hat with my fingers. When the bus started to move, heat erupted inside of me, but there were no tears.

CHAPTER 6
PHANAT NIKHOM TRANSITION CAMP
TO AMERICA*

The rice paddies stretched away on both sides of the orange bus, fields of green met the blue sky, thin lines of eucalyptus trees divided the paddies, thatched-roof field houses stood on stilts in the far distance. The entire journey felt like I was looking at a television screen (I had seen one at the one-baht moviehouses: a big room with a dirt floor and a TV propped up in the front). The scenes outside the windows did not look real to me: the houses looked like little dollhouses waiting for little doll farmers; the grass looked like plastic grass waiting for plastic gray buffalos, and the children looked like little toy children walking behind toy adults. I held up my index finger and I could block out a whole human being. This bus ride is my first memory of not belonging to Thailand.

Through the window, I could see the breeze in the waving of the young rice stalks, whole fields shimmering in synchronized motions. The people in the bus were talking in whispers or else sitting silently looking out the windows. Some of the people were sick because they had never been in a car before. I was not sick; I was too busy trying to remember the feeling of being in a car for

* The camp was known formally as Phanat Nikhom Processing Center.

the first time. I thought it was like flying. My right hand, without my realizing, waved to the stalks of green rice. I waved and waved.

"Are you saying good-bye?" my father asked.

I shook my head. I knew that I would always remember the green rice paddies of Thailand waving, waiting like a movie outside the orange bus, with the sticky plastic seat hot against my dangling legs.

I thought we were going to America. I did not know that we were headed to Phanat Nikhom Transition Camp to America. My memories from the time in Phanat Nikhom are ones of a time of preparation. The Hmong had been like the land, fertile and green, waiting for new growth. Because we were an old people, our lands had grown wild. In this camp, our big trees would be cut down, our large stones thrown out, and new seeds would be planted. The Hmong people were pushed together, pushed apart, pushed out in Phanat Nikhom.

I stood with one hand holding my hat, scrunching the lace tightly in one fist. I looked at this new place. The ground was strewn with rocks and bits of cement; the dirt was rust colored, and the soil was dry and hard. Dust flew around the huge tires of the orange bus and the footsteps of people scrambling for their belongings. The air felt thick. A barbed wire fence surrounded us. On the other side of the fence there was a small dirt road, and then banana trees beyond that; very far away in the distance there were big mountains that looked gray and green. We were on a road leading to America, and then we were in a place surrounded by a high fence that was as sharp as knives. The heat seemed to come from everywhere at once: the dimming sky, the rectangular cement buildings—painted in shades of white, blue-green, and dark gray—and even the orange and brown pebbly ground. I could feel the hot air going through my clothes, drawing out the water from inside my body. My throat felt old and wrinkled.

I looked at the grown-ups.

They looked around the enclosed camp and talked to one another. Is this where we live now? Yes, in the long cement houses that look like boxes with tin roofs. Do many families live in one? Yes, but first find out where your family is assigned.

I tried to swallow my saliva so that my throat would stop feeling dry, but there was no more to swallow. I was tired. My eyes could not look at all the people talking and the barbed wire and the mountains anymore. I felt my chest start to heave like I was going to cry.

My mother called my name. She wanted me to hold her hand right that minute: Could I not see that the buses were moving? Was I not afraid of the large tires? There was a high guard tower, a man in a uniform with a gun stared down at the families without smiling. His mouth was working. Was there chewing gum in the camp? I hurried to my mother's side and took her outstretched hand.

The first night we were in the camp, I could not go to sleep no matter how hard I tried. The insides of the houses were empty space. There was no split bamboo or pieces of wood to stand as walls between families. The building we were assigned smelled like the toilets that I had dreaded back in Ban Vinai Refugee Camp. In fact, it *had* been used as a bathroom. There was always human waste between the buildings and amid the cement blocks and large rocks throughout the camp. My mother and father and the other grown-ups had cleaned the long one-room buildings as best they could and hung pieces of cloth to mark where each family would sleep. There were big lights on wooden poles high up in the sky on the outskirts of the camp to light the barbed wire fence. The buildings had no doors, only spaces where the doors might have been, for each family's sleeping place.

Moonlight mingled with electric light and entered our sleeping room with a pale kind of watery glow that left shadows along the cold exterior walls. The lights combined and I could not tell which came from the moon and which came from the wooden poles standing tall over us. There were noises: a baby cried, a sound like cars speeding by, the buzz of lonely night creatures. I tried to guess where the things that reached us came from, but it was no good because it was difficult to tell exactly how far the things that reached us had traveled. The cotton walls that hung between the families billowed in the night, the sound of wind colliding with cloth. I tried to match my breathing to the sound so that I could breathe like the wind. I tried and tried but could not hold my breath for long enough. The hard cement floor was cold, and although my mother had spread our plastic mat and covered it with a thin blanket, I turned from one side to the other looking for sleep.

Everything was uncomfortable. Dawb and I slept in the middle between my mother and father. Was my father asleep? I wanted him to tell me a story—perhaps the one about the brother and sister who were mean to their mother so she turned into a frog and jumped into the river and swam to the land of the dragons, leaving them lonely and regretful and wishing for fins so that they might follow after her. I nudged him on the shoulder.

"Father, Father. Are you sleeping?"

He mumbled in his sleep. Everybody was tired from the trip on the orange bus. I promised myself that one night I would be the first in my family to fall asleep.

I woke up in a gray dawn, my body calling me to consciousness before I was ready, before the sun's full ascent into the morning sky, because I was in a new place. I had never slept in a new place; every day before I had awakened next to my mother and father or, if they were awake already, Dawb, in our bamboo platform bed in our sleeping room in Ban Vinai Refugee Camp. I opened my eyes to find my father was already up. I went to the empty doorway and looked for him. The night before I had not noticed the doorway directly opposite ours. I had not realized how close all the buildings were to each other. I could see another family sleeping. Our area (I could not call it a house) was on the outskirts of the camp, only a little walk away from the barbed wire fence and the guard tower. The rocks and the cold morning earth chilled my feet. I looked down to see curled toes, pink against the debris of torn dirt and cement. I looked up and saw my father.

He was standing with his back to me, next to the fence, facing the mountains in the distance.

I called to him, "Father!"

He turned at my voice and motioned for me with his hand. I ran back inside. I slipped my feet into a pair of white tennis shoes that I did not like. The Thai government had handed out one pair to each girl or boy who was leaving; it was their gift to us for leaving their country. I was out of breath from skipping when I reached my father's side. In those days I only knew how to skip from one place to the other, from one person to another, one knee in the air and then the other. I did not walk unless my hands were held securely by a walking adult. The guard was in his tower, his gun strapped to his back, looking down at us. Were they afraid we would run away? Where would we go? Ban Vinai Refugee Camp was so far away, and Laos was not a happy place and no one knew the road to America. I stared back at the guard. Would he wave back if I waved? I wanted to wave but I was too shy, so I focused on skipping my way to my father as fast as I could.

He stood silent and still. I inserted my left hand into the warmth of his right. With his left hand he tested the sharpness of the metal on the fence. I kicked it lightly with the white tennis shoes. I watched as the sole of the shoes tangled with the barbs, the rough gray of the fence that separated us from the tall mountains in the far distance, mountains that loomed taller than all the hills I'd ever seen in Ban Vinai Refugee Camp. Mountains that brought to my imagination the country across the raging Mekong that the adults all talked so much about returning to: a place full of morning dew and low-lying clouds, of fresh air and the call of birds and bees and insects and the lonely whistle of high winds through tall trees.

My father said, "Your grandfather was buried on mountains that look like those."

There was no need for an answer. I had never been on a real mountain. I had only heard of it all my life. And I knew that my grandfather had died a long time ago, when my father was just a baby. I thought it was a good thing, that even if we are only babies when our fathers die, we always remember the places where they are buried. Some day we could find our way back if we wanted to, to say thank you, and to say hello, and maybe to tell them: this is my daughter and she has never met you and she did not know where you were buried but I am showing her now so she will help me remember.

In Ban Vinai Refugee Camp, my father told me I would go to school in America. Phanat Nikhom was not America, but it was a transition camp to America. We had only been in the camp a few days when my mother woke me up one morning and said that I had to get out of bed and get ready for school. Dawb was already up and dressed. My mother got me ready: she combed my hair with my father's black plastic comb; used a warm, wet cloth to wipe my face; made me brush my teeth with my small yellow toothbrush from a cup of cold water; and dressed me in a light pink cotton shirt with a matching skirt. My mother tucked the shirt into the skirt. Dawb wore exactly the same outfit except hers was baby blue and one size bigger than mine. We were probably nearly identical, but I thought we looked completely different; I was the pink sister, and she was the blue one.

My mother gave each of us a pencil and a thin book with lines on each page. My father had gone to school already, she explained. She, too, would go after she walked us to our school. I wondered what a person did in school. I was still sleepy. I did not want to carry the book or the pencil. I gave them to Dawb to carry for me. Our school wasn't far from the place where we slept; it looked exactly like the building we lived in.

I did not like school in Phanat Nikhom. Inside the one-room building there were rows of wooden benches. A blackboard was in the front of the room. At the door, my mother instructed us to be good and reminded Dawb to watch out for me. She was good at school despite the fact that she had been sick and had become slower in casual talking. Although Dawb was a year and nine months older than I was, and one of her legs was shorter and weaker than the other, and she walked with a small limp—she had always taken care of me.

I remember one time in Ban Vinai when there was a horrible storm, and though we were not supposed to be outside, we were. We were alone and had to cross the open sewer to get to our house. I remember falling into the water from the slippery rock in the middle. I regained my feet, waist deep in water, and started to cry. Not because of the wind and the rain and the water (I loved all three) but because I was scared and my red sandals were running away from me in the current. Dawb jumped in after me, pulled me out, and ran in the water after my shoes. She ran and fell and ran and fell, and I was going to tell her to stop because I could see she was getting swallowed up by the murky water, but she just kept on going. I sat on the banks and cried. I had decided to go find Dawb, when I saw her limping toward me, her long hair plastered to her shivering body, with my shoes in her hand. She even tried to smile at me. I smiled at her and I hiccupped, but the tears had stopped. I always felt better when Dawb stood near me.

On this first day of school, Dawb, like many times in our lives, promised my mother she would hold my hand, and she did. In the classroom, she pushed me up onto the bench before she tried to get up herself. She tried to shove off the cement floor with her stronger leg, but the bench was too high. She gave me her hand, and I pulled and she pushed, and finally we got her up beside me on a bench that was clearly not made for our short legs. We dangled our feet side by side in the air. I kicked mine to see if it would reach the bench in front of ours. She stopped me with her hands.

"You can't be a kid like that in school," she said.

I looked around the room to see other refugee children just like us. We were all different sizes. There were some who had never been to school like me and were my height and others who had been to school for longer than even Dawb and were much taller than her. Everyone was mostly skinny. When the Thai teacher came in and smiled and started talking, I fell asleep.

The teacher could not keep me awake. Dawb nudged my shoulder when I started leaning on her arm. I tried to stay awake, but my breathing would slow down, and I would be asleep again. When school was out, Dawb and I walked home together. She told my mother and father about my long nap.

That night, my mother tried to get me to go to sleep earlier. She boiled water for my bath so that I would get tired. I knew that my parents were worried that I would not do well in school in America if I could not stay awake at this practice school. The herbs did not work. I listened to my family talking and then falling asleep, my eyes wide awake.

Every night I lay on the floor and I watched the cloth walls billow in and out. After a week or two, the teacher felt that I was not ready for school. She talked to my parents, and they agreed to send me to the daycare center with the babies and other children younger than me. A few of my older cousins served as helpers there. They bathed us in large cement tubs and then told us it was playtime or naptime. I hated naptime. I could not go to sleep no matter how hard I tried. I stared at the ceiling while the other children slept.

I wanted to be back in Ban Vinai Refugee Camp where the people I loved could tell me stories. I wished Grandma was with us so she could take care of me. I did not want to attend a child care center for babies. I told one of my older cousins how sad I was. I bit the insides of my mouth and tried not to let my lips tremble. She gave me my notebook and pencil and told me to draw quietly by the light of the doorless entryway (it seemed there were never any doors in Phanat Nikhom). I would lie in the doorway with my legs in the shade of the daycare building and my head and arms in the sunlight. My feet would feel cool against the cement in the shade, and my head would feel warm and tingling in the sun. I propped my chin up with both my hands and stared at the pencil and notebook in front of me on the cement floor. I did not know how to draw. I did not know how to write. I had seen other people draw. I had seen other people write. I thought writing was the easier of the two.

I wrote cursive circles on the sheets of paper, careful to keep my "words" between the blue lines on the page. Slowly the thin notebook filled with make-believe stories that I had been told, with stories that I wanted to tell about how it had been in Ban Vinai Refugee Camp, and stories about the times before I was born. I tried to tell the story about how a squash got thrown in a wild garden and how different Hmong clans came to be from this one act alone. It was mysterious and incredible the places that I could have come from because Hmong people didn't have a home, which meant we could have come from anywhere at all. I spent much time writing these stories out in my nonsensical lines of connecting zeros. Maybe, in those lines, there was a fervent but stupid wish for an America that would make my body so tired that I could sleep at night like everybody else and not have to sit outside curving lines in shade and sun.

Time became a blur of days in the sun, heat coming off the cement floor, heat coming down from the sky, seeping into my hair, warming its way into my head. I disliked heat. The only respite was in the clinic outside of the camp, and I hated that more.

The clinic was a cold place where the nurses asked my mother and father to hold me still for needles filled with liquids that looked like water, like candy, like sugarcane juice. I cried pitifully. My mother and father did not help me. Although they held me steady, I called to them to free me, help me escape.

They only shook their heads and whispered, "Be silent. They will hate you if you yell and cry. It will hurt more. Be a good girl and stay very still."

I swallowed, closed my eyes, and made my body stiff, and the Thai nurses in white clothes laughed at me. I opened my eyes and tried not to look hateful so they would be nicer to me. Only it hurt the same. It was the way to America, my mother and father said, holding my hands as we walked to and from the bus that took us from the camp to the clinic. America was a place where they would not let illness in the door or admit little girls who could not hold pain. I hated pain, but I would not be left outside America, especially here in this place where I could find no rest. I started biting my bottom lip when I smelled the clinic.

After school, I often would stand near our building, lean my back against the wall, and look at the entrance to the camp. The refugee buses kept streaming in regularly, people from other camps coming in, getting ready to go to America. All the camps would be closing in Thailand and everybody had to go somewhere or else go back to Laos and maybe be killed. More Hmong refugees streamed into Phanat Nikhom every day.

Australia, France, and America were offering homes to Hmong people who could pass their tests. America's was the hardest because the fathers had to identify the pictures of white soldiers and tell what their names were and how long and hard the men had fought under the American leadership. My family was going to America. My father and my uncles had studied very hard for the American test; they memorized all the facts from the soldiers who had been on the American payroll. There was no acknowledgment in the test to enter America that more Hmong than the thirty thousand who had been paid to fight had fought. We fought during the war and after it, fleeing into the jungle, just to hold on to our family and survive.

My mother and father said that Grandma would come soon, with Uncle Hue's family. Grandma's children had conspired to get her to leave Ban Vinai Refugee Camp. They knew the camp was closing, and they thought that of all the options available, America was the best. They had heard that children of refugees could go to school in America. Letters from America said that the country was paved in cement and that grass was green. They tried to explain the possibilities to Grandma, each of them in his own way, but she refused to hear them. They all registered to come to America; they assured each other it was not a separation, merely a way to get to the same place, one at a time. Uncle Hue agreed to come last and sign Grandma on with him because he was the most patient of her sons. My father knew this the day we left Ban Vinai. All the adults knew it—only Grandma and the children did not.

A month after we arrived at Phanat Nikhom, on a regular hot day, a big orange bus just like the one that had taken us to the camp came rolling in. When my grandma stepped down from the bus with a scowl on her face, her fierce angled eyebrows pushed close, my heart stood still. I walked to her and pressed my face into her stomach—her money bag was in the way—and tried to wrap my arms around her wide middle. The smell of menthol and herbs seeped into my nostrils. She held me close for a moment. On the outside she looked the same: her curly hair was pulled back from her face, and she was wearing a polyester shirt and her blue flip-flops. Inside, she must have felt betrayed, hurt, and afraid.

She would say years later that it was in Phanat Nikhom that she stopped being a woman and was turned into a child. "Ban Vinai Refugee Camp was not so bad for old women like me. We had feet so we could walk. In Phanat Nikhom, my children became busy, and there was no walking for me to do. It was a place to practice being in America . . . where if you are old and you don't have a car, you are like a man or a woman in a wheelchair with weak arms. You wait for others to push or pull. A child who does not have the face of youth."

I did not know how my grandmother was feeling, I was only eager to hold her hand again and to show her the room where we slept. I had grown to like the sight of the billowing cloth walls, and

I wanted her to like them with me. I told her that Phanat Nikhom had mountains in the distance. I told her that it reminded my father of the mountains where Grandpa was buried. I told her that maybe she would like this place because it would remind her of my grandpa. To all the things I told her, she only nodded.

After Grandma came, I no longer had to go to the child care center when I fell asleep in school. A few minutes after the teacher began talking, I would slip into sleep, and Dawb would nudge me awake with her elbow against my arm. The teacher would point outside, and I knew it was my cue to walk out of class. Grandma waited outside the school building for me under the overhang of a roof, the sliver of shade in the noon sun just wide enough for her to stand below. I skipped my way to her, one foot in front of the other. I handed her my notebook and pencil and skipped ahead of her to the barbed wire fence where Thai women waited on the other side with goods to sell in round bamboo woven baskets.

The baskets were full of simple things like duck and chicken eggs, dark purple eggplants, deep-red banana blossoms, and bunches of pale-green watercress. There was one woman there I particularly adored because she made the best, at least to my mouth then, *khao pad*, Thai fried rice, in the world. I stopped on my side of the fence, stared at the woman on her little stool on the other side of the fence, and waited impatiently for my grandma to catch up.

As soon as Grandma and I approached, the woman, without our asking, dribbled oil into the hot pan on her little portable coal ring. She cracked an egg. It sizzled, and she added a spoonful of rice, mixed the two, sliced a tomato, and seasoned the food with a few leaves of cilantro, a sprinkling of soy sauce, sugar, and MSG, and the air started smelling good. I followed the smell, my body moving to the barbed wire fence. Grandma warned me not to get too close; the wire would cut me and it would bleed and hurt, she admonished in her deep voice. I pulled my body back and kept my feet still until the food was spooned onto a hard plastic plate and a metal spoon placed beside it. Grandma fumbled in her money bag, the one tied around her waist, and came up with the correct coins. The Thai woman handed over the hot plate to my grandma through the fence, both of them careful of the heat and the sharp barbs.

We sat, Grandma on a rock and me on the hot ground, my dish of *khao pad* on my knees, and I ate while she stared at the misty gray mountains in the distance. They looked tall and fierce, full of creatures and magic. I wondered who lived on them. I knew that long ago, my family had lived on such mountains. I knew that my grandfather had been buried on such mountains. I knew that my grandmother had been born on such mountains. The mountains were our faraway, long-ago homes. I wondered if one day I would walk upon them. I wondered if I would fall from them, my feet only used to the flat of Ban Vinai and now the expanse of Phanat Nikhom. I wondered if my grandmother would ever return to them. But I didn't ask her if she would. Somehow, I knew that the asking would make her sad.

I don't remember us talking, Grandma and I, although I was a talkative child. I don't remember her telling me stories, something she liked to do. Our time together in Phanat Nikhom was strange. The adults were busy trying to learn the things they would need to know in America. How to say: "Hello. How are you? I am fine, thank you. Hello. Where is the restroom? Is it left? Is it right? O.K., thank you." The children who went to school were busy, too. Dawb learned the alphabet and the different colors. She loved to say "yellow this" and "yellow that." The younger children were at the child care center learning to enjoy playtime and naptime, things that American children were taught to do. Grandma looked at the mountains silently, and I sat at her knees, at first busy with my food, and then later, with fear.

One of my uncles became sick, and was taken to the clinic. My mother and father took us to visit him. The room was crowded; there were hospital beds, some with curtains dividing them, others without. In the bed beside my uncle's there was an old woman asleep. On her stomach was a plastic cover, and although the room felt cold to me, there were flies that flew around her sleeping form. My older cousins said her intestines were coming out. They said she was dying. I looked at her. She looked fat and perhaps if she were on her feet, tall. Her skin was a pale sort of unsteady gray. She was dying, and she scared me because I had seen the deaths in Ban Vinai Refugee Camp. I could not make sense of the short time that a person was called sick and then called dying and then the sounds of the crying for the dead rising around the camp. I tried not to think about death, but it was impossible.

I wanted my parents and Dawb and Grandma to live forever. I didn't want anyone in my family ever to die. Everyone I knew in my life, who loved me and who I loved, was alive. I made them all promise me they would never die:

"Will you die someday?"

"Yes."

I would start crying.

"Stop crying."

"I can't. If you die, I will die, too."

"Be quiet and I will live with you for a long time."

"Forever?"

"Yes, forever."

But the old woman was dying, and I became afraid. On our visits to the clinic I looked at her from the corners of my eyes. She was always alone. Where were her grandchildren? Did she have a granddaughter like me? Were they far away from her? Could they not see that their grandmother was dying alone?

My uncle got better and returned to the camp. It was a sunny day. My older cousins were talking: the woman in the hospital had died. She was in the camp funeral hut, a small thatched-roof house, the only one in the camp that was not cement. It was located on the outskirts of the camp, set apart from the rest of the buildings. The doors to the funeral hut must have been tied back. Perhaps like other buildings in the camp there were no doors.

All of my cousins dared each other to enter the tent. I was the youngest. Heads turned to each other and then to me. Everyone was brave enough. I was afraid, but I wanted to be brave, too. They said that I was a baby and that I should go to my mother. I shook my head no. Dawb was going to go. I could run faster than her, and if I got very scared, I could always hold her hand. Everybody wanted to see the dead body; no one wanted to fight with me. The cousins shrugged and said fine. Dawb wanted to know if I was sure. I wasn't sure, but I nodded. Everybody had to promise that they would never tell the adults, no matter what happened. It would be our secret. I accepted the terms of silence.

It was my first secret, and I was going to see my first actual dead body. I felt like I was growing up and becoming braver already.

My older, quicker cousins led us to the funeral hut. They all walked carefully up to one side, and then each of them passed through its open doorway. Heads peeked quickly in, and then fast feet started running, kicking up dust. It did not look so hard. We had organized ourselves by age and height; I was the last to go. Dawb wasn't very fast, but she went to the door and looked in and then ran carefully, limping a little, to join the rest of the cousins standing a distance away. I was confident. When I skipped to the doorway, I stopped and looked into the hut.

The light from the afternoon sun entered the room from the doorway and all around, from the little holes in the split bamboo wall. The corners of the one-room hut, areas where the sun did not penetrate, looked particularly dark in contrast to the spots of sunshine dappled on the floor. It was mostly empty. My eyes took in the body, no details, just an outline on a sleeping platform, not terribly exciting. There was no movement, no flies buzzing, no smell. I imagined her round stomach with the intestines coming out.

"Kalia! Kalia! Kalia!"

I jumped at the sound of my name. I started to run, just like they had, but my eyes were still on her body. I didn't see the rock protruding from the ground in the middle of the doorway. It surprised my feet, and I tried to grab the air as I fell to the ground.

I had always been told that when a person falls in the presence of a dead body, the body takes the living person's spirit. All my life I had heard this from my older cousins and the adults—even Grandma believed it. In Ban Vinai Refugee Camp I refused to go where there were any dead bodies because of this. At Phanat Nikhom, my curiosity had gotten the better of me: I had fallen. I was stunned by the implication.

I couldn't cry out. I stayed on the ground trying to feel for my spirit; surely, something had gone out of my body. What and where? Dawb ran to me. I saw her coming in slow motion, her shadow longer than her body, limping toward me as fast as she could, one leg first and then the other trailing slightly behind.

Her voice reached me before she did. "Get up, hurry."

I could only hold my hands out to her. She pulled me up and brushed my bleeding knees. I was damp with cold sweat. My cousins were waiting for us far away, safe from the dead woman's body. I knew it: something had gone out of me and in its place a deep fear had settled.

But there was the promise. I could not tell anyone. I had to keep my word. I felt like crying, but that would have made me a pathetic baby, so I decided that I was o.k. When we returned home, my mother wanted to know what had happened to my knees. I said I had stumbled over a rock. She asked if I had been skipping. Yes. Someday I had to learn how to walk like a regular person, she said. I answered that someday I would, but that day wasn't happening just yet. She looked at me, shook her head, and then cleaned my knees with cold water, washing the dirt away with her fingers lightly brushing over the damaged skin. All the while I was thinking: I would not break the promise, pleading: please let my soul come back to my body.

That night, a neighbor's child cried, my father turned over in his sleep, the cloth walls billowed. I could see the blend of electric and moon lights coming into the doorless entryway. She stood in the shadows. Her hair merged into the night; the whites of her eyes were steady. She stood in the dark looking at me. I closed my eyes and turned into my father's back. Silence. I waited and I counted: one, two, three, four, five, six, seven, eight, nine, ten, eleven, twelve, thirteen, fourteen, fifteen, sixteen, please, please, please, *please* let her be gone. I felt the sweat come. I felt the sweat dry. I slowly opened my eyes, and again, she stood there. I could not see her stomach or the intestines, but I knew they were there. This was how my fear of the dark began. Before, I had only wished I were tired. After that night, and for many other nights thereafter, I couldn't close my eyes because I knew the dead woman was waiting for me in the shadows to call my spirit to the land of the dead.

I worried that I would never make it to America. Like the Hmong people who had died in Ban Vinai, I would die in Phanat Nikhom. Like the little girl neighbor who had died so suddenly, I would be pale and still. Unlike the deaths in Ban Vinai, they would not be able to go to the hills to bury my body because of the barbed wire standing in the way. I would be buried under the pebbly orange of the ground, to be left behind with the old woman, my soul hers forever. My soul would never climb the mountains to where my grandfather was.

In the mornings, I would wake up and a new day would begin just like the one before. My parents would go and learn more things about life in America. They learned how to turn on a stove and how to flush a toilet. One day, my mother came home with a chicken sandwich for Dawb and me to eat. Her teacher, a pretty Thai woman who always wore white, had taught her how to make the American food. My father explained to us that when we got on the airplane to go to America, we would have to wear seatbelts. His teacher, a Thai man with curly hair and a big smile, had used strings to practice wearing seatbelts with their class. Dawb and I also went to school. When I fell asleep, I was released into Grandma's care. Every day, I asked my grandfather's spirit to protect me, or at least to tell my grandmother of my fear.

I wanted my grandmother to put on her shaman's hood of red cloth and fight to get my spirit back from the dead woman—as she had done in Thailand when I had needed to pee all the time. I dreamed of how she would carry her shaman's sword in one hand and hold it up to the dead woman, saying in her strongest voice, "Hand over my granddaughter's spirit to me right now!" Or, if that didn't work, Grandma could bargain with the dead woman, say that I was sorry, explain that my falling was an accident, remind her that I was only a little girl, tell her that I would be more careful if she would let my spirit return to my body so that I could close my eyes to the dark again.

If I had been a smarter girl, I would have just told my grandmother. I would have explained that I had fallen before a dead body, and not said anything about the other cousins. She was fierce and strong and she loved me, and the dead woman would have been no match at all. As it was, I dreaded every dusk, fighting the sun's departure, a force much greater than a skinny six-year-old.

I spent my nights praying to the moon to shine through the walls, to take away all the shadows in the world so that the dead woman would have no place to stand and wait. Some nights, I tried to stare her down. But then morning would come and I would know that I had lost.

There were nights when I was so scared that I would cry out. My mother and father knew something was wrong.

They asked me, "What are you afraid of?"

They said, "There is nothing to be scared of."

They promised, "We are here, you are our little girl, no one else's, and we will protect you."

I could only answer in a small voice, "The dark scares me."

I knew they would protect me if they could, but I believed we were dealing with a force that was too big for their world.

They tried to hush my fears; they said, "There is nothing here."

I pointed to the place where she stood. They shook their heads. They saw nothing.

Each night, my fear battled my exhaustion. Some nights my father would have to gather me up and take the bamboo mat outside for us to sleep underneath the big fluorescent lights of the camp, near the barbed wire fence. His arm pillowed my head from the hard ground. The guards and their guns looked down at us. The shimmering stars glimmered down on us. The dead woman did not come then. I looked at the bugs buzzing about the lights high above the ground. I looked and looked until my eyes closed against the fear.

Each time I sat on the ground at her feet, the *khao pad* on my knees, Grandma looked to the mountains. She wished for something, and I looked at her and wished for something, too. We both wanted to be free again—she from this barbed wire place with no trees and going to a new country, and me from the dead woman's nightly visits. Both our spirits were lost, unsure of the way to freedom—this thing that we did not know we had ever owned until it was taken away by our faith and our fear and the things we could not control.

The six months in Phanat Nikhom was a time when fear dominated. I was happy when I heard that it was almost time for us to leave for America. I thought ghosts couldn't travel across oceans—though I didn't really know what oceans were. The four of us, my mother and father, Dawb and me, still needed to pass the final health examinations before we could leave the camp. All my aunts and uncles, my cousins, and my grandmother had passed theirs already. We were not worried. The day we had to go for our examinations, the same day I received the last of my shots for America, did not go the way we had expected.

In the cold clinic where I had first seen the dead woman, Dawb and I waited in a room as my mother and father were called in for their tests.

They came out smiling reassuringly: "This is the last time you will ever have to come here."

When Dawb and I followed the nurses, we held hands. In the examination room, the nurses told us to let go of each other's hands. I did what the nurse wanted me to do: stepped on a scale, opened my mouth wide, said "ahhhhhh" with my tongue sticking out, looked into the flashlight, and followed it with my eyes. I stood very still and tried not to wince too much when they gave me my final shot, the cold liquid burning my arm.

When I felt the needle slide out of my skin and the pressure of a cool cotton swab, I took my gaze from the ceiling and I looked at Dawb across the room. She was doing the same things that I had been. She didn't even blink when the needle went into her arm. The nurse who gave me the shot smiled and gave me a piece of red candy. I was still admiring the piece of candy in my hand when Dawb's nurse took her out of the room. When I was led to the room where my father and mother were sitting, Dawb was already there. She had failed the test. Was it because of her limp? No. The nurse who examined her said that there was something wrong with her eyes and that it could be contagious. It was unwanted in America. Her eyes were pink. We were sent back to the camp with the stipulation that her eyes become clear before the end of the week or else we were not going to America.

After a week, Dawb's eyes, which looked normal to me before the clinic visit, continued looking normal. When the day of the appointment came, there was only one thing to do. We knew Dawb wasn't sick. Other than the limp, she was the healthier of us two. My father came up with an idea. I would go to the health examination in her place. If I had passed the test already, I could pass it again. Dawb and I had the same haircut, and while we didn't look alike, we were both skinny Hmong girls. The nurses would not know the difference, we hoped. I wasn't scared. Fear was for the nighttime. This was broad daylight and there were no ghosts. My father took me by the hand, and I went with him to the clinic. I did not say a word. At the clinic, the nurses looked at my eyes and touched my throat with cool fingers. They listened to my heart and asked me to breathe in and out deeply; then they gave me a piece of red candy. We were going to America after all.

When the day came for us to leave, my mother took a long time to pack because the rest of the adults in my family came and talked about the little things. Was there this in America? Was there that in America? I wished they would hurry. I did not want to spend an unnecessary night in Phanat Nikhom. I was getting tired of getting ready for America. I just wanted to hurry up and get there. If by chance the dead woman could cross the ocean after my spirit, I would make sure she had no room to hide in America. I would keep all the lights on, all the time, day and night. Why couldn't my mother hurry up with the packing? I was ready to get to it. I did not see any problems. Grandma would follow us to America with Uncle Hue and his family. It would be a short separation. We would be going to Minnesota, and they would be going to California. The distance between California and Minnesota was unknown, but if there were no fences in America, why couldn't we visit whenever we liked?

My mother began with the larger red suitcase. I was restless and didn't know why she was packing so much. I felt that in a new land you needed new things. She said for me to sit down and be a good girl. She packed two big Hmong kitchen knives made of iron just in case the knives in America could not cut through bone. She carefully wrapped an old shirt around her traditional necklace of pure silver, the most expensive thing that we owned (a replacement that my parents had saved up every little bit of money to get because she had lost to the currents of the Mekong River the one her mother gave her at their wedding in the jungle), along with her two traditional outfits, one velvet, one cotton, both black. She folded the red and green sashes that belonged with each outfit along with the two traditional deep purple head wraps. She said that when Dawb and I grew up we would wear them. She folded my father's Western suit, which Grandma had bought him in Ban Vinai Refugee Camp when she knew she could not keep him from leaving. She packed the pieces of brown embroidery that her mother had given her. She said that they had crossed the Mekong River with her and that she would keep them forever. Dawb and I only had a few outfits each, and she folded those and placed them in the red suitcase as well.

The brown suitcase with the hard wood cover was for the things that might break during the plane ride to America. She packed a pot to make rice and another to make soup. I asked her if there was even rice in America and would we really be eating soup at all? Didn't Americans just eat chicken sandwiches? I didn't like the taste of chicken sandwiches. My favorite food was ground beef and diced tomatoes seasoned with lemongrass, mixed with warm rice. My mother was pretty sure America would have rice and that I could continue eating my beef and tomato soup. The last things she packed were our two photo albums, pictures of the four of us and some of the larger family as well. The albums were not full, but my mother said that the empty pages would be filled in America. I told her to hurry, please.

"It has taken us eight years. What are a few more hours?" she said.

Those words reached me, settled deep inside of me, and calmed me.

I don't remember saying good-bye to my grandma or to anyone else before we came to America. I have no memory of leaving Phanat Nikhom Transition Camp, as I do of our arrival there, or as I do the leaving of Ban Vinai Refugee Camp. Perhaps one place had felt like home to me and the other hadn't. In the minds of children, maybe in everyone's minds, we do not remember so well the places that taught us fears that we did not, could not, know how to articulate in a world where there was already so much to worry about, to work around, and to try to understand. A bus took us to Bangkok International Airport. I was happy because I was not alone. There were many more people than just the four of us. The bus to America was full of many Hmong families, pregnant mothers, little boys and girls my age, some still suckling on their mother's breasts, and others looking almost grown up with their hair pulled back, with straight spines, all of us in our newest clothes. Old grandpas and grandmas with steady eyes that blinked back the past and tried to focus on a future they couldn't see. The saddest surely were the young and old people on that bus with no families, desperate to find people who would care in a place far away from the memories of despair.

CHAPTER 7
A RETURN TO THE CLOUDS

I looked up at the sound of heels clicking on the hard floor. Men and women in airport uniforms and Western suits walked past us. A flurry of motion, they didn't look down at us. They were beautiful. They walked quickly, and their clothes didn't move, and it felt like a silent dream to my tired eyes. I followed them with my gaze, first one person and then another. My nose had bled intermittently throughout the flight from Bangkok to Tokyo. I was in my mother's lap. My chest rose and fell in deep waves of exhaustion. All in a line, we refugees from Thailand sat along the wall of a long hallway in the airport, some sick from the plane ride, others just tired, their heads leaning against the wall. The older Hmong children were excited and afraid. They talked quietly among themselves. The younger children did not feel excited or afraid: we took in our surroundings. We saw how all the people were in motion except for us, and we knew that we were the travelers with the longest way still to go. We asked questions.

"Why are we sitting on the floor?"

I told my mother that my bottom was cold.

She shushed me.

She tried to explain. She said that in America we could sit on chairs, but we were not there yet; we were in Tokyo waiting for a plane to take us there. She pointed down the hall, to a wall made of glass.

She said, "Look," pointing to the tiny lights shining.

Outside, the world looked solemn and black except for clusters of lights, small blinks of red, blue, yellow, but mostly white.

"That is where the people live, in a big city," my mother whispered.

Between looking at the lights that shined like stars in the distance and at the people who resembled the film stars I had seen at the one-baht moviehouses, I couldn't close my eyes, though my body was getting heavier all the time.

My mother said in a quiet voice that I shouldn't look at the people—they were not looking back at me, did I not see? I nodded and divided my eyes between the feet of the women in heels and the men in dress shoes and a city lost in lights.

My body didn't want to move, but I had to pee. I nudged my mother.

"I need to go pee."

I had seen the flushing toilet in the first airplane. I was scared the pee had been dropped down to earth. What if some little girl thought it was rain and opened up her mouth because she was thirsty? She would get sick. She could die! My mother laughed and said that there was a big tank underneath the airplane for the pee. Wouldn't the plane get heavy? She said the plane was strong. I was not convinced. Nothing was strong forever.

"I need to pee."

My mother looked at my father. He was holding Dawb. He looked down at my sister. Did she need to pee, too? She shook her head. I hated that her bladder was stronger than mine; she never needed to pee when I did. My mother pushed me up from her lap. My father got up from around Dawb, who scooted closer to my mother. He handed my mother the blue plastic bag that all the

Hmong men were carrying on our way to America. Dawb had told me that the letters on all the bags were U and N. My mother said the bags carried important papers that we needed in order to enter America, papers saying we were refugees of war. What war? A war in Laos that the Americans fought with the Vietnamese and the Hmong helped and it all happened before I was born. The war where everyone had died? My mother nodded. My father held his hand out to me.

I placed my small hand in my father's big one and watched as his fingers closed over mine. He started walking, and I only skipped a little because he wasn't walking very fast. I looked back at the line of refugee Hmong people as we walked away from them. I smiled up at my father. We were moving with all the busy people. I wondered if we looked like movie stars, too. It was O.K. if we didn't because my father was like my God then. It didn't matter what we looked like—I was happy to be with him in this shiny, new place.

When we were still in Ban Vinai Refugee Camp, men and women who believed in God visited and tried to get Hmong people to share in their belief. My family was not interested because we already had our own belief in our ancestors and the spirits of the land and the Buddha, but many of the children grew curious. I was one of them. I once asked my father to explain God to me. He compared people's belief in God to our allegiance to our ancestors. The idea that God helped people was hard for me to grasp

"But our ancestors help us."

"So does God for those who believe in him."

"Then why don't we?"

"Because we already believe that our ancestors gave birth to us."

"But you gave birth to me. Does that mean you are my God?"

He didn't say yes or no. My father was how I understood God to be.

In that hallway to the bathroom, I saw the first glimpse of my father as just a man trying to take care of me.

The people walking by did not look at us. My father tried to stop them; he didn't know where the bathroom was, and his little girl needed to pee.

A man passed by.

My father said, "Excuse me, excuse me."

My father's voice, usually deep and even, sounded strange to my ears. In English, his voice lost its strength. The steadiness was gone; it was quiet and hesitant. Did all Hmong people lose the strength of their voices in English? I hoped not. I noticed that the people, even the women, were taller than my father. In the camps, he had been a good height for a man. In that hallway, he said the words again and again and the people didn't seem to notice he was speaking to them. We stood there trying.

Finally, a woman who was dressed like she worked in the airport stopped to hear us. My father cleared his throat. His grip on my hand tightened.

"Can you help us?"

She nodded.

"Where is the restroom?"

My mother and father were taught to ask for the restroom, not the bathroom. The Thai teachers in Phanat Nikhom tried to teach them to be very polite in a new country with a new language—they could not be who they were, they had to be what they were taught.

The woman in the airport uniform pointed to the wall where there was a sign with a man and a woman. There were arrows. My father nodded his understanding. The woman walked away.

"Thank you."

He said this to her slender back.

Click, click, click, her heels said to the floor.

My father's hand was hot over mine, and he didn't look down at me as he followed the signs with the pictures that led us to a room with white, flushing toilets and mirrors along the walls.

My father did not know it then, but I was very proud of him. He could speak English, no matter that his voice sounded weak to my ears. If he could take care of me in the airport in Tokyo, I believed he could take care of me in America. I smiled up at him, but he was too busy following the signs, trying to take care of me, to notice.

We were all led onto a different plane, much bigger than the first one. I sat by my father, and Dawb sat by my mother across the small aisle. I thought our plane rides were free. I didn't think about money at all, but both my mother and father were already worried about it. Money would become something we would always think about in America. How would they ever pay back the cost of the plane tickets? It was eight hundred dollars for each adult, and the people who had given them the piece of paper to sign had said that Dawb and I would be the price of one adult. The Thai officials told my parents that they should be thankful because the tickets were only half as much as they would be if they were round-trip tickets—we were lucky that we only had to pay for one-way tickets to America.

I was hungry. I whispered to my father. He said that there was no more food. I asked for my mother's pink plastic basket. On the flight from Bangkok to Tokyo, she had given Dawb and me balls of rice and pieces of boiled chicken from the basket. She was always afraid that we would get hungry, and I hadn't eaten because I hadn't felt hungry. I thought I could wait to eat in America. Weren't airplanes fast like birds? But America was far away, and my stomach growled. Couldn't I at least have some water? My father said the Japanese people had taken the food and the bottle of water my mother had packed. The pink basket was completely empty. I would have to wait until the airplane ladies gave us American food to eat. He reminded me to be patient. Would they have rice and chicken in America? He told me he could not promise me. I told him that I already knew I wouldn't like American food. He asked if I knew what American food was. I shook my head. He said any kind of food was better than being hungry. I nodded. If I couldn't eat, would he tell me a story? No. He shook his head. We should rest for America. I shook my head. He told me to look out the window.

I looked out the small circular window. I held my hands against the glass, and it felt cold to me. It bothered me: walls that pretended not to be there. I pressed my face against the glass; my nose would not flatten. For a moment, I thought about becoming beautiful, and I lost myself to a dream of growing up in a land I didn't know how to imagine, to skirts full of blooming flowers and hair long and straight and red, red lips the color of mangosteen. Grandma had said that I had a good bridge to my nose, unlike hers. A good bridge to the nose was a sign of beauty. So I dreamed I would be beautiful, and in the dreaming I remembered her nose, and I missed her.

I could not see anything out the window. I imagined that there were babies flying in the dark clouds, trying to look in at me. I hoped they didn't want to be my baby. I looked at my father, but he had his head against the chair and his eyes were closed like he was sleeping, but I knew he wasn't; his hands were held together, and his thumbs moved on one another.

"What is outside?" I whispered.

"An ocean," he answered.

Everybody said that to get to America you had to cross an ocean. I knew that an ocean was water where the big dragons lived. I wanted to know if it was the same size as the Mekong

River, the river that all the adults in my family talked so much about, so tirelessly of: the Mekong River this and the Mekong River that, that night when we saw the lights, that night when we waited so long, that night when the water was so strong, that night that would last for the rest of our lives . . .

I looked around and I saw the Hmong people get up and go to the bathroom. They did not seem to be worried about the weight of pee in an airplane. Everyone looked small in between the aisles of chairs. They walked on unsteady feet, careful because they were so high in the sky. I worried about Grandma crossing the ocean with Uncle Hue and his family. Would Grandma look out the window and be worried too?

I fell asleep looking out the window, my head against the cold glass pane, black clouds and black Hmong babies and black night, and a dark ocean outside my small oval to the world.

My mother woke me up to eat. There was a small table that came out of the side of my chair in a secret place I hadn't noticed earlier. I saw the food she placed before me on the tray. I shook my groggy head. I didn't want to eat. I would rather sleep. I didn't feel hungry anymore. My mother said if I didn't eat something I would be hungry later. She wanted me to eat just a little. I glanced over at Dawb, who was eating. I knew she would love America and American food. Of course she was eating. She ate with her hands. There was a piece of chicken. I sighed and agreed to eat. I would try my best. I copied Dawb, eating with my hands instead of using the spoon and fork and knife that came with my meal. My mother and father talked in whispers. I noticed that they did not eat their food. I looked at Dawb. She looked at me, her small eyes, the shape of a teardrop, looked glassy and wide below her new bangs, which were cut straight across, a black fringe at her eyebrows.

I remember the day my father cut Dawb's hair to look like mine, shortly before we left Ban Vinai Refugee Camp. Dawb had

had long hair since she was small and everybody said it was beautiful, black and straight, but she didn't know how to care for it so my mother and father said it would be easier if she had short hair like mine. They had heard that America was a progressive country, and they thought that short hair was a sign of moving to the future. They wanted both their girls to be ready for a new land and a new life.

My father wanted her to be ready, his little girl who had held on to life so strongly, who continued her fierce journey, even as she walked the earth with a limp. His right hand gripped the pair of scissors and there was the sound of cutting away.

The memory was like yesterday. In the dim light of the airplane, Dawb looked like a bigger version of the serious me. Her hair looked like mine. We both had hair to the middle of our necks. We had bangs in front that were supposed to be straight, only I couldn't sit still like Dawb during the haircutting so mine weren't as straight as hers. Her eyes laughed at me over the food. I didn't know why she thought something was funny, but I giggled anyway, picking at the chicken with my fingers. She motioned with her hand for me to look at the American man (that's what we called all white people intended for America) beside her.

I leaned forward in my seat, careful not to hit the tray, as far as the seatbelt would let me so I could see the man better. I couldn't help it. I had to laugh. He was dipping his chicken into yellow sauce that looked like diarrhea! I tried not to be loud. Dawb kept her eyes on the food. She didn't make any noise at all; only her eyes laughed. My mother and father looked at us, from her to me, and in serious voices told me to stop laughing. I swallowed the bit of chicken in my mouth. I promised myself right there and then: in America I will never eat that yellow stuff, babies' diarrhea, no matter what happens.

I fell asleep again, after the food was cleared by a beautiful woman in a uniform, so graceful she could wear high heels in the sky. Dawb and I had just shared our first laugh on America and America didn't even know it. What a special moment it was. I fell asleep, happy.

My mother said the trip to America was only a day and a night. She kept saying that it was hard to believe that we had crossed an ocean, that we were really making our way to the other side of the world. Personally, I was disappointed by the speed of a plane that could not possibly fly as fast as birds, as babies in the sky. In the hours of sitting and then falling asleep and then sitting again, I could only think: how easy it was to impress adults.

When my mother woke me up, without her normal gentleness, we were in America. My father said we were in a place called San Francisco International Airport. When we got off the plane, it was daylight. There were American adults kissing. There was a man and a woman with their faces pressed close, their arms around each other. I didn't blink at all. I was wide awake. I walked closer to the kissing couple. I looked up at them because I had never seen kissing before, and they did not notice me until my mother called my name, walked quickly to me, and pulled me away. In the camps, grown-ups never kissed like that, and when they kissed little babies, they only kissed them on the cheeks, the forehead, the chin, and sometimes the bridge of the nose. The American couple laughed at me; she was blond and he had dark hair. I was still not blinking. My mother smiled at them as if she was afraid they would get angry.

When she walked me back to Dawb and my father, she looked down at me and said, "You will see many things that you have never seen before, but just because you have never seen them before does not mean you can stare like that—especially if they are people."

She took a deep breath. I thought she was angry with me, but she said I was young and that I would learn how to live in America. Even as she said the words, her eyes scanned the world around us in a careful way, in a way I had never seen before from my mother, like everything was too real and it couldn't be.

In San Francisco the Hmong refugees were divided into different groups and put onto different planes. We would all go to different places in America. Only a few families were directed to the same plane as my family; that one was smaller than the one we had crossed the ocean in. It would be our last plane, and it would take us to Minnesota. I had decided I did not like planes at all.

When were we going to get to Minnesota and California? San Francisco was close to California, my father said. Then how far is Minnesota? Neither of them knew. Dawb was sleeping, sleeping, sleeping: breathing in deep, closed off to the world. Would she ever get tired of sleeping? I wanted to take a bath. Would my mother give me a bath when we got to Minnesota? She and my father were talking again. They were both worried. Who were we going to live with? my mother wanted to know. My father said that there was family in Minnesota; we would figure it out once we got off the plane. His hands were in his lap, and his thumbs kept on moving. They both assured me that I would get my bath in Minnesota. I tried to be patient for America, for Minnesota, and for my bath.

Our plane landed. A man's voice came on. People started moving around. A beeping sound. The airplane hitting against heavy air. The sound of tires running over pavement. At last, we were still. The engine of the plane was cut. Belts were unbuckled. We were in Minnesota; our lives had changed forever.

We got off the plane. My father walked down the stairs to the ground with the blue UN bag in his hands. My mother followed with her empty pink basket on one arm. Dawb walked out next, looking tired, and I walked out last, looking at America. I have no actual memory of the sequence of events of our departure from that final plane. My body was probably too exhausted. My mind was probably asleep.

The date was July 27, 1987. It was night in Minnesota. It was not as cold as the Hmong people in Phanat Nikhom Transition Camp to America had said it would be. There was a cool wind that blew my hair around my face. I was six years and seven months old. Uncle Chue and his family had been in America for a week already, and they came with their sponsors to welcome us to the new country. Our sponsor, my father's best friend, came with his family as well. They had left Ban Vinai Refugee Camp before I was born, so they knew America well and would help us. Uncle Nhia, Grandma's oldest son, the one who had disobeyed her in Thailand and the one whose disobedience didn't kill her, waited for us at the airport with his family. The night we arrived, we met family first.

The adults were crying, but many of the relatives were strangers to me, so I just held my mother's hand. I tried to hide behind her back.

After they had cried all their tears, it was decided that we would live with Uncle Nhia's eldest son, a cousin I had met only as a baby, and his wife and three children. My cousin lived in a townhouse in the McDonough Housing Project (the older people just called it "Meenano"). My mother and father and Dawb sat in the back of a gray Subaru. Our two suitcases were placed in the trunk. I sat in the front of the car with my cousin and his wife. My sister-in-law held me on her lap, and we didn't have our seatbelts on. The adults talked. I looked at the lights.

Even now, in the warm summer nights, when the wind is warm and sweeping, I look inside of me, somewhere that nestles in my heart, and I can find that night, safe and warm, close to my stomach, beating in my heart like it is alive.

We were on a road with many cars in front and behind. The window was open. The wind came in and out of the car, past us, inside of us, if we opened our mouths and swallowed very fast and quietly so the adults didn't interfere. I was not impressed with the car or our speeding down the highway, or even the taste of the wind in my mouth. Of all the things that thrilled me and filled me that night, the lights held my attention.

We were in America at last. The world was dark, but the lights on the high poles showed the way. The cars had lights too, red and white ones that blinked in front and back. The world was big and I was small and there were lights everywhere, and for the first time since we left Ban Vinai Refugee Camp and lived the six months that had felt like years in Phanat Nikhom Transition Camp to America, the dark was no longer full of the dead woman waiting for my soul. That night, I believed that if I followed the lights, I would never get lost in America, just as my mother and father had believed in the lights of Thailand, just as that night in the Mekong River would live forever inside of them—the night we got to America would live forever inside of me.

The wind and the night and the lights. I had the feeling that my family had arrived at a place that was more perfect than we knew how to imagine. America was before me, my mother and father were close by me, and the world was open.

In the dark and on the fast highway I could not see the plywood of American homes or the metal fences of American yards. I could not imagine the homes we would live in or the gardens we would tend. I could not have imagined, in my furthest reaches, the life we would live. All I did was feel.

We got to my cousin's townhouse. The car climbed a small hill to get to all the houses that looked alike, long squares against the dark night. The only thing that set their door apart from the other doors was the number. My cousin had a key and opened the brown wooden door as far as it would go.

He said, "Come into the house, come into the house."

My mother helped me take off my shoes. The shiny floor was hard and cool against my toes, unbelievably smooth. The other relatives from the airport had followed us. The adults all gathered to talk about life in America and the family still in Phanat Nikhom. They were trying to catch up on all the years of separation. My father asked of their lives here, and my new relatives asked how we were there.

My father's response was simple: "Life in the camp was the same as when you left it. Nothing changed. You moved to the future. We are walking from the past."

The responses of the relatives were troubled and festive and loud and long and full of warnings and directions and reflections. They were too complex for me, too hard to remember in the moment, in the future, even now, as parts of the past. My father looked as confused as I did.

They settled on a place before "here" and "there": Laos and the war and the mountains, names of faraway villages, a river and a creek, the sound of the morning, the silent howls of the old, the fast, the best dogs in the night. The people that no longer are, a teacher, a friend, a loved one. The talk grew loud and restless, voices going back in time.

Future or past, I didn't care. We had our first meal in America. I ate a bowl of white rice and a crispy fried chicken wing. There was Pepsi, our name for all the soft drinks in the world. I made good effort on a full can. My cousin Lei, who was almost adopted by Laotian people during the escape from Laos, offered to give me my first bath in America after dinner.

In the bathroom, I took off my clothes. They smelled of Thailand. Lei turned a knob and water flowed out, cold and hot water mixing together to form perfect water. I knew I would bathe for the rest of my life; not just short baths but long ones. She wet my hair, and she put Head & Shoulders shampoo in her hands, and she washed my hair. The smell of Head & Shoulders still reminds me of that night. The water was perfect, and I closed my eyes, and I listened to the water falling at my feet on a surface so smooth and kind.

That night, we slept just as we had in Thailand. We had all bathed and our smells were different. My mother's especially. She no longer smelled of green Parrot soap—there were no small, oval, green bars in America, at least not in the bathroom. I had to cuddle close to pick up the warmer smell of cream that came from her. Dawb smelled like me, which was just water mostly. There was the light smell of Head & Shoulders shampoo coming from all of us. And although we were sleeping on the floor, I knew that we were two floors off the ground, nothing but the cement underneath holding us up. The idea of sleeping on air in America was new; no adult had said it. It felt like something magical. My cousin and his wife and their children slept in the other bedroom down the short hall, where they had mattresses stacked on top of plastic and metal milk crates. My mother and father, Dawb and I, slept on blankets laid out on the hard tiled floor. We were in America, but we slept the same way we always had: Dawb and I between our mother and father. I fell asleep listening to Dawb's regular breathing and the fervent voices of my mother and father, dimming voices talking about our new life in America.

PART III

The American Years

CHAPTER 8
BEFORE THE BABIES

The McDonough townhouses had been built after World War II for returning soldiers and their families. The first low-income housing units in the state of Minnesota, the buildings were made of concrete. Everything was cold and strong, meant to last a long time. And so they had, and they had waited for us, soldiers from a different war, not returning to families but to remnants of them.

Located in St. Paul, the John J. McDonough Housing Project housed many Hmong families. The housing project was smaller than Ban Vinai Refugee Camp, but it was on high ground, and in this way it recalled the other places the Hmong had lived on, cried on, and died on. When imagination struck, I fancied that the grass hills were really mountains, the resting place of our ancestors. In the silent moments when my hands and feet weren't busy, I knew our townhouse was different from the homes of the American children on television and along the highways.

All the buildings in the project were rectangular and made of cement, all were the same shade of tan with brown roofs and had small windows covered with steel screens. The symmetry of the place was similar to the sameness of our lives, each family caught up in school and English, each family visiting thrift stores and driving used cars, living on the monthly welfare and disability checks from the government. The truth was dawning: the lives we were living in America were far from the life that the adults had imagined from the camps in Thailand.

My family lived at 1475 Timberlake Road, Apartment C. It was a small unit for families with few children. Our segment of the townhouse consisted of two bedrooms, one bathroom, a small living room, a kitchen, and a bare, cold, concrete basement. The bedrooms had no closets, just spaces pushed into the walls with a rod across the front. Onto thin, rusty wire hangers my mother hung our better clothes from Thailand. Into plastic hampers she folded our pants and the few pieces of everyday clothes we'd gotten from church basements. The bathroom was tiny and the site of perfect showers, but otherwise uninteresting. The living room was my favorite room. It held a black-and-white television and two couches from the early 1970s, one a dark forest green that smelled of cigarettes and the other a musty orange with cat and dog hair embedded in the tough fibers. The kitchen belonged to my mother, who stood often at the sink or the stove. It held our first American-bought appliance, a rice cooker from Japan that we got from an oriental store. The basement belonged to no one. It was dark and empty. Sometimes I stood in the open doorway, looking down the shadows that cloaked the stairs, feeling the cold air seeping up and into the pores of my skin, shivering before the darkness, challenging and shirking away from its unhesitating reach. Each time I stood at the top of the stairwell and looked down, I wondered: why were rooms made to hold darkness in America when lights could be shined on everything?

It was as if our time in Thailand—the way we had lived and played and waited—had not been a part of the world.

My family was part of the biggest wave of Hmong refugees to enter the country; many of us were settling into California,

Wisconsin, or Minnesota. In 1980, the u.s. Census recorded 5,204 Hmong in America. By 1990, that number would grow to a substantial 90,082. But the story of the Hmong lives in America hadn't changed very much by 1987. On October 20, 1980, the *St. Paul Dispatch* published a story titled "Hostility Grows Toward Hmong." On June 11, 1987, the headlines read similarly, "Hmong Gardens Vandalized for the Third Time This Spring." My family arrived in July; we were just beginning. On the streets, sometimes people yelled for us to go home. Next to waves of hello, we received the middle finger.

My mother and father told us not to look at the Americans. If we saw them, they would see us. For the first year and a half, we wanted to be invisible. Everywhere we went beyond the McDonough Housing Project, we were looked at, and we felt exposed. We were dealing with a widespread realization that all Hmong people must do one of two things to survive in America: grow up or grow old. In the case of the noticeably young, the decision was made for us. For those who were older, the case was also easy to figure. Those marred by the war, impaired by the years of fighting, social security and disability were options. For my mother and father, already adults who had waited on life long before it was their time, the government stepped in and told them: the welfare clock was ticking. She was twenty-five. He was twenty-eight. They knew they wanted a chance to work, but they did not know how to keep that chance safe, so on the streets, before the slanted brows of mostly white men, they held us close for security.

On the hills of the McDonough Housing Project, the sun high in the summer sky, Hmong people practiced walking in America, children struggling with their parents holding on to them harder than ever. Dawb and I could no longer walk as we always had. The hands holding ours were more determined than before, and also full of pressure. When I skipped, my mother told me falling on the pavement would hurt, so I struggled to match her rapid nervous gait. When Dawb limped, my father placed himself before her, protecting her with his body, and I watched her learn to stand strong for him. At night, the children looked at the white ceilings and remembered how it had been long ago and far away. We wondered if our parents, on the high mountains of Laos, had to relearn the basics of walking when they were our age, when the bombs fell and the craters broke into the earth, the paths of their lives shattered forever.

That very first summer, I encountered the challenge of not getting what I wanted most: to see my grandma in California. I also wanted her to sit with me on our small front porch, talk with me from the windows of the townhouse, and tell me about how it had been when we were still together. Money, something that I had begged like a monk for, in the dress of innocence, became a stumbling block. She'd arrived in America in late August with Uncle Hue's family. On the phone, her voice trilled in the distance, and though I could not see her tears, I felt them on my own face. Dawb clamored with me for this thing that we both dearly wanted: please let us all go see Grandma. Our mother and father shook their heads. It was not an explanation—it was a new fact in our lives. We did not have enough money.

Facts are not enough for children. We asked questions.

They tried to explain facts: "Money is not something the heart makes."

We were not convinced, but we knew that they wanted to see Grandma, too, so we accepted it. On the telephone, with Grandma's tears in her voice, our tears on our faces, we promised each other a future in America.

We said, "One day, we'll find our way to you. This country is big. But it is not as big as our love for you."

She cried. We could not hear what she was trying to say. We cried with her. I got teardrops on the receiver. I wanted to believe that the tears would reach her, but I knew they wouldn't. Only human beings can reach each other; tears are just water; salty water that I cannot control, so they slip out of my eyes, down my cheeks, to my lips, to the tip of my tongue, until I wipe them away on my sleeve.

I started dreaming about money, dollar bills that folded into cylinders, looked like trashcans, and rolled around in my head, loud and angry, smooth and gentle. After my dreams, I made decisions. When I grow up, I'm going to have money. When I **grow** up, I'm going to never need money. When I grow up, I'm going to treat money so well that it will always want to stay with me. When I grow up, I'm going to hate money so much that it will be afraid of me and stay away from me. Money was like a person I had never known or a wall I had never breached before: it kept me away from my grandma. I saw no way to climb this wall. Sometimes I thought so much about money that I couldn't sleep. Money was not bills and coins or a check from welfare. In my imagination, it was much more: it was the nightmare that kept love apart in America.

The welfare check arrived in our mailbox near the first of the month. We were a family of four, so we got $605 a month. Rent was $250, and our sponsor was teaching my father how to drive because a family cannot survive without a car in America. My parents had bought an old brown Subaru on monthly payments. After we paid for the car insurance, electricity, and natural gas, we were left with only $150 to spend on gas for the car, on Dial soap and Pert Plus shampoo, on extra lightbulbs and vacuum bags for the old Eureka we received from a church basement, on Vaseline lotion and powder detergent so my mother could wash our clothes in the bathtub. Then there was the money we had to save to help pay for clan dinners to talk about life in America and for emergencies like sickness or death. We'd learned a lesson from our history: hard times were inescapable, but when they came, Hmong people would have to help Hmong people survive.

In our new life of not looking closely at Americans, of walking carefully on paved streets, of living without money, my family sat in front of the black-and-white television and watched soap operas. My cousin's wife, who did not know English well, came over with her children and translated the dramas for us. The American people on television kissed and kissed and kissed, and I slipped my hands over my eyes and then carefully spaced my fingers apart and looked between them. My cousin and his wife had young children that cried all the time and drank bottles of cow milk; I worried that they would become like cow children. I watched the television, and the days passed, one after another.

At night, the families gathered for long conversations, which were always about surviving in America, the same topic that the adults in my family started the first night we arrived in the country. It was a conversation that would continue for the next twenty years. How do we survive in America and still love each other as we had in Laos? We must have yearly family picnics to discuss our problems and progress. What are safe things a family can do to save money? If a family purchases a one-hundred-pound bag of Kokuho Rice from a Hmong store (only around twenty dollars then) and goes to Long Cheng's Butchering Complex to buy a pig for one hundred dollars to put in the freezer, the family will not starve. Which program was the best one to help a man find a job, the Lao Family Organization, formed by General Vang Pao, or the Hmong American Partnership, led by Hmong men who were on their way to being established already? Go to Hmong American Partnership, because they are less political than Lao Family. Politics had destroyed our lives too many times. To make lives in America, let us all try and focus on the things we can control: ourselves. I grew drowsy during these conversations.

Life without money became more than the things we wanted or could not do. It became the things I smelled and touched, the people I loved. We shopped from secondhand stores. Together, we discovered the aisles of Goodwill and Savers. We learned about church basements. The piles of badly folded clothes and the smell that hung in the air, dust and mold mingling in dry places that had not seen sunlight or fresh air for a long time. Instead of colorful skirts, my mother wore solid-colored pants, and instead of soft-fabric pants, my father wore jeans. My fingers crumpled the fabric of their changing wardrobe, and my eyes noted the absence of color.

Amid all this, my mother and father tried to protect our visions of America. They said the used clothes were road maps of successful paths out of being poor, signs toward our happy futures in this country. They said watching television was a luxury. We should pay attention and learn something. Their smiles and laughter were for us, to cover up the nothing in our lives.

I missed my grandma, and I saw the used clothes on my parents. I felt the weight of the road before us. The only road signs I liked were the red ones put out by the ice cream trucks when children came answering its melody. When the ice cream truck started calling the children, my mother gave Dawb and me quarters to buy the sweet treats. We handed the man in white clothes our quarters and he handed us Kemps banana-flavored popsicles—cold in the palms of our hands, in the hold of our eager fingers. Every day the ice cream man came with his song and his road sign. Every day I waited eagerly.

One day, I asked my mother how it was that we did not have money to visit Grandma in California, but she had quarters for ice cream.

She answered me flatly, "Because I do not like to see you watching other children run to the truck. Because even from the window, a child can taste the sweetness of sugar. Your throat swallows when other children lick their ice cream."

The truck came every day, and then the days got a little cooler and the call for ice cream became less frequent. The only road sign that I liked in America went away as summer became fall.

I have an image of my mother and father on a bridge over a highway. They are looking down at the busy people on the road, but they have nowhere to go. The sky is a rumbling gray, perhaps in anticipation of the fall rain. They are little more than two out-lines, standing together, not touching, facing the same direction, standing still. In their thin jackets, the sizes all wrong, too big and too long, they watch people with work to do and places to go, young children buckled safely in back seats. That first year, and for many years after, my parents spent a lot of time yearning to be strangers. I felt it then, and I feel it now. It is hardly ever enough to simply be alive. This image, played time and again that entire first year in America, is how my father learned about the types of cars that didn't leave families behind on the road, which cars, even when old, ran strong. This is how he became an advocate of the Toyota and Honda brands. This is how my mom's fear of driving began. Everybody was so trained, so fast, trusting one another, but things could go wrong—the sound of far-off ambulances and police sirens. I watched my mom and dad stand on the highway bridge from a distance, safe on the sidewalk of my youth.

When the days and nights grew colder, and summer changed to fall, my parents began talking about Dawb and me becoming edu-cated people. They stopped talking about money almost entirely. They became hopeful. For my mother, the thinking was simple: we all had to go to school so we could all learn about America. For my father, the thinking was more complicated, snagging more emotions and giving rise to more questions than answers. He said we could no longer wait. We could no longer play all the time— even if it was just in our heads. We had to practice growing up to be good people. The Hmong had traveled farther to America than we had to any other land. We would live here longer than we've ever lived in another country. The only way to live in America was to learn of its possibilities, and the way to do that was school.

My parents knew that Dawb had been good at school in Ban Vinai Refugee Camp and Phanat Nikhom Transition Camp to America. They had one strong learner. They were confident that I would do well, too. When they saw me gnawing my lips, contemplating school, they reassured me. I had learned how to speak early. I asked hundreds of questions a day. They told me a story about a cat. I asked: Does the cat in the story have one mouth? Two eyes? Paws for hands and feet? What about a tail? They didn't know education well but they knew it was tied to curious questions. I would do just fine in school.

A cousin took us to register at Battle Creek Elementary first. There was a white woman with curly hair wearing a red turtleneck and a sweater with a reindeer on it. She wore white stockings and black heels. Her skirt was made out of denim. She was the tester, and she told us to say our ABCs. I had to go first. I said, "A, B, C." Then I stopped. She said for me to say my ABCs again and my cousin said for me to say the letters again, so I repeated them again, "A, B, C." The woman tried more times and then she shook her head. She held up cards with different colors and I smiled each time she changed the card. Say the color. I said them in Hmong. She shook her head. She held up numbers, but I didn't know them, so I smiled some more. She shook her head, so my cousin took my hand and pulled me gently to his side, and pushed Dawb before me. Dawb said her ABCs. She said every color was "yellow." She said the numbers in English up to ten, and then she offered to keep on saying the numbers in Hmong and Thai. Battle Creek Elementary let us in. They placed Dawb in second grade and me in first.

We had only been in Battle Creek Elementary for a few days. It was recess time, which we had practiced for in Phanat Nikhom at the child care center, so I knew what to do. I was playing with a ball, a red rubber ball that bounced up and down against the hard concrete. A boy approached me; he had dark hair and was taller than me by at least two heads. He said something, but I didn't know what he wanted. When he pushed me, I knew what he wanted but I was not sure I wanted to give it to him. It was too late. I fell against the cement. I started to cry from the surprise and then because my elbow started to hurt. He picked up the ball and bounced it at my feet.

I didn't see Dawb run up. All I saw was the boy on the ground, flat on his back, and Dawb on top of him, pulling his hair, saying again and again, "Why are you mean to my sister?"

She was speaking in Hmong. My back hurt and my elbows were bleeding. The boy began pulling at Dawb's hair and yelling in English. I didn't know which part of him to hurt first. Dawb had his head. I looked at his feet. He had on white hightop sneakers and was wearing jeans over scrawny legs. I was about to try to step on his leg when the teachers came and blocked me. They grabbed Dawb, and then they turned and grabbed me and took us to the office. Battle Creek Elementary did not want us anymore.

Our sponsor, my father's best friend, had a daughter who was my age. We became kind-of-friends. Because she was born in America and spoke English, we could not become very close friends—I thought the Hmong children who had lived in America for a long time were not as Hmong as us newer kids from the camps—except this didn't matter when we were playing. She went to a school close by, and the adults believed that it was a good school. My cousin took Dawb and me to register there, but they didn't want us because we couldn't speak English well enough, and they didn't have the special teachers we would need. This is my first memory of feeling embarrassed.

My cousin took us to register at another school, Ames Elementary School, because they were accepting many new Hmong kids, and they had special classes for children who didn't know English. Dawb and I held hands when we went to register, and we were surprised when they didn't even test us—they just said for Dawb to go to second grade and for me to go to first. We weren't at Ames for very long either. I didn't learn a thing. Dawb was learning, but her teacher said that she did not participate enough.

We ended up at North End Elementary School. It was not far from where we lived. Dawb and I were in the same class. The whole classroom was Hmong children from Ban Vinai and Nong Khai refugee camps. The class was a combination of ages. A Hmong man worked with the teacher to help her talk to us all. The teacher wore glasses, had dark hair, and repeated herself softly when we didn't understand. I decided she was a good teacher and was sad when she had to leave to have her baby. The Hmong man explained that we would have a substitute teacher and then a brand-new teacher once one was found. The substitute teacher came to our class for a few days. She read a book for us called *Mrs. Nelson Is Missing*, and the Hmong man translated the story. It was the first book that made me cry.

We had a new teacher who had a rule: no chewing gum in the classroom. Dawb had a pack of gum my mother had gotten for her while we were out shopping for dish soap at Kmart. Dawb decided to share her gum with me in class. I was careful not to move the gum around in my mouth. Dawb was eating hers, moving it around with her tongue, smiling at the sweetness. The teacher saw. Dawb was scared and swallowed her gum by mistake. The teacher jerked Dawb by the arms from her seat and pulled her to the front of the class so quickly and hard that she pulled

Dawb's feet straight out of her winter boots. Dawb didn't cry at all or make a noise, but I knew that it must have hurt her arm and that she had been shamed in front of the other kids.

We came home and we told my mother and father and showed them the bruise. They loved Dawb, but there was nothing to do. We must all follow the rules in this country. They agreed that this was the only way we could protect ourselves and those we loved.

I started hating school a lot more the next day. Dawb was scared of the teacher, and she couldn't learn anymore after the gum trouble. When we had spelling tests, we all waited in a line and when we got to the front of the line, we had to spell "two"; if we passed, we got candy, and if we didn't, we had to go to the back of the line again and then try to remember how to spell it. It was a long line—plenty of time to repeat "t, w, o, t, w, o, t, w, o." When my turn came, I said the letters loudly and passed easily. I didn't know how to spell the word, but I knew how to say "t, w, o." Dawb couldn't spell or say the letters because she was so nervous. Every time she got close to the teacher she got all confused.

I saw Dawb trembling. I saw the way she leaned into her stronger leg, how her body turned higher on the right side. After her third try, I got an idea that I borrowed from my father; I remembered how he had me go to the health examination in Phanat Nikhom instead of Dawb. I got up from my desk and sneaked to Dawb. I whispered the idea to her. She nodded. I gave her my candy, and I took her place in line. There were so many of us, they didn't know the difference even though Dawb had blue boots and wore a blue shirt and I had pink boots and wore a pink shirt. I got to the front, said, "t, w, o," and they gave me a candy. The translator man checked Dawb's name off the piece of paper. It was so funny—we had fooled the teacher. We had broken a rule that she hadn't made, and in this had protected each other. School would not be so bad if Dawb and I stayed together.

At home, we settled into a routine. My mother went to adult evening school. My father had passed the competency test for high school, and the welfare people wanted him to work. They told him that he was a man in America and that a man's job anywhere is to take care of his family. My mother wanted my father to continue going to school. She told him that if he didn't learn more English, he would have to work that one job for the rest of his time in America. She said that we had been poor in Thailand and being poor for a little longer was not impossible to live through. They didn't have young children—just Dawb and me and we were in school. She convinced my father to apply to a community technical college to learn about operating heavy machinery. He called the welfare man.

"I have only two little girls," my father said. "My wife goes to school. I don't know English. We have only just come to this country. I want to work and support my family. You are right. I am a man and I will take care of my family. I ask you for a chance to learn more so that I can get a better job. I am not scared to work. I understand that in life we all work. Please help give me time so that I can take care of my girls as best as I can in America."

I could not hear what the man on the other line was saying, but my father talked in circles for a long time before he said, "Thank you. I will remember this gift that the American government has given my family and me."

After my father hung up the phone, he walked around the house. He walked from the living room to the kitchen, climbed the stairs to the two bedrooms and the bathroom, and then came back down. He went outside and stood in the little yard with the low brown fence, and he looked at the trees on the hill. He looked at the hills of America just as he had once searched the mountains of Thailand, searching for the place where his father was buried in Laos.

The snow, which I had delighted in, melted into the soggy brown grass. Already a year was ending in America. My parents talked about how time moved much faster in this new country. They said they missed the weather of Laos, where it was like spring all the time and the rivers teemed with fish. Each day had been a gardening day and going to school was a far walk away from home. I was not particularly impressed by the idea of walking to school far away, especially when they said that teachers in Laos hit the hands of little children with rulers if they were dirty or couldn't recite their lessons properly. I grew to feel that Laos was their country, as Thailand had been mine. America was supposed to be for all of us, only we were lonely, lost, and struggling every day at a life that constantly looked to the future for happiness.

Our second summer in America was quiet. My mother had learned that buying a gallon of ice cream for three dollars gave more treats than buying popsicles from the ice cream truck. My Kemps vanilla ice cream cone, the food I loved most in America, took forever to melt in the Minnesota sun, and my tongue waited on the edges of the wafer cone for the drops of sweet, thick liquid cold to enter my mouth. The silent stretch of the summer had settled deep into me. By my second summer, I had learned how to live without the thing I wanted most. Emotions are captive to facts. Grandma was in California. The missing had become constant, the tears on the phone a routine.

Another fall came and with it the inevitable return to school. It felt like one day Dawb and I were going to school together and then the next day we weren't—as if the whole summer had not happened. The people at school said that I was a second grader, but I was still in the same classroom with the same people. Dawb was placed into a third-grade classroom with white children and only one other Hmong girl, who had been born in America and could speak English.

When Dawb and I were divided, I lost the few English words I had grown comfortable with. English was hard on my tongue. I was learning the meanings of words and how to write them, but my voice sounded different to me in English. I didn't like the way I stuttered and breathed through the words, so I tried never to speak it unless it was necessary, in which case I started whispering everything that came out of my mouth. I got by with nodding and shaking my head and smiling.

In the third-grade classroom, Dawb was doing well under the care of a teacher with brown hair and big green eyes. North End Elementary School had a spelling bee, and Dawb won. She learned how to speak English quickly and without an accent. Without knowing all the words that belonged to the language, she could sound out their parts, the letters that made them corresponding with her voice, in a way that I marveled at. She won fifty dollars from the spelling bee and gave the money to my father to buy him a new pair of shoes. It was the first validation of the dream: education was the answer to our lives' questions.

I think the winning of the spelling bee was how Dawb became smart, how she changed from the little girl who let my father cut away her long hair to the one who would stand back in stores and wait for me to ask for candy because she would no longer cry for it as she had for noodles in Thailand. She learned what I'd always known: if one of us got something, so would the other. The American doctors cut half-inch soles to fix her left shoes so she stopped limping when she walked. Her life was becoming better in America.

Though Dawb and I were not learning to speak English at the same rate, we were both learning to write in English. Because writing did not take voice, I liked it better. We wrote letters in English to Grandma in California. I wrote the same things every time:

Dear Grandma,

Please have one of the cousins read this letter to you. I am in Minnesota and I miss you a lot. I go to school now. You are in California. What do you do with your every day? When we have enough money, I will come and visit you. Some of the kids who live here have grandmas and I have you but they don't know it. I miss you a lot. I will love you forever even though I am in Minnesota. Do you still remember me? Please say you do.

Love Your Granddaughter,

Kao Kalia Yang

I knew that Grandma did not know English, so I didn't expect her to write back, but I believed that wherever California was, my letter would reach her, and she would know that I had not forgotten her in America, despite all the new things that I had to remember in school.

I sat with my father (my mother was at night school) at the parent-teacher conferences and listened as my teachers talked and my cousin translated. My handwriting was sloppy. I had not even learned how to form the printed letters well but already I was trailing my letters together in cursive. I rushed through my math. I rushed through all my work. I had to color better. I colored as if I did not see the black lines on the page. My teachers could not pinpoint how much I was learning of English; they knew I had responses but I never shared them. In my head, I answered their commentaries with my own: My handwriting was sloppy because I wanted to make it beautiful to look at, not easy to read; I liked to rush through the numbers because I knew what to do with them— never mind that I made mistakes along the way; I saw no point in coloring: the pictures were already drawn and our coloring was not helping very much anyway. I listened as my teachers diagnosed my biggest problem in school: my silence. Did I talk at home? Could my parents make me talk? Inside myself, I had no answers.

Because I had always been a talkative child, my parents didn't understand my silence. The problem at home was never that I didn't talk enough, but that I talked *too* much. They asked me what was wrong. I didn't know. They said I could tell them anything and that they would try to help me. I told them that I had no voice in English. I said sometimes when I wanted to talk, I couldn't find my voice, and then when I did—the person, a kid or a teacher—would already be gone.

My whole family worked to help me.

When my mother came home from school late at night, we read my library books, sounding out letters together. In the beginning, we were equally good. Gradually, I became better than her. I explained the stories on the pages, "It's about a beautiful princess and a prince that was a toad. Yes, like a frog but uglier."

My father tried to help me with math. He did it the way he had learned it in Laos. Even the way he wrote his numbers was too curvy to be American. I tried to understand the way he wrote more than what he was writing. He lost patience with me.

He said in a voice that left no room for answering, "Do you want to learn or not?"

Each night, he returned home and we tried again, as we had the night before, going in circles.

Dawb tried to help me, too. She practiced my spelling test words with me. I didn't need her help with words. Remembering was not so hard to do. The way to speaking English was harder than just knowing the letters that made the words.

Standing beside the wall of the school watching the other children play, I wished I was like them. In the beginning, they used to ask me to play with them, but I was too shy. As time passed, they stopped asking. I paid a lot of attention to the weather. I picked up small pieces of rock, and I tried not to look lonely or watch the other children closely. There were always one or two kids in class that the other children did not like. They were lonely, too. I tried to be nice to them. I gave them pieces of candy when I had any. I shared my pencils. A few were nice back; a few weren't. Being alone at school gave me a lot of time to play in my head.

I started writing short stories in the second grade. I still have a story that I wrote in my bad handwriting on gray, recycled paper in big, bold letters: "The Story of a Watermelon Seed."

The story is about a watermelon seed that was planted in the ground by a little girl. Each day, the girl watered the watermelon seed and talked of how delicious the seed would become once she grew bigger. From the day she sprouted in the earth, the watermelon seed knew that she would be eaten. Because she was not a dumb watermelon seed, she refused to grow. She tried to spit out the water. She tried to crawl up from the hold of the ground. But she was weak without hands or feet to help, so she couldn't move, and despite her trying to stay the same size, she kept growing every day. A whole season passed and the watermelon became ripe and big. One day the little girl said, "Tomorrow I will come and I will eat you, watermelon." That night, the watermelon tried hard to die. She made a wish to the moon: When I die tomorrow, please take one seed and let the wind blow it far away so that not everything will die with me. The moon heard her. When the little girl came with a knife the next day, the watermelon closed her eyes and did not feel the cutting of her thick skin. Not just one seed, but all of them fell to the ground. The moon had told the wind what to do. The wind picked up the seeds and blew them all away from the hungry mouth of the little girl, and they escaped into the world to live as their mother had wanted.

There's a comment on the story in red pen, in cursive letters. It reads, "Kao is not so bad at all. She is getting something with the language. Surely she is learning how to use it on the page. The problem is, she won't speak it."

In school, I was learning how to write but not to talk. At home, we were all learning things in opposite directions, too. We no longer talked about money. The feel of my mother's and father's clothes no longer bothered me. The fact that Grandma was in California stopped making me feel like crying. The food we were all eating was no longer just Hmong.

Each morning, my mother got up early to make instant noodles or peanut butter and jelly sandwiches for Dawb and me—she had learned how to make the American food in night school. At night, my father tried to tell me stories when he could, new stories that he made up about little caterpillars who would not eat enough green leaves and only ate tree bark and grew brown and lost their chance to become beautiful butterflies. He tried to be very subtle; he said that if a student was only learning one thing about the world—for example, how to write in English, and not to speak it—the student was like a water bucket with a hole: knowledge would always leak out. She would never be quite as smart as she could be—as beautiful as the monarch butterflies that visited in the spring, carrying only the dull gray of summer moths. In the food and in the stories, our home emphasized America in different Hmong ways.

It wasn't just us. It was the whole wave of Hmong people we were surrounded by. Each family was taking up a special hobby. For some it was fishing. For others it was soccer and volleyball. For our Yang family, it was watching wrestling. It became our idea of family fun. Every time there was a World Wrestling Federation (WWF) special match, my cousin called the cable company and paid special fees so we could watch.

We went to Uncle Nhia's McDonough townhouse to watch. The women, my mother and my aunts, cooked dinner. We had fried chicken wings, rice, and salads made Hmong style, where the lettuce and the tomatoes and the eggs are allowed to wilt into the dressing—mixes of ranch and Thousand Island and soy sauce. After we ate, everybody gathered to watch the TV, each with a can of soda pop in hand. The little kids sat close to the TV; Uncle Nhia had a twenty-one-inch color television—the biggest screen in the family. Wrestling was very exciting; we understood the fight, good guys against the bad guys who always cheated to win. It was a simple lesson that my family believed in: just because a person was good did not mean they would win in a war. We cheered and cheered for the good guys. When they lost, we comforted ourselves as best we knew how: "At least no one died."

Good people had to fight for their lives.

One cold night, my father took Dawb and me to watch a WWF special match between Hulk Hogan and Rick Flair. My mother was not feeling well, so she stayed behind. My father reminded her to lock the door and promised he'd bring us back immediately after the match. It was only down the hill at Uncle Nhia's house, only about three blocks. Dawb and I were jittery with excitement; we'd never walked in the snow underneath a star-splattered sky before.

It was past midnight by the time the match was over. Outside the dark window, we could see swirls of white. We didn't know about snowstorms. My father held our hands and we set out joyfully. In the beginning, it was amazing, pieces of white coming at us, strong and fine like baby powder. We were halfway up the hill when we couldn't see anymore. The snow and the cold started biting our faces with tiny teeth that left our skin numb and hard.

I couldn't open my eyes. I couldn't open my mouth. The wind was blowing and it was hard to walk and Dawb had one weak leg so she was just stumbling. At first, my father tried to find a way back to Uncle Nhia's house, but he didn't know which direction to turn. There was no one around. Everything was white; we couldn't see our feet or our hands. My father couldn't carry both of us. He held us close to his body and he kept walking: climbing, climbing, and climbing. We knew we were going up because when we fell, we slipped downward. Except for his hold, we would have been lost to the cold. Even in his hold, I thought my frozen legs had died in the snow. I gave up walking. Dawb tried to say something, but I only heard the wind and felt her trying to speak. She gave up, too.

The only one who did not give up was my father. He kept us huddled close to the ground and moving. I don't know if he thought about how heavy we were or how strong the snow was. Maybe it took an hour. I don't remember getting home. My mother said that my father fell against the front door. She had been looking out for us but couldn't see anything. She heard the thump. She opened the door carefully and there we were: a puddle of wet rags on the doorstep of America.

From the moment we arrived, I knew that my family had survived a great war to bring me to this country. I understood that the conditions in Thailand and the camps were hard for those who knew more than I did. But for me, the hardness in life began in America. We are so lucky to be in this country, the adults all said. Watching them struggle belied this fact. We are so fortunate to be young, new lives opening before us, they believed. And yet the life in school that opened before me made me feel old in a world that was struggling to be young. A silence grew inside of me because I couldn't say that it was sometimes sad to be Hmong, even in America.

CHAPTER 9
COMING OF THE SON

There was happy news. Grandma was coming to visit us in Minnesota. She had been saving the money the government gave her. My mother and father and aunts and uncles had all been saving a little bit of theirs, too, a few dollars every month. Together, they had collected enough for a plane ticket. It was a very American thing to do. It was something that we read in books and saw on television: families waiting for grandmas to visit. When the news came, all the futile first questions dissipated in a nine-year-old heartbeat: Money was a monster and a wall, yes, but the adults in my life had battled it down. Wasn't it great to be in America, after all?

On the day Grandma was scheduled to arrive, all the Minnesota cousins woke up early and prepared for the airport. It was our first return to the airport since we had arrived. I couldn't wait and asked a hundred times for us to go early. My father promised me we would, and we did—all Uncle Chue's, Uncle Nhia's, Uncle Eng's bigger children, and Dawb and me. My mother and my aunts stayed home to cook a big meal to celebrate Grandma's coming. At the airport, all our cars were parked on the highest ramp level, number seven. We took the elevator down to the third floor, to the skyway connecting the parking ramp to the main terminal. Along the glass corridor, we chased each other into the airport. Who was going to see Grandma first?

A chorus of, "Me! Me! Me!"

People stared at us and we didn't care.

We went to the gate to await her flight. We watched every plane that came in and each person that came out. My cousin announced that Grandma's plane had landed. We became quiet. When the door opened and the first person emerged, we craned our necks. We stood in a line between the other people waiting for their friends and relatives. We waited and waited, but she didn't come out. The other passengers came out in a line, were greeted by their people, and then they left. Where was Grandma? They didn't know. No one knew. She was lost. Where? Was she alone? Was she scared? She couldn't speak English. Everybody was panicking. And then an airport worker came to tell us: there had been a layover in Utah. The flight attendant who was supposed to make sure Grandma had gotten on the right flight to Minnesota had been confused. Grandma would be here within the hour. The airline was so sorry for the inconvenience.

The late afternoon shifted into dusk, twilight flooded from outside through the glass panes of the airport. My cousins and I sat on the floor along one wall on the airport carpet; there was no coldness seeping in from hard floors onto our bottoms. The people walking by us didn't look down at our dark hair and anxious faces. My eyes followed them. When was Grandma ever going to get here? I put my head against the wall, and I concentrated on the red and white runway lights until my vision blurred into overlapping circles of throbbing color.

Dawb woke me up. Grandma's flight had landed. The news wiped my sleep away. Together we ran to form a line with other people waiting for their families. We waited, turned our heads and followed each person who walked off the plane to see who they matched up with in the crowd. We tried to put passengers with the waiting people. They have the same color lipstick: they are mother and daughter! They are both young and brown-haired: they must be married! They both look mean: they are from the same family! Would people know that Grandma and I were from the same family? The waiting was nearly over. I felt my throat swelling. I had not cried when Grandma and I had parted in Phanat Nikhom Transition Camp to America, but I knew I would cry when I saw her this time.

She was the last person out of the plane. It took me longer than my cousins to recognize the old woman in the wheelchair. In the camps, only sick people and very old people were in wheelchairs, and in Thailand, only people who might die. Tears spilled out of my eyes.

I could barely make her out because of my wet vision. I wiped my eyes with the backs of my hands.

My father nudged my shoulder. "Grandma is here now. Don't cry."

I nodded and bit my bottom lip because it was trembling. Dawb and my cousins had crowded close to the wheelchair. She wore a black hat of fake fur on her head. I looked at her earlobes and found the broken one. I always forgot which side it was on, left or right. But once I saw it, I was reassured; this was my Grandma. She wore a bright polyester shirt that she told me later an aunt had brought back from a church pile. She had on a black skirt with simple-looking flowers on it. Her wide feet were hidden in black canvas shoes, the kind you can get on sale for two dollars at Kmart. Her wide face was tanner than I remembered. Her bottom lip trembled in the fluorescent light.

Everyone wanted to hug her. She sat in the chair trying to hug everyone back. When there was enough room for me to reach her warm body, I pressed my face to her heart. Around her neck was a string holding a few index cards, which poked into my cheek. The smell of tiger balm, menthol, and Hmong herbs penetrated my nostrils. I heard her heartbeat answer my hug. My arms tried their best to hold as much of her large frame as I could.

After my hug, I reached for the cards around her neck. I read the words and the pictures on them. I wanted to take them off and throw them far away. There was one that said, "Please take me to the bathroom," with a picture of a toilet to let her know what it meant. Another read, "Please call my grandchildren" and two phone numbers, one in California and one in Minnesota. There was a drawing of a phone on that card. There was a card asking for a drink of water. There was none for food. She said that a cousin in California had made the cards for her.

Grandma said that I should be careful not to wrinkle the cards because she would need them again when she returned to California. She said that she had thought she would never see us again. Nobody had told her that Minnesota was so far away; that it would take a whole day on an airplane. Her wrinkles were wet with tears. I could not say that America was not for me. Everybody said that I was young and that America was a good land for young people to become educated and live better lives. Thailand wasn't for us; the Thai people didn't want us there. The only words I could say to her to make her feel better came out jerky, like a small sorry.

"I love you, Grandma."

"I know you do."

This would become her answer to my love: simple knowledge. I did not have to apologize for wrinkling up the cards in my wet hands. I did not have to say that I was sorry for making her come all the way from California to Minnesota.

The airport worker helped Grandma out of the wheelchair. We all tried to hold her hands. We all walked out of the gate area.

There was an escalator that led to baggage claim on the ground floor. I loved the escalators. I didn't like the elevators because they made my heart feel like it was going up and my stomach feel like it was going down, but the escalator took my whole body, stomach and heart, up and down. At the top, I waited for Grandma to catch up. When Dawb, who was holding one of Grandma's hands, led her to the stairs instead, I skipped to hasten them along.

"Why aren't you taking Grandma down the escalator?"

Grandma shook her head. She had fallen on the escalator at the San Francisco airport when their plane to America had landed. She didn't know how to stand on one. Her long skirt had gotten sucked into the metal stairs. She had been holding a little cousin's hand, and she tried to pull the skirt free with one hand, but it wouldn't come out. She fell down. The airport employees had to turn the escalator off and help her get up. Grandma laughed when she told us the story. She said many things in America were not made for her slow feet. I volunteered to walk down the stairs with them all. She said I could go on the escalator if I wanted. I shook my head. I skipped down the stairs and waited at the bottom, smiling up at her. She smiled back. There were things in America that she would never get used to, but that she tried them made her remarkable to me.

Grandma stayed with us all summer. I wanted all the kids in the McDonough Housing Project to see that we had a grandma and that she loved us (although she disliked my shorts immensely, saying they were no better than underwear). At night, when the streetlights came on and the summer bugs flew up to crowd about the lights, Grandma sat outside our door and I sat at her feet so the other kids could see. I held her hand and I played with it. The straight fingers were different from my own small ones with their twists and turns. Her skin was dry and felt thin, like living paper.

I wrote my name in English on top of her hand with my fingers, Kao Kalia Yang, the name she had given me when I was born. When I got tired, I leaned against her leg and looked at the lights. My grandma was the light, and my emotions flew around her like the winged insects.

It was the first of many summer trips that Grandma would make. I got used to the cards around Grandma's neck and the wheelchair. I got used to the necessary introductions every time she visited. That first trip is how I still see her. It is how she lived in the world. She was a woman who would travel far for those she loved, on a journey that must have been scary, unpredictable, and lonely. She quickly became the most remarkable person I knew. I saw every day how my mother and father suffered, the long hours they spent trying to be American enough to get into the system so that they could feed us and our dreams. My grandma did not try to be American. She spoke only Hmong. She told stories from long ago. Most importantly, her scent and her clothes remained the same: full of herbs and full of colors, and my childish love for her bloomed into a flowering admiration.

That summer of Grandma's visit my father was going to school for a certificate in machine operating at Century Community College. I liked the college because they had small crabapple trees by the parking lot, which Dawb and I climbed, picked the small pebbly fruits, ate them a little, stuck out our tongues in distaste, and then threw them at one another. Whenever my father took my mother to practice driving in the parking lot on a weekend we ran on the grass and played.

We ran around. I am a Vietnamese, and I am chasing you with red bullets! Dawb runs behind a slim tree. I am a Vietnamese. "Blahbleeblablo," I am speaking Vietnamese at you! She sticks out her tongue at me. I throw handfuls of crabapples at her. I chase her, and because of her limp, I catch up on spurts of short breaths, and I laugh like a Vietnamese soldier, "Hohohohohoho." I make my voice deep, an imitation of my father's, and say in my scariest tone, "I am a Vietnamese, and I am going to kill you! You will never get to Thailand! You will never get to America!" Dawb crumples to the grass, and she doesn't get up. I've won again!

Then, we hadn't met enough Vietnamese people to know the dangers of generalization, to see beyond the narrative of loss. It would take us the next decade before we ventured beyond an understanding of enemy lines, how it was that the Hmong would play no written roles in the war of our existence in America. Then, we were only two sisters playing a game we knew well.

Dawb and I were an inseparable team. My father said that we would be partners for life because we were born together and we would live together longer than with anyone else.

No one told me that my mother was pregnant. I had a cousin who was pregnant, and I thought it was exciting. Her stomach got bigger and bigger, and everyone was nice to her, so I was nice to her, too. But my mother was acting the way she always did; she cooked and she cleaned and she went to adult school. She picked clothes for me to wear to school in the mornings, and when she walked Dawb and me to the bus stop, she would say to me the same words she'd been saying to me forever, it seemed: "Try and talk a little today in school."

She smoothed my bangs. She turned to Dawb. They talked. She waved, careful walking on the sidewalk back into the impenetrable brown of the townhouse in the McDonough Housing Project. I was not nicer to my mother because I did not know she was pregnant. My mother and father had ceased talking about babies and sons. The hushed tones they'd once used about the possibility of sons, they applied to survival in America.

It was clear to everyone, including me, that the presence of a brother was really beyond the control of my mother and father. The long-ago discussions lingered in the back of our minds. Whenever we went to visit an uncle and there was talk of sons and legacies, my father was quiet.

In Thailand, he'd asked me frequently, "Do you want a brother?"

I shook my head no.

"Why not?"

Now, in America, I didn't want to say that I had seen my mother try to have sons for him in Thailand, seen the blood and the water wagon that took her to the hospital, heard the yelling, and how I remembered, and maybe would never forget, the image of my father carrying my mother's limp figure away from me. I shrugged away his questions.

Except for the times when I saw my male cousins help their fathers do things that I couldn't do, like lift a heavy bag of rice into the house, I tried not to think much about sons. Whenever there was talk of sons in our family, I tried not to listen too closely. But of course I did. There was a cousin who was growing into everything his father wanted. I thought silently to myself:

If I were a boy, I would be everything that my father had always wanted in a son. I would be handsome and kind. I would have compassion and intelligence. I would look like the young man he was and act with the confidence of a father behind me.

But mentally I put up a stop sign. I wasn't a boy. I was a girl, a girl whose hair was growing longer and who was learning how to cook and clean. My mother was working hard to raise a proper young woman.

In my heart, I knew that he couldn't have loved me more—even if I were a boy. I understood that changing into a boy would not alter the way I loved him either. Still, when I saw my cousins lift heavy bags of rice into their homes, and when I saw my father shoulder the burden of our rice—Dawb and I standing close by—hoping to open doors, a part of my heart ached for a difference that couldn't be.

The cool of autumn was in the air. The long grass was still lush and green in our small yard. The few trees in the McDonough Housing Project were turning their leaves. A shade of yellow, so bright with orange and sun that they looked like they were laden with ripe apricots. Except for the arrival of school, fall in Minnesota had become my favorite season.

September 19, 1989, was the last day I was the baby in my family. It was the first day I became a big sister and the long-awaited son entered our lives. I had been taken out of the Hmong classroom and placed into a regular classroom, except for reading hour when I had to go to an English as a Second Language closet (because it was small and there were no windows, it really must have been a closet) with seven other Hmong children in similar circumstances. Each day, when the hour came for me to get up and leave for the ESL closet, I felt embarrassed, odd, and different, but there was no changing it, so I pretended to be casual. Dawb was a fourth grader, and she had proven she no longer needed ESL at all. The closet was only for children like me, who were not learning English as well as they could be.

Our teacher was a serious woman with brown hair. In my class there was one other Hmong girl, a born-in-America one who spoke English very well. She was smart. Sometimes I beat her at math on the blackboard, and sometimes she beat me. I could not speak English like she did, I did not talk in class like she did, I did not have friends in class like she did, I did not wear glasses like she did, my hair was not long like hers, and she was not mean to me and I was not mean to her, but we did not like each other. Our teacher had no idea of these internal feelings.

September 19 was a school day. We were in line for the bathroom. I was first. The Hmong girl came and said very loudly that she needed to pee. She was moving around like she really had to go. I whispered in Hmong that she could go in front of me. She responded in English that she could wait her turn. I whispered in Hmong that I didn't mind if she went first. She shook her head. I nodded mine. The teacher was in a bad mood. She yelled both our names and told us to go to the classroom that minute and wait for the others. I was shocked. We had not done anything wrong. Now, the Hmong girl will never like me, I thought. Now, I will never like the Hmong girl. It was a horrible day in the third grade.

On the bus home, I sat next to Dawb. She was telling me about how she had played Oregon Trail on the computer during technology lab. I didn't want to tell her about getting in trouble for doing nothing wrong, so I just asked her if she had the key to the house. My mother had given Dawb a key on a string for her to wear around her neck, so that in case of an emergency, we could get in. What kind of emergency? I had wanted to know. My mother had not answered my question.

Instead, she had given directions: "In America, parents get placed in jail if they leave children home alone. If we are not home, you should go to the neighbor aunt who lives two doors down. Only use the key if she isn't home. You should lock the door and not open the curtains. Pretend no one is home. Don't answer the phone. Don't answer the door if someone knocks. You should call Uncle Chue and tell him you are home alone."

When the yellow school bus stopped at our stop, I ran out and skipped to the door. My backpack felt heavy on my shoulders. I was cranky. I hit our door with my open palms. No answer. I kicked it. No one came to the door. I waited for Dawb to catch up. It took her a long time. She knocked on the door with her knuckles. No answer. She knocked again, louder this time. No answer again.

"What are we going to do?" I asked her.

"We have to go to the aunt next door now. I don't think we should use the key. They aren't home. This is not an emergency."

Dawb took my hand, and we walked to the aunt's townhouse. She opened the door immediately, smiled, and called us inside. She had been expecting us.

She said, "Your father stopped by today. Your mother and father are at the hospital. They are having the baby. You two can stay with me until they come home or until your Uncle Chue comes to pick you up."

Somehow her words did not register with me. Dawb was smiling very big and was full of questions. Our aunt had no answers. Her son, a year older than me, invited me to play blackjack with him. He had taught me during the previous summer. We liked to gamble for pennies. We went to the living room and started to play. We played with his pennies, and I lost every time. Like his mother, he was kind. Each time I lost, he gave me all the pennies back, so that we could play again. We played until the aunt called us to eat.

When her phone rang, we were still at the table. She said it was our cousin Lei on the phone for us. Dawb ran to the receiver.

"No. You're kidding. I don't have a brother! No. Tell me again! I don't have a brother!"

I looked at Dawb jumping near the telephone, and I was no longer hungry. She hung up the phone, and I began thinking. How can I have a brother? My mother was not even pregnant. How can a baby just come? Didn't he see our lives? Why did he want to join? How can I have a brother? I didn't even see my mother's stomach get bigger. I didn't have any brothers. I didn't want any brothers. The old questions remained: What would a boy do for our lives? What would he do *to* my life?

Dawb was happy. Everybody was happy. Our aunt was smiling. Even her son, my friend, was happy for us.

He said, "You are going to have a brother! Are you excited?"

He seemed more excited than I was. It was a surprise that I had not wanted, and even though it was happening, it didn't feel real to me. I wondered what he would look like. Would he look like me? My mother? My father? Or Grandma? Maybe Dawb? Would he cry a lot? Would he eat a lot? Would my father still love me the same? Somehow I knew my mother would. But my father—hadn't he always wanted a son? He had always loved me, but that was because he had no son. I was like a son: I sat on his shoulders and had gone with him everywhere on the motorcycle in Ban Vinai Refugee Camp, and now in America, when he went fishing with my uncles, I always stood next to him, like their boys did.

The phone rang again. It was my father. He spoke to my aunt first, then to Dawb, and then he wanted to speak to me.

"Hello."

"Be a good girl. Stay with your aunt tonight. Your mother and I will come home tomorrow. You have a new baby brother now. He is very small, and his lips are red, only the size of a small chili pepper, but he cries loudly. You are a big sister now."

"I am?"

"Your father is very happy."

"Good for him."

I wanted him to know that I was not sure if I liked this idea of a new baby in our house. He said that I would get used to the baby and that I might even like him. It was too late now. We spent the night at our aunt's house. She made a sleeping place with blankets in the living room, and Dawb, her son, and I watched movies until we all fell asleep.

The next day, our aunt took us back to our house so that we could shower and dress while she made rice and boiled chicken with special herbs for my mother to eat when she came home with the baby. She said that a Hmong woman had to eat this food for every meal for a whole month after she had a baby. I wanted to know why. She said that pregnancy was a lot of work, and my mother would need the good, pure food to get strong again. I asked if I could eat with my mom since I was going to be a woman someday. Yes. I was in the process of tasting the chicken broth when Dawb announced, "They are coming!"

Dawb ran outside. I put my spoon in my aunt's hand, and I ran after Dawb. We reached them at the same time. My mother was carrying our brother in her arms, walking slowly. He was not asleep. I could tell because he was looking at me with small, dark eyes, but as if he were sleeping, my mother said very quietly, in a whispering voice, "His name is Xue. Someday, when he is old, we are going to call him Zong Xue."

They had given him a strong name. In Hmong, *xue* is the word for knowledge, for skill. *Zong xue* means forest of knowledge, forest of skill. I wanted to hate him a little, but I was unsure of what hate felt like. I listened to my heart: no erratic jumps, just the regular pounding response. I couldn't find the hate inside of me. But I didn't love him immediately, as Dawb did. But he was small and weak, and I couldn't hurt such a baby. I even wanted to hold him. My mother and father were smiling, happy the whole time. I asked them why they never told me my mother was pregnant. They said I was too young. I didn't believe them. They just wanted to keep me from knowing. I was too young to know that my mother was pregnant, but I was not too young to be a big sister? There was no sense in that.

I tried to look for changes in the beginning. Xue, the son they had waited so long for, the baby boy whose spirit made it to our world when six others had not. Xue, the tiny round head and the red lips like a chili pepper, whose breath smelled like fresh sugarcane and warm jasmine rice steam. My mother treated him gently, gentler than she treated me, like he was softer and more fragile, but I was not jealous. It made sense. He scared easily. If I was loud, he whimpered in his sleep. If I was rough, he winced, little brown eyebrows furrowed in a wrinkled forehead. My father treated him like a regular child. I paid attention to the way my parents talked and treated me. I noted that there were no significant changes.

It didn't take me long to conclude that Xue's coming into our lives changed many things but not the way my parents loved Dawb and me. My uncles, my grandma, and the whole family were excited for us; they all called and said how happy they were at the arrival of a little son at last. I started feeling proud, as if I had something to do with the calling of Xue's spirit from the clouds into our world. If I had been a gift when my mother and father didn't dare dream of presents, Xue was a miracle that they had hoped a long time for.

Like the year I was born, 1989 was a big year for babies in my family. All my aunts and uncles except for one pair had a baby that year. It felt like everybody wanted to have a baby in America. The adults continued to say that we were lucky to be here in America, to have new lives opening before us, but they added a different phrase for the new children.

They all said, "These new children are Americans."

All these new children would know was America. They would have no refugee camps in Thailand to compare life here with. The stories from Laos they would only hear, as I had heard them, from the adults. The war and the tragedy and the difficulty of our early lives, they would feel only via our filtered memories. It was our duty, all the big brothers and sisters, even the mothers and fathers, to make sure that these young Americans had a better world than we'd ever known. It was a big obligation, and I took it seriously.

Xue shapes the memories I carry from that time. He cried at night. My mother and father were always walking him around the house trying to shush him. He cried during the day. My mother would sit with him on her lap close to a small electric water heater they had bought just for him. There was no more real fire to hold babies by, as there had been in Thailand and Laos, but in America there were substitutions for the real things. Sometimes my mother told me to sit very still, and she placed him in my arms. He wiggled and looked at me, and I smiled down at him. It took him a long time to learn how to smile back. I don't remember taking care of him as a baby, only that he was in my life. Maybe I was too busy in school, trying to become educated, overwhelmed by my growing silence.

I was becoming good in different subjects: math, English, social studies, science, and art. My report cards were full of 4s for "great" and 3s for "good." I had learned how to be a good student in America, except for an important thing. I got 2s for "needs improvement" for all things that had to do with making friends and talking. I realized I was forgetting how to talk, and things got immediately more complicated. There were Hmong kids who were not any better than I was in English, but they were trying to speak English left and right, which made them look young and silly and new. There was a part of me that felt old. Instead of talking, I focused on listening.

In third grade, the serious teacher with the brown hair didn't care. The other Hmong girl in class spoke English well, so maybe that's why the teacher noticed that I was not talking. There were American kids everywhere. I was embarrassed trying to speak their language in front of them because sometimes when I whispered something wrong, a few of them laughed. The teacher encouraged me to speak and frowned when I answered her questions without words, when I shook or nodded my head instead of using my voice. She made me feel that my silence was a bad thing. I tried to respond to her in whispers, which I kept as short as possible. I neglected the embellishments of my life to keep it simple:

"Kao."

"Here."

"Yes."

"No."

"Fine."

"O.K."

"Thanks."

"Welcome."

"Bye."

My vocabulary list was short, and I never volunteered to speak. Inside, I grew angry at myself: Why didn't I speak? Why couldn't my voice sound normal in English? It always felt stuck in my throat, and it showed on my face that I was trying too hard. The words came out with rust all over them.

Despite my silence, I knew my grasp of English was growing. I no longer needed Americans to repeat themselves or speak slower. I understood, only I didn't respond, so my understanding didn't show. The American people at school did not trust that I knew what they were saying.

At home, I had to use my English. It was not a matter of choice. My mother and father had become shy in America, especially when it came to English. They were taking care of us in the important ways: buying us food and clothes, making sure the welfare check came, and being careful about money so that we could have plastic rulers to do our math with and winter boots for the Minnesota snow. But whenever there were interactions with random American people, at Kmart when we were looking to buy electrical outlet plugs so Xue couldn't get his fingers into the sockets, or at Wal-Mart when we needed to know the aisle for the replacement vacuum cleaner bags, Dawb became the speaker. If Dawb wasn't there, I would have to speak.

It's hard to watch your parents stumble before other adults. We wanted to protect them and our visions of them as competent people who knew what we needed and the best ways to love us. So we took the fall into the language. We did not think about how this would change our roles as children or their abilities as parents. It was one more necessary step in surviving as a family.

My parents knew that I was not speaking much at school, but they both knew that I was learning English. They had seen me write letters to Grandma in California. They had noticed when I laughed at the funny parts of *Tom & Jerry*. But the thing that gave me away most was my anger. Whenever I got angry, I spoke in English, unless I was angry at them, in which case I would want them to know everything I was saying, so I would try my best at being angry in Hmong:

"Dawb is a lazy bum, and you never ask her to do anything. You always ask me because I do it. I make it too easy for you! You are being unfair! You are parents, and you are not doing your job well!"

I did not know enough bad words in Hmong to satisfy my anger. The words I knew justified it but did not show it. My parents had made it a point not to say any bad Hmong words in front of us. In English, though, I was learning. Every time kids got mad at school, they usually said "fuck" and "bitch" and "shit." When I was angry, when my feelings were hurt, or I felt injured and weak, I used these words in a fierce whisper just for me. My parents hated it. They, too, had learned the meaning of these words. They said that if I wanted to use English, then use it for a worthy cause: our survival.

My parents tried their best at English, but their best was not catching up with Dawb's and mine. We were picking up the language faster, and so we became the interpreters and translators for our family dealings with American people. In the beginning, we just did it because it was easier and because we did not want to see them struggle over easy things. They were working hard for the more important things in our lives. Later, we realized so many other cousins and friends were doing the same.

I remember being at the grocery store with my father, buying diapers for Xue. They didn't have his size on the shelves. I hated to speak English outside the house. Even to my cousins I did not like speaking the language. My father was still looking on the shelves. A deep breath. I'm a big sister. It is the least I can do. I had started calling my father "Daddy."

"Daddy, I'll go ask them if they have any in the back."

"I'll go with you."

I put my hand in his, and we walked over to the clerk at the customer service counter. I was self-conscious that my father was going to hear me talk. I could barely see over the top of the counter. I stood on tiptoes, with one hand on the counter for balance. I tried to look brave. I was hesitant and quiet when the words came out.

"Do you have a box of number one Pampers? We didn't see any on the shelf."

I shook my head to support my words. I couldn't trust myself in English; my mother and father could barely trust me.

My father said in a louder voice, "Pampers number one."

He held up one finger. He didn't trust himself in English, either.

The fact that so few people trusted themselves in English was a big problem for my whole extended family. Over time, the kids were invited to the family meetings on how to improve our lives in America. We gathered at an aunt or uncle's house; they usually called the meetings because they were worried that their children were wasting opportunities to become educated people in America. All the young cousins were to learn not to become like the bad older cousins—bad usually because they had friends and went out with them and had started speaking English at home, and sometimes when they were angry with their parents, they would go into their rooms and slam the doors and say that their lives were horrible and that they wished they hadn't been born. The adults would point out the good role models for us to follow at these family meetings—good usually because they went to school every day and came home on time and spoke Hmong at home, and sometimes when they were happy with their mothers and fathers, they talked about how lucky they were to be in America and have opportunities to make a good life. High school was the highest educational level of the children in our family then. When we went to these family meetings, I usually sat with the cousins who were close to my age. The meetings were always the same. They began with the same words, in Hmong, by an uncle (they took turns):

"We almost died in the war. Many Hmong people died in the war. We are fortunate to have made it to America. Many died trying to get to this country of opportunity. Now we are in America. There are schools for children to go to. There are universities. Your mothers and fathers are not educated people. Maybe you go to school and you see that your classmates have parents who are doctors and lawyers and you wonder why your mother and father do not work and have disability checks and cannot help themselves, let alone help you. We are not doctors and lawyers. We never had the chance. We do not speak English. You can."

They would say how much they loved us and hoped that we became great people in America. They said they understood that some of us may feel embarrassed at school because we got free lunches and our parents were on welfare. Sometimes they cried. At these meetings, I learned that what made our parents sad was not so much the hardness of the life they had to lead in America, or the hardness of the lives they had led to get to America, but the hardness of *our* lives in America. It was always about the children. And so the pressure built.

The children would sit and listen. I always thought the talks went on for a little too long and that they were much the same each time, but I enjoyed these gatherings because the family was together. Even then I knew that not many American families got together and tried to speak to each other about becoming better people in America. It was something special that my family did. Some of my cousins didn't enjoy the talks at all, especially the ones whose parents had called the meeting. They felt it was public ridicule. They complained about the comparisons among children.

We had one cousin, the one my family had lived with when we first came, who had graduated from high school. We were all proud of him. He looked older and wiser and more stylish to me than any other cousin because he carried a yellow notepad and a pen at the family meetings. Sometimes he wore a suit. He said he was going to go to college if the family would support him. Of course we all would—even children nodded. Then yes, he would go. He would go to a community college and then transfer to the University of Minnesota. He would blaze a trail for us in America toward education, so that when it was our turn, we could follow his lead. He had learned the term "role model" and used it with authority and a resounding eloquence that made the adults pause in pride. Dawb really listened to this part of the conversation. I could tell because she would nod her head as he said each word, her eyes following his pen on the paper as he marked each point he had made.

At home Dawb told me that we had to work hard so we could go to the University of Minnesota, too. It was a great school, she said. It was *the* University of Minnesota—smart Americans went there, like her teachers. Only the luckiest and smartest Hmong people could go. We had to work very hard so that we could make our father proud. Dawb said it was ambitious and that we shouldn't tell our parents or Grandma or anybody else that we wanted to go there. She understood how it was when people did not turn out as expected. I didn't contradict her. I wasn't even sure I wanted to go forward with the plans at all. Dawb said that people might laugh if we told them. That part, I agreed with. Dawb pressed on, said that we could remind each other if one of us forgot that the University of Minnesota was a great school. She said that maybe we could qualify and get in if we studied hard and really learned English. I knew there were no problems with her English. She was trying to be kind by saying "we." I saved my words: I didn't tell her that I didn't really care about the University of Minnesota or college. I wasn't even in junior high yet.

I think each of us cousins still remember the words that were spoken at the family meetings. We could see the dreams of our parents in their words. It was often hot, and the windows would be open, and the panes would fog up as the night wore on. The aunts prepared food: warm rice and fried chicken wings, beef vegetable stir-fry seasoned with oyster sauce, and pots of red chicken curry and green salad, and always an assortment of pop. My favorite was Sunkist, and I always had a can, although I could never finish it, only drink it halfway and then sit and look at the adults and the good cousins and bad cousins and know that I did not want to be either. I knew that if I couldn't carry the pressure of being good then surely I would be bad. But I didn't let on.

Sometimes at the meeting the adults went around and asked each child to stand up and say in front of the entire family what they were going to work hard to be in America, what they were going to do to make the trip that their mothers and fathers had taken worthwhile. The air got heavier, and our bodies were on alert. Before the meetings, my mother would tell us that if we were asked, we should modestly say, we girls especially:

"I will try my best in school. I cannot know what I will become. Thank you for telling us to be good children."

I think my mother wasn't the only one telling her children what to say at the meetings. I remember the different cousins standing up, trembling a little, clearing thick throats, speaking their dreams and ambitions in shaky voices, but I have no memory of doing so myself. A part of me knew that these meetings were more for the boys of the family than the girls. We were told to be good girls. We were told to dream of school. We knew that the boys would carry on the family name, be called to life and death for the Yang name we all carried.

My father told us that we were his future in America, that it didn't matter if we were boys or girls. He had called our spirits from the clouds, and we would be his future on the earth (never mind that our children would carry other men's last names and live in legacies he couldn't own). We were in America and the small size of our feet would not determine how far we could travel in life. Xue was only a baby, he said, and added, sincerely, "I will be very happy if one day Xue could grow up to be just like you two. No less, no more, just like his sisters."

Grandma visited us the summer after Xue's birth and saw this first son in our family. Xue didn't reach for her, and she didn't reach for him—they were like strangers to each other. She did not stay long enough to know him the way we all had—there was little time to bond—and so Grandma left kissing Dawb and me, holding us close, and looking at Xue only a little as he smiled from my mother's arms. A part of me grew protective of the little boy and the unspoken expectations of the man he would have to become. I wondered if she found him as cute as I did. After the hug, I held Xue's little hand and we both waved good-bye.

I don't remember Xue learning how to sit or crawl or stand or walk. I have no memory of his first words. I know only that he was a sweet baby. I played word games with him: He couldn't have been two yet when I told him that "oh my sugar, oh my honey" was a bad thing to say. Every time he did something that I did not like, I would say, "Oh my sugar, oh my honey!"

I said it so often that he learned to repeat it after me.

Each time I took a toy from him or made him angry, he would yell at me, "Oh my sugar, oh my honey!"

I laughed and then pretended to cry, sitting on the floor, my legs pulled close to my chest, my hands around my head, sniffling loudly into the dark of my body. He looked at me, his small lips trembling, his hair spiky, his eyes round. Approaching me slowly, extending his small hand to my hair, stroking it gently, he said in soft words I told him meant *sorry,* "I love you."

Xue was only a year and a month old when my mother gave birth to my sister Sheelue. When she came home from the hospital, she had light brown hair, the skin of her eyebrows were pink, and her little hands curled in fists. Like Xue, she was an autumn baby, and like Grandma's meeting with Xue, Grandma's meeting with Sheelue was not emotional. My father said that Sheelue looked like Grandma; she said it was the wide face.

She held the baby for a little bit and said, "Her name means love in Hmong. Let us all hope that she grows up to be a lovely one."

I don't know if Grandma resented all these names given to new babies without her—in Laos and Thailand, she had given out the names of her grandchildren. In America, some of the names were American, like Tommy, the name of a cousin Sheelue's age. Grandma couldn't even say them, so she had to make Hmong versions. For example, Tommy was called "Ah Tong." At least Sheelue's name was Hmong, although in Laos or Thailand, no one would dare call their child "love."

Although my parents didn't tell me until my mother's stomach had gotten round, Sheelue's coming did not surprise me. Xue had taken my place as the baby in the family. Despite assurances that I would always be their baby girl, I didn't really believe them.

We had been in America for nearly four years. My mother passed her high school equivalency test after two tries, and my father got his machine-operating certificate. They were both eager to work and began looking for jobs. Dawb was in fifth grade, and she made resumes for them. She had never seen one before, but it was necessary for work in America, so she said she'd give it a try. In Laos, my mother and father had both gone to school in their villages, but then there was the war. In Thailand, there wasn't much. Dawb sat at the table, her feet dangling, and wrote out two resumes by hand with a black roller pen. They were one page each, written carefully in Dawb's new cursive. My mother wanted Dawb to write that she would try her very best to work to feed her children. Dawb said that "to try" is not enough on a resume in America. Dawb would put instead that my mother would do great work to feed her children. My mother was scared of this line, but Dawb said it sounded much more confident. "Mommy, on television the only people who get jobs are the ones who *say* they are going to do great things, not those who try."

After the resumes were done, my father gave them to a cousin who had access to a typewriter. My mother did not have her driver's license—having the babies had interrupted her lessons with the car, so they needed jobs where they could work together. This meant that my father could not put his degree to use. They were desperate to accept anything; the welfare people began calling right after their schooling ended, and the calls made them feel bad about continuing to be on welfare. We didn't say anything, but they knew that we had grown embarrassed by our free lunch status and by the McDonough Housing Project. They wanted us to have pride in their work as they did in ours.

They found work as assemblers at Phillips and Temro Industries in Eden Prairie, Minnesota, about thirty-five minutes west of St. Paul. They were not good jobs. My parents had to stand every day, all day. Their work consisted of putting little pieces of wiring on coolant systems. There was a quota for how much a person had to assemble each day, so they both had to work fast. My father developed carpal tunnel syndrome in his hands. The machines were loud, and they both wore earplugs. My mother eventually developed hearing loss. The long hours meant they couldn't keep up at home.

They told us that we had to help them more, to try and act more grown up. Dawb was twelve, and I was turning eleven.

They said, "We will work at night so that we can take care of Xue and Sheelue during the day when you two are in school. When you come home, you will take care of the babies, and we will go to work. We know it is illegal to leave children home at night in America, but we cannot do anything now. In this country, we have to work in a factory, not in a garden where we can carry our children on our backs. Welfare is hard to be on—there is never enough money. The money that there is we take only as charity. You two are growing up and when you get bigger you will want to wear nicer clothes. Help us make life possible in America."

We did our best to help. One night, I remember Xue pushing me awake because Sheelue was hungry and crying, and he didn't know how to prepare the bottle. Dawb took care of the hungry baby while I carried Xue with me down to the kitchen to warm a bottle. I was still scared of the dark, and although Xue was just a small baby, his being with me made me feel better, even if I had to carry him on my waist and only work with one hand. We were lucky that Sheelue didn't cry very much. When she was full, Xue and I would sit and listen to Dawb read from our growing collection of secondhand books (twenty-five cents at the thrift stores). There was no time to learn how to take care of a baby; we learned by doing.

The thing that I enjoyed the most about my growing list of responsibilities was learning how to cook. I made simple food, like ramen and eggs. I had to be careful because the pots and pans on the stove were too high for me to see into their bottoms, so I had to stand on tiptoes and stir slowly. One time I moved the spoon too fast and the hot water spilled out and burned the left side of my face and my ear. I cried because it hurt, and I cried because I thought the damage would be forever: I could never be an ear model one day, wear hearing aides and earrings on television if I needed to earn a living. I had seen the old wounds from the war on my father's knee and on my aunts and uncles. My mother and father asked Uncle Chue to do his whispering magic trick to cool the skin. It worked, but the healing took a long time. To my relief, young skin penetrated by heat, not bullets, repaired well. I became very careful when I cooked.

The thing that I liked least about my new responsibilities was washing the babies after they pooped. I didn't care about the smell so much, or the dirtiness, but I was always scared that the babies would fall out of my arms underneath the running water of the bathtub when my hands were slippery with soap. We used baby wipes, but my mother was scared of diaper rashes, so we always washed after we wiped. It was what my mother did, and I didn't want to do less. I never felt that my hold was strong enough to hold a wiggly baby. Luckily, I never let go, no matter how much they twisted and turned.

I crooned, "Don't move, o.k.? I'll be fast."

They would wiggle some more, so I had to change tactics.

"Feel the water. It's perfect."

I tried to get them to like the water as much as I did. First Xue, and then Sheelue, learned to love the water as I did, to marvel at its perfect temperature, its liquid weight and its feel.

There was no room to complain in our home about work. It was the only way we could have a life in America. It wasn't just us. It was what all the Hmong people were doing.

I always believed that while the work that each family did was different, everybody worked just the same. There were pieces of shrapnel lodged in different places in the bodies of the older people in our family—even my father has a piece in his knee—so sometimes they could not stand up for long. Their backs hurt from the years of carrying their packs in the war, which prevented some of them from sitting in place for long. Uncle Chue had fallen out of a truck in Thailand and had broken his skull. When he recovered, he forgot much of his formal education. On the highways, in the early dawn, I made out the faces of Hmong mothers and fathers on their way to work, going side by side with the yellow school bus crowded with Hmong children.

The adults continued having nightmares. They cried out in their sleep. In the mornings, they sat at the table and talked to us about their bad dreams: the war was around them, the land was falling to pieces, Pathet Lao and North Vietnamese soldiers were coming, the sound of guns raced with the beating of their hearts. In their dreams, they met people who were no longer alive but who had loved them back in their old lives. There were stomach ulcers from worrying and heads that throbbed late into the night. My aunts and uncles in California farmed on a small acreage, five or ten, to add to the money they received from welfare. My aunts and uncles in Minnesota, in the summers, did "under the table" work to help make ends meet if they could, like harvesting corn or picking baby cucumbers to make pickles.

And the adults kept saying: how lucky we are to be in America. I wasn't convinced. I saw them walking in the snow drifts, their backs bent, their hands curled to their sides. I felt the humiliation of not knowing English, and a bubble of hurt began.

But when I saw how hard they all worked to keep us in school, to put warm food on the old tabletops, I could not, no matter how discouraged, say: This is not enough. This is not the life I had wanted for myself or you in this country or any other. We've come too far for this. Haven't we?

But then the inevitable question entered our lives, time and again: if our life was good enough for all these new babies, including a son, why wasn't it enough for us all? These new children were Americans. This was life in America, and it was not so bad after all. The happy news kept coming with each baby, with each year. I found myself slowly becoming softer inside, opening my heart and my mind further and further to make room for all the new lives unfolding in America: Xue, Sheelue, Shoually, and then Taylor came into our lives.

Long after them, Maxwell would follow, too late to meet Grandma. He was a gift from her, a reminder that our lives were not so bad at all, that our love for each other was stronger than the circumstances that held it together.

CHAPTER 10
THE HAUNTED SECTION-8 HOUSE

At the ends of the rainbows you can find anything. A rainbow is really a dragon coming out to drink. It can be big or small, the colors easing in and out, first red and then lighter red and then blue and then lighter blue and then violet. Before I learned about reflections and the color spectrum, I learned that rainbows were really just dragons in disguise coming into the world. The first time I saw a dragon drink water from my feet, the sun high in the noon sky, no clouds, a sprinkler in my hands, drops of water falling around me, I knew something powerful: I could see dragons in a world that only dreamed of them.

It felt like we had lived in America for a long time already; nearly two-thirds of my life in this new land. I was thirteen years old, and Grandma was coming to Minnesota, like she did every summer. She hadn't seen our new house or Shoually, the newest baby girl.

We had moved out of the McDonough Housing Project. We lived in a small white house built in the 1950s on a small hill in a quiet part of St. Paul, three blocks from Como Park Elementary School. It was a normal one-and-a-half-story American house in a normal American neighborhood with trees along the streets. The only special thing was that the house was government-subsidized.

For some reason the people who had owned it before didn't like it. They'd given it to the government, who was letting us live there for $350 a month. I stood in the yard, bigger than any other yard I had ever walked on, and I marveled at the rainbows from the sprinkler, a perfect angle of water in the air, sun drops falling low over the grass. I wondered why any family would leave this house behind, on its quiet street, with its cold rooms and the echo of voices ringing when we were loud.

And no one was as loud as Shoually. Shoually had dark hair and a tiny head. It was hard to see her face because of the hair. She might have been born on July 4, Independence Day, but that summer the clouds lingered in the sky in a way that made the heart stand still looking up: puffy white clouds that floated on top of each other slowly, drifting in perfect blue. I understood why she hadn't wanted to leave the clouds behind until the very end, when her hair grew so long, until it covered her eyes, and she couldn't see the beauty of the sky anymore. She came down to earth because she needed a haircut, so she chose July 16, 1993. In the new house, her new world, she cried loudly and fiercely and baby echoes resounded gently between the quiet around us.

Our lives were progressing nicely. Dawb and I were moved from free to reduced school lunch. Mom and Dad were paying back our debt to America for the one-way tickets from Thailand. Finances were still tight, but we'd gotten used to managing on a small budget. Shoually came into a busy, working family. Her name, like our life, was a blend of all the things we had and all the things we yearned for. It was an American take on my grand-mother's name: Youa Lee. She would be wise like Grandma, with oceans of past in her, and be American in her ability to use this knowledge in her life. My father was full of ambition that his new daughter would become strong like his mother, like our lives were beginning to be.

In the new house, there would be different things to show Grandma. This stove doesn't work like the old one, Grandma. No flames will come out of it the round metal will get hot. The water in this bathroom doesn't have two knobs for cold and hot, Grandma. It's all just one knob now. You have to balance it out carefully in the middle, between the red and blue water drops, so you don't burn yourself. This is the new room we share, Grandma. The bed is different so the sheets are different; the other church sheets were getting too thin, so Mommy got us new ones. Here, I will help you turn on the stove, Grandma. Here, I will help you turn on the water, Grandma. Here, Grandma, let me.

Each time Grandma visited, there was more and more to help her with. She kept trying the new things, but it was getting harder. Then of course there were introductions to the new children. But it wasn't just the new children; even the old ones were changing. We were all getting older, Dawb and me, and Grandma, too. She had always seemed old to my eyes, but I started treating her like an older person in that house. I did more and more things for her. When I was busy, and she needed something she came to me, unlike when I was younger and needed something, and went to her. Like the cup on the shelf: Before the section-8 house, I would go to her, and she would walk over, slowly reach up for me, stand on her tiptoes, one hand balanced on the counter. In the new house, the shelves were higher, and when she needed a cup, she came to me, and I ran over. I opened the drawers, stepped on them, and climbed my way up to the counter to retrieve the ceramic cups for her coffee.

Unlike her meeting with Xue and Sheelue, Grandma had been excited to meet the daughter who was named after her. For all the distance that separated them, her son and his wife had remembered. It was bittersweet. Shoually, her hair all cut off, and her dark eyes, round and black as the depths of a lake on a still, moonless night, shimmered up at Grandma as if she were the moon. Their good-bye when fall came was full of echoes.

The big tree in the backyard let down its leaves. Dry and casual, they flew in the yard in whirls at night. They flew into the metal fence and stuck. Our backyard was framed by fallen leaves.

We had lived in the house for the entire summer. It was a small house with two bedrooms, a bathroom, a kitchen, and two stairways, one leading up to a cedar attic, the other to a damp basement. Before we moved in, my mother and father **had** gone over to clean the house. Underneath the carpet of the stairs leading from the attic, they'd found a white envelope with a hundred-dollar bill inside. We'd used the money to buy pizzas, a small celebration of our new home. We figured it had been a secret hiding place, forgotten in a busy move. We'd learn later what it was really for. But that summer, there was no fear, no suspicion. Thailand and ghosts were far away, almost a decade in the past. In America, there was science and the church, no ghosts except at Halloween.

The first time I saw the little boy I was rushing to my parents' room to get a diaper for Xue. They were both still working second shift so that they could take care of the children when we were at school. It was late and the lights in the bedroom weren't on. I saw a blur, a small figure in a striped shirt, running after me. I paused in the dark, looked behind me, saw the hallway light stream in. Was it Xue? No, Xue was smaller than that. It was my eyes. It was me. I grabbed a diaper and ran as fast as I could. I told Dawb and the children's eyes grew big. I shushed myself. A trick of the light, it must have been.

Dawb saw him next. Again, a figure running into the dark of our parents' room. Dawb, braver than I, chased after him. She saw him hurry into their closet. Without turning on the lights, she followed with her hands, feeling the clothes, the slippery polyester and the dry cotton, taking in the smell of mothballs. Nothing. She mentioned it to the family as an aside, casual and calm. We didn't give it much thought.

At night, in our bedroom, with my eyes wide open, I heard sounds. A ball falling down the attic stairway. Then a noise like a child falling after. I wasn't the only one who heard this. My mother heard it. Dawb heard it. My father didn't say whether he did or not. He was the most critical. He didn't want to leave scared children behind every night.

He said, "There's nothing to be afraid of in this house. Your grandmother's shaman spirits will protect you. Your grandfather's spirit won't let a thing hurt you. We have a right to be in this house. We are not intruding. There's nothing to be afraid of."

One night our cousins, Uncle Chue's children, visited for a sleepover. We spread out plastic mats from Thailand (purchased at the local grocery stores) in a colorful array on the living room floor. We watched soap operas from China, dubbed in Thai, all night. My mother lingered with us; my father went to bed early. It was close to three in the morning when he walked into the room. His hair, thinning, was standing on end. His eyes were wrinkled, not from age, but from muscles worked too hard, too fast.

"Did you hear me call out?"

Everybody shook their heads.

Their bedroom door was open, the hallway light streaming in. He hadn't been fully asleep yet. He saw the little boy in a striped shirt standing in the doorway. He entered the room, merged into shadows along the wall, walked closer, approached the side of the bed, and grabbed my father's arm. The boy pulled, jerked, and twisted. Pain shot through my father's arm. He struggled, yelled, fought for us to hear. He could make out the sounds of dubbed Thai voices from the movie we were watching, but no one came to help. His arm was breaking. He grabbed with his left hand, found a tiny arm, a wrist, fragile. He twisted: the breaking of bones. My father got up, the little boy danced in the shadows on quick feet, and made a dive for the closet. When the light flooded the room, there was nothing. A careful look in the closet: nothing.

And so we all came to believe in the haunting of the section-8 house. From the neighbors, we found out that a little boy about four years old had fallen down the stairs of the cedar attic chasing after his ball. He didn't survive. Money was placed at the foot of the stairs to appease his spirit. We spent this money for pizza. Grandma had visited, and her shaman's spirits had kept him at bay. In her absence, he'd appeared. My father was the last to believe. The question of what to do next was the hardest one of all.

We couldn't afford to buy a house, and we couldn't reapply for a new section-8 house either. There were no apartments that would take in seven people (at least not one we could afford). Most importantly, to speak of this to Americans would make our family look very primitive. There must be some explanation, only we couldn't think of one. My parents said that Grandfather's spirit would keep us safe. My father burned incense and joss paper. He explained the situation to Grandpa on the smoke of the scented incense.

"My family lives in this house now. We have the paperwork. The government said we could. We pay honest money to live here. Father, please protect my family. Nothing can hurt my children."

Nothing happened for nearly half a year. Teenage temper and frustrations took hold. Dawb got zits and grew depressed. Although there was too much of the old country and new responsibilities tying us to our home to make us attractive prospects for the Hmong gangs, we felt their minor pulls. Dawb saw her friends go out and play together after school. She wanted a starter jacket and eyeliner and a few hours off. Mother and Father grew wary. They shook their heads. She knew the schedule; she knew that I couldn't take care of the children alone. That wasn't our life. She brewed. She stormed. We tried not to be critical or mean. Dawb and I felt the same pressure. I, too, was hitting teenage status and angst. I grew chubby and felt uncomfortable in my skin, not only my voice. Everybody was working too hard, even the children. Raised by us for half the time, they learned of our frustrations and comforted us as best they knew how. Little arms around necks, little hands wiping away tears, saying that everything was O.K., that they were sorry we were sad. And then we grew sadder because we'd made the children sad. There was no room to grow beyond each other. Then our grandma in Laos died, and the nervous energy of our home gave way to grief.

My mother's mother died on a weekend. Dawb and I were home with the children. Our mother and father were at an uncle's house. I did not know how to love this grandma except to believe that her love for my mother was like my mother's love for me. Because the village in Laos had no phones, my mother used to send audio cassettes to her. My mother would teach me what to say into the old tape player we had bought from the thrift shop: "This is Kalia, your daughter's daughter. I am now [eight, ten, twelve] years old, and I only have a few words to say to you. I am well and I hope you are well, and we are in America but I have no money to send you. I only have a few words to say so you can hear my voice."

I had seen some pictures of her, sent from Laos, and Dawb said that the bones in my face were like hers. In the photos my uncles sent from Laos, I saw a life that was lived close to the ground, as ours had been in Thailand. My mother went over the photographs with Dawb and me, tried to tell us who each member of her family was and how they had loved her before, in a life that was like a dream to her now because she had been married to my father for longer than she had lived with her own family.

On the day that my grandma in Laos died, my mother was not home. The phone rang and Dawb ran into the kitchen to pick it up. I had no idea what was going on—I was watching the kids in the living room, waving an old sheet that my mother did not want anymore up and down, up and down, for the little kids to run under. Dawb came back into the room. She came close to me. I raised my eyebrow.

"What?"

She whispered in English, "The grandma in Laos is dead."

My arms were tired, so I stopped waving the sheets. The laughter of the children ceased, and it occurred to me that I did not know how to feel. I remembered my fear of death, but this death was happening far away, in Laos. I began worrying about how my mother would feel. Dawb looked somber. I took my cue from her.

When my mother and father came home, Dawb didn't say anything. I wondered why.

"Wouldn't it be better to tell her?"

Dawb shook her head.

When my mother went to the bathroom, Dawb whispered the news to my father. He waited for my mother to come out of the bathroom, then asked her to step into their bedroom, the one they shared with Xue, Sheelue, and Shoually. I don't know what he said, but we all heard my mother's loud voice, not the one she used in anger, but the one she used when one of us was on a table or a beam and she thought we were going to fall. She didn't believe him. She was going to call her sister herself. I heard her run out of their room to the kitchen. The voice turned into a wail.

The children got scared, and Dawb and I pulled them close to us, into our laps. "Shhhh. Everything is o.k."

My mother was crying, "My mother, my mother, my mother."

I went to the door of the kitchen, and I saw her crouched against the wall, crying into her arms. She was not even talking into the phone. The call that she wanted to make to her sister never went through.

I realized then that my mother had left her mother, the woman who had loved her best in the entire world, to walk with my father toward this life with us. I felt worried that perhaps I'd been selfish. I felt sorry for the decisions a Hmong woman faced, the decisions that *this* Hmong woman—who I had never seen as such simply because she was my mother—had made. Why does love in a war always mean choosing? Her mother or my father? The country that gave birth to her or the one that would give birth to me? The little girl she had been or the woman she would become? For the first time, I knew the sadness of choice in my mother's life. I had a glimpse of the world she was working hard to protect me from, to keep me young in, this education and pursuit of a life she never had a chance at. I had the freedom to stand strong in the wake of love and to perhaps choose my own mother—instead of a man.

The house seemed to shake with her cries. My father walked into the room and placed the dangling receiver back on its hook. I knew her life would never be the same again: she didn't have a mother anymore.

The next morning I got up to find my mother in the kitchen, cooking. She did not offer any words when she saw me. She looked shy and faraway; her mother's death, a woman who was a stranger to me, had entered our lives. The rest of the family came in and we ate. The rice was a little hard, and I swallowed it down with warm chicken broth. I ate the way she ate, spoon to mouth. She looked out the window until the little children drew her attention to them. My father tried to talk like normal. Dawb looked somber. My mother said that she would be o.k. because she had children to live for.

She said, "Mothers do not die on their children if they can help it."

Her eyes were swollen for many days. I knew that she cried, although I never saw. Maybe she got up and cried in the living room late at night, when we were sleeping, or in the bathroom, when she looked at herself in the mirror and realized that the woman in the mirror was an orphan.

The days passed, and every once in a while she would offer an explanation for her sadness, saying, "There is nothing left for me in Laos now. She was the only reason I would go back. The last time I saw her it was in the war. I was married, and we were visiting, our only visit. I saw her walking away into the jungle to carry water." She shook her head as if to wake herself from the dream. "My mother was the only woman who always took care of me without my ever having to show that I needed care. She knew what I needed before I did."

But our needs soon took my mother away from her grieving. That, and a new pregnancy. Taylor had decided to come into the world to give my mom more reasons to live.

During all this we forgot about the little boy with the striped shirt. But he didn't let us forget for long.

One night, in the dead of winter, when my mother and father were at work, the children and Dawb and I were sitting in the living room. Shoually's eyes started following something moving before her field of vision. I noticed and tried to divert her attention. Casually, I put my face right before her eyes and stuck out my tongue. Normally, she'd laugh. That night, she didn't. She waved my face away with her small fisted hands. Dawb noticed. Xue noticed. Sheelue noticed. A silence grew in the house, so thick the air felt choked. We all moved onto the same couch. A beating started, like a human heart, all around us. Dawb got up and looked out the window; the lights of the houses around us were off for the night. Should we call Uncle Chue? What would we say to him? It was already close to midnight. Mother and

Father got home at around twelve thirty in the morning. We could wait for forty minutes, couldn't we?

And then a panic started. Xue had just turned four. He had on shorts and a t-shirt: a little boy with round, intelligent eyes and a ready smile. His small lips quivered.

He said, "Ai [the children's nickname for me], I'll go with you to the kitchen and make a bottle for the baby. And then we'll come back here."

I figured that no matter what we did, Shoually would need a bottle soon. Sheelue and Dawb huddled on the couch while we went, his little hand in mine. I was so glad I had a brother. At the fridge, he stood guard while I bottled the milk. We ran back.

The breathing got harder. Dawb said that we had to leave. Without knowing to where or what to do exactly, we all made a move, the baby in Dawb's arms, to the door. I wore Mother's boots and an old jacket. Dawb wore Father's. Xue and Sheelue grabbed various shoes and put them on. Xue had on my jacket, all the way down to his knees, and Sheelue wore Dawb's. The baby cradled in Dawb's arms, underneath the coat, we tramped out of the house. We had nowhere to go. The snow was piled up to my thighs. The shoveled walk led to the dark garage. In a line, me at the end, Dawb at the beginning, we went into the garage. The cold seeped in between the thin plywood and bit into our exposed skin.

We stood shivering, looking back at a house that was surely looking out at us.

Just as we thought we were going to die of cold, a car came into the driveway. Our mother and father had come home from work a little early. They took us by the hands, and we went into the house. That night there was no rest. My father started an apartment search the next day, calling mostly Hmong apartment owners. All we could afford was something around $450. We had to move before spring when the new baby would enter our lives.

It would be the last one, my mom and dad said. They were getting too old. One son was enough. There were already four daughters. Depending on this one, whichever way it went, no more babies from the clouds.

In a small flurry of desperation we moved out of the haunted section-8 house. No one wanted to look back. For my mother, it was the news of her mother's death. For us, it was the little boy in the striped shirt and the fear he brought to our world. The more people there were in a life, the faster it goes. Life was a fleeting thing. Our family had gone from four to eight. The whole Yang clan was growing; more and more older cousins were getting married and there were babies coming in from many directions. The babies were cute and funny, and all the time was getting eaten up by them. We could not deal with a lonely ghost boy haunting our lives.

Each time a new baby was born, we went to see it, and the adults talked about how they were fortunate to have babies and how lucky that they were born in America, not in Laos or Thailand—places where so many Hmong people had died. They would never understand why American people talked about how expensive babies were and how poor people shouldn't have so many. How was it that such smart people couldn't understand that the best way to live life was to give life. And then they spoke of how there was no one to take care of children in America, and how hard it was to work and take care of young babies, and yet how hard it also was to look away from a child's face after you have seen it. Time had been something we feared, but with the babies the things that held time together—the years, the months, the weeks, the days—melted and flowed toward the future.

We tried to forget the haunted house. But we learned that leaving is not the same as forgetting. Memories live on, behind us, under our closed lids and in our dreams. They are just like the dragon that had come out to drink near my feet. Before I learned about light particles and the color spectrum, I had believed in the dragon, and so it had lived and would always remain deep inside me. Like my grandma in Laos, and how she visits my mother in dreams. Like my grandmother in America, and how she used to walk free on the grass hills of Thailand, and how she had once reached high on the shelves of America to get me a cup, a spoon, a plate—the things that I needed to grow up. Once we are, we will always be.

CHAPTER 11
OUR MOLDY HOUSE

In 1995, the only homes that anyone in my family had owned no longer existed. They lived on only as fragmented memories. These memories were jarred by movies. Hmong production companies were bringing to life old Hmong legends, such as the Yer and the Tiger story, telling the stories of love lost during the war, taking the Hmong people back to Laos and Thailand, to thatch-roof huts and the yellow dirt of mountain paths. Everyone in the family pointed to this plant and to that mountain vista, talked of the homes they had once lived in and, in floods of memory, painted images of home. Though sometimes full of colors, these homes could not quite rise into life, since they were held in check by memory.

We had been in America for almost ten years. I was nearly fifteen, and Dawb had just gotten her driver's license. The children were growing up. We needed a new home—the apartment was too small. There was hardly room to breathe when the scent of jasmine rice and fish steamed with ginger mingled heavily with the scent of freshly baked pepperoni pizza—Dawb's favorite food. We had been looking for a new house for nearly six months.

It was in a poor neighborhood with houses that were ready to collapse—wooden planks falling off, colors chipping away, sloping porches—and huge, old trees. There was a realty sign in the front yard, a small patch of green in front of the white house. It was one story, with a small open patio and a single wide window framed by black panels beside a black door. There was a short driveway that climbed up a little hill. No garage. It looked out of place in the east side of St. Paul. In fact, it looked out of time. The house should have been on the prairie, in the early days of Minnesota. It looked like it belonged to Laura and Mary Ingalls and a time when girls wore cotton skirts with little flowers and bonnets to keep the sun away and carried pails with their sandwiches inside. The team of two old trees in the front yard dwarfed the house. From the car, my imagination took flight. I never thought I would get a chance to live in a house that belonged to storybooks.

I asked my mom, "Are you sure this is only $36,500?"

"It was really $37,000 on the paper, but Dawb asked the man to lower the price for us, and he agreed."

"It looks like at least $70,000 to me."

I couldn't wait to get out of the car. We had been looking for houses a long time—some we had liked well enough; most we couldn't afford. Now, this one that looked like a real antique, was only $36,500. The deal was incredible. It felt like a miracle.

Together, we had scoured the city looking for a suitable home. My mother, father, and Dawb in the front, and the rest of us in the back, all our knees touching. We had looked all summer long, driving up and down the avenues, the corridors, the smaller streets, and the busy thoroughfares of St. Paul. On days of fruitless hunting, my father would drive us past the mansions on Summit Avenue for inspiration. We were awed and discussed the merits of owning the structures before us, humongous and intimidating, haunting and invincible. We marveled at the bricks and the green lawns and the ivy climbing up the walls and windows.

Dawb and I posed creative arguments for why owning such behemoths would never work for our family. These were the homes that we saw on television, the ones with the ghosts and the gun dramas, the ones with the 1980s movie stars and their loose-fitting suits. These were the homes with the secret drug addicts and the eating disorders. We'd much rather live in places where men carried beverages in brown bags and walked lopsided up and down the sidewalks and a child could kick an empty beer bottle just as conveniently as a rock. We had fun with our talk, but sometimes Mom and Dad got annoyed. These houses were supposed to inspire us to work extra hard in school.

The small house before us would work. It would be our first piece of America, the first home we would buy with the money our parents earned. We were full of eagerness. Some of our cousins had purchased houses already; others were looking, just like us. It felt like we were joining the future with the past, our dreams and our lives coming together. This would be the home that the children would dream about for years to come.

Up close, we could see that the wood of the house was falling apart in places. White paint had been applied to the parts where the old paint had chipped. The floor of the porch was rotting. The black panels on either side of the window made it look bigger than it was. But that afternoon there was a feeling like the house was special, like it would be ours for a long time. I walked through the front door, into a space that was small, like an elevator. Then I made a left and entered our first home in America: 437 East York Avenue.

The house had the simplest design I had ever encountered. After the elevator-sized reception area, there were three bigger rooms all connected, each with a small bedroom to the right. There was a single bathroom in between the second and third bedrooms. The first room was a designated living room. The second was an "anything-you-need-me-to-be" room (that would be used to full capacity as bedroom, playroom, study room, and eating room). The third was a kitchen with enough room in the center for a round dining table (a remnant of the old owners). Off the kitchen there was a door leading to an enclosed porch area that my father liked because there was an old pencil sharpener nailed into the wall. The realtor had said that the sharpener still worked. Also off the kitchen there was a small room with just enough space for a washing and drying machine and the requisite heavy-duty sink. The total area of the house was 950 square feet, and it was built in 1895. It was called a two-and-a-half bedroom house because the middle room had no closet. The entire structure smelled old, like the thrift shops we were frequenting less and less.

My mother and father were in disagreement over the house. My mother kept on hoping for better. My father's position was that we had to make do with what was before us. But they both felt that they could not afford better for us.

My father said, "We can hide from the rain and the snow in here."

"Ah-huh," we answered in various octaves.

"Someday maybe we can do better."

We all knew he was referring to education. Someday when Dawb and I became educated, and the kids grew up and did well in school too, and my mother and father no longer had to work so hard just to get enough food and pay the heating bill. That is the someday my father was waiting for. It was the someday we were all waiting for.

We moved into the house in the fall, my first year of high school. Dawb was already attending Harding High School, an inner-city school where nearly fifty percent of the student body was multicultural—many of whom were Hmong. Naturally, I would attend Harding with her. She had helped me choose my classes; I would take all the International Baccalaureate classes that

I could get into, and where I couldn't, I'd take the advanced place-
ment or college prep courses. I had gone to a small junior high
school, a math and science magnet, in a white neighborhood with
few Hmong kids. There I had done well in my classes; I discovered
a formula I thought quite sacred: do the homework, go to class
every day, and when in class, follow the teacher with your eyes. I
was still whispering in school, but the teachers took it in stride. I
felt ready for the life changes that high school would bring my way.

I was feeling a strong push to reinvent myself. Without my
realizing, by the time high school began, I had a feeling in the pit
of my stomach that I had been on simmer for too long. I wanted
to bubble over the top and douse the confusing fire that burned in
my belly. Or else I wanted to turn the stove off. I wanted to sit
cool on the burners of life, lid on, and steady. I was ready for
change, but there was so little in my life that I could adjust. So life
took a blurry seat.

I knew that the parameters of our life would continue, but I
pushed against the skin that contained me. There would be school
or work during the day and then a return to the children and
babysitting. The drama of a changing body had taken me by surprise but had taken care of itself smoothly. I received my first bra
in seventh grade. I had gotten my period in junior high school and
had learned to sleep without moving very much the first few
nights of each cycle. Dawb drove around the block, often with me
beside her in the passenger seat. We were both growing up, we
were big sisters, and we took care of the children, and my mother
and father were convinced of our status as good daughters with
good grades. High school was important because it meant that we
were closer to college. It did not resonate in my family that high
school was a time to be young or to be old or that it was a time to
sneak peeks into different worlds. Such ideas hit against the
closed lids of my consciousness.

Dawb and I had decided long before that when the time came, we would strive for the University of Minnesota. We were hearing of Hmong doctors and lawyers, both men and women, all excelling in America, building successful lives for themselves, their mothers and fathers, grandmothers and grandfathers. I had never actually met a Hmong doctor or lawyer, but they had clan names I recognized as clearly as I did my own: Vue, Thao, Vang, Xiong, Lee, Lor, Moua, Cha, Hang, Chang, Khang, Her, Chue, Pha, Kong, and Khue. Dawb and I wanted to add to the success of our clan in this growing list of Hmong people who had made lives for themselves and their families in America. We wanted to make the life journeys of our family worth something. Our ambitions had grown: we contemplated changing not simply our own lives but the lives of poor children all over the world. And the key, we believed, was in school. But how far we could strive in school was unknown. We didn't tell anyone about our secret dreams.

Dawb had teachers who supported her all the way through. She had the kind of intelligence that a teacher could see (she looked every part the interested learner), could hear (her English had no accent), and could support (she soaked up information and processed it into her world for her use). I was lost, perpetually biting my lower lip: I didn't speak well or easily, and the link between what we were learning from books and living in life was harder for my mind to grasp.

In high school, this changed. I met a teacher who changed the way I saw myself in education. Her name was Mrs. Gallentin, and she opened up a possibility that I was special. She taught ninth-grade English, where we read *Romeo and Juliet* and *Nectar in the Sieve*, as well as other literary classics. I sat near the front of the class and absorbed the books. Mrs. Gallentin had a red face and a dry sense of humor. She had little patience for kids who giggled or were fussy in their seats—students who didn't pay close attention to lessons and did not do their assignments on time. I had overly curvy, confident handwriting that was hard to read, and I did not have a computer, so reviewing my work was a slow process. She may have noticed me initially because of this, and her interest was compounded by both my silence and my serious approach to literature.

Mrs. Gallentin became impressed with me because I could tell the important parts of a book. I knew how to anticipate the questions on her tests. At first, I was convinced I could read her mind. But after a few thought experiments in class, I realized I was picking up understanding from the books, not from her. It was in this class that I wrote my first real essay in response to the question: Is the story of Romeo and Juliet a story of love or lust?

It took me all night long to think about the essay. I had no personal experience with love, or lust. Some of my friends said that they were in love, but I was not convinced. The phone conversations they had with their boyfriends were mostly just listening to each other's breathing. After many false beginnings, I wrote about what mattered to me. I wrote about the love I felt I knew: Love is the reason why my mother and father stick together in a hard life when they might each have an easier one apart; love is the reason why you choose a life with someone, and you don't turn back although your heart cries sometimes and your children see you cry and you wish out loud that things were easier. Love is getting up each day and fighting the same fight only to sleep that night in the same bed beside the same person because long ago, when you were younger and you did not see so clearly, you had chosen them.

I wrote that we'll never know if Romeo and Juliet really loved because they never had the chance. I asserted that love only happened in life, not in literature, because life is more complex. As soon as I wrote the essay, I started worrying about it—what if she didn't like it, what if she didn't agree, what if I had it all wrong.

That was my first understanding of how writing worked, how it mattered to the writer, personally and profoundly.

I had written the essay out by hand first. I stayed up all night typing the essay on our gray typewriter at the dining table (it was the only surface in our house that was steady enough for us to really spread out our books and papers), slowly, with my index fingers (mistakes were costly). The sound of slow keys being clicked, first the right and then the left, eyes looking from keyboard to the page. Flexing careful fingers every few minutes. Trying to find a rhythm and a beat in the clicking of the keys, the mechanical whirl at the end of each line, the changing of paper. It took me a long time to think it through and follow the letters to the words, but the writing calmed something inside of me, it cooled my head: like water over a small burn in the pit of my mind. I watched eagerly as the third then fourth then fifth page filled with typed letters.

My mother and father came home early in the morning. They had changed their work schedules entirely to the graveyard shift (the nominal increase in their wages was necessary to maintain the new house). They saw my eyes closing over my work and became convinced that I was their hardest working daughter. My heavy eyes followed the way they walked so tired around the kitchen, and I grew confident that I really did know love—that I had always known it. By morning, the exhausting work of writing was done. I turned it in to Mrs. Gallentin.

Mrs. Gallentin caught me in the hall later that day and said that my essay was beautiful. She said that I wrote more than an answer to the question; I was telling her the ways in which questions come from life and end in life. I had never thought of myself as a good writer. I liked stories, and in elementary school I had written gory tales about intestines coming out. I thought I was good at math and science (what my junior high school had been good at), but Mrs. Gallentin said that I had talent for literature. I didn't see it, but it pleased me to hear her say this. In the course of a semester, she opened up a real possibility that I could excel in high school and college because they were all about good reading and good writing.

I began to see a truth that my father had been asserting for a long time, long before America. In Ban Vinai Refugee Camp, I had sat on my father's shoulders, my hands secured in his hair, and I listened to him talk about how we might have a brother, how we would become educated, and how our lives would go places far beyond the horizons we saw—in America. I looked at our lives, and how could I not believe? Beyond all the spoken wishes, a dream had even come true: eight years into America and we owned a house of our own. I wanted to recap this journey with Grandma. I waited enthusiastically for her summer visit.

She didn't come.

In 1996, welfare reform was in the news. The program was ending. Families living on welfare had to learn how to work "within the system." This meant that my uncles in California could no longer farm on the side and raise their families with the help of the government. This meant that my grandma's sons were in danger. What's more, she herself could be at risk. She was not a citizen; there was no way she could pass the citizenship test or speak enough English to prove her loyalty, to pledge, "I will fight for America if it were ever in danger." It was fighting that all the Hmong in America had done with the lives that had fallen to the jungle floor, the spirits that had flown high into the clouds again, that had fled life and refused to return—despite all the urgings, the pleas, the crying. But we were refugees in this country, not citizens. It was not our home, only an asylum. All this came crashing down.

In American history we learned of the Vietnam War. We read about guerilla warfare and the Vietcong. The Ho Chi Minh

Trail and communism and democracy and Americans and Vietnamese. There were no Hmong—as if we hadn't existed at all in America's eyes.

And yet Hmong were all over America. An exodus from California began. Minnesota was softer in the process of change. Welfare programs would not be terminated as quickly. Measures would be taken to ensure that old people received their benefits. A bill was being considered that would allow veterans of the Vietnam War, Hmong with documents, to apply for citizenship, and take the examination in Hmong. There was crazy studying everywhere. Aunt and Uncle Chue hovered over pages that he read with his French accent as she tried to make out the letters of the alphabet one at a time, through her thick reading glasses.

My own mother and father questioned themselves out loud, "What if we try to become Americans and fail?"

On the phone, Grandma said, "Lasting change cannot be forced, only inspired."

For the Hmong, inspiration came in those that were born in this country, the ready-made Americans in our arms, the little faces of boys and girls who spoke Hmong with American stiffness.

We could not remain just Hmong any longer. For our children, we could not fail. We had to try, no matter what. Even if it meant moving. Thousands of Hmong families moved from the farming lands of California to the job possibilities in Minnesota companies and factories. Aunt and Uncle Chue, despite their lack of English, studied for the citizenship exam, took it, failed, despaired, studied some more, and tried again. Eventually they succeeded, and they inspired my parents to try for citizenship, too. We had no more lands to return to. After nearly fifteen years, my family knew this. The camps in Thailand had closed. Hmong people there were repatriated, sometimes without knowledge, back into Laos. Families went missing in the process. Lives were lost. Children were killed. Ours were only beginning to raise their eyes to a country of peace, where guns at least were hidden and death did not occur in the scalding of grass or rains that drizzled death. We could not handle any more death. In wanting to live, we were willing to try becoming Hmong Americans.

A new chapter of our lives unfolded as we strived to become Americans. We sank our roots deep into the land, took stake in the ground, and prayed to the moon that one day the wind would carry us away from our old moldy house, into a new stronger home that could not be taken away, that would not fall down on us, that would hold us safe and warm.

Grandma and the uncles from California came to live with us in Minnesota. I felt caught in the larger context of being Hmong. We were only one family in the over two hundred thousand that lived in America. We all came from the same history. I burned for our stories, our poverty, and our cause. I was only in high school, and there was very little I could do. My father chided my impatient heart.

He said, "Patience is the slow road to success."

My father was a poet, and had a poet's heart. He carried love songs about the falling apart of a country. He made music of the loneliness in Thailand. He sang traditional song poetry about the earth grumbling and the sky crumbling, the leaves of the human heart fluttering all the while. I was his daughter, and I could not see poetry in the mold that grew wild on our walls—no matter how much my mother, Dawb, or I scrubbed, it never stopped, no matter how many layers of paint we applied. I couldn't understand why the Hmong people had to run for their children, how their children had to make lives, again and again, in different soils, to know belonging. Why it was that our house, so cute on the outside, rotted on the inside.

Why couldn't Grandma live with us now that we were all in one state? Why couldn't she live with any of her sons permanently? Because their homes were small. Because at one home, her heart yearned for another, and because all their homes together could never be like the country of her home in Laos, in the imagination and the stories she told all of us. In the world we lived in, our grandma carried her bags from one house to the next, sharing all our beds.

All this made me sick. My stomach cramped, and I could no longer eat. My bones hurt. I was tired. In the night, my heart squeezed itself, and I woke up incapable of crying the pain away. I remember one night, falling asleep looking at how the car lights from the street reflected on my wall. I could hear the pounding of my heart in my ears, very loud and deep, like a hollow cry from my chest. I felt like needles were twisting their way into my chest. I remember thinking that the pain was teasing me but realizing soon that it wasn't a joke. The air in my lungs caught in my throat. I struggled for escape, my hands reaching for my heart, beating frantically within me. I remember trying to cry out but finding a lack of air, a thickening tongue. I kicked desperately on the hard wall. First one, then a sad two, a final three: thinking in red: Mom and Dad, help me, I'm dying. I'm Hmong and I'm your daughter and I'm dying in the room beside yours. The thoughts were on repeat. Sweat. I could feel it breaking out on my forehead. Skin: I could feel the cold settling in. Heaving inside of myself. My eyes growing tight in the darkness, light streaming in. The door opened, slamming with force against the wall. My mom and dad rushed to my side, and I remember seeing myself twisting and turning, all out of color and out of breath, but still moving with nervous life. My father tried to hold me and I could hear my mom's voice panicking and Dawb running for the phone, and then I felt expiration come. I stilled. Air flowed in. My vision cleared. It was slowly over.

No ambulance was called. It was too fast. What seemed like forever was little more than five minutes on a dark Minnesota night. No one knew what happened. In the doctor's office, days later, I said: perhaps it was a heart attack. The doctor didn't think so: I was too young for a heart attack. My mom and dad were eager to believe the doctor. We didn't want to pursue the idea, and so we came home happy that it was all over.

In the month that followed, I lost twenty pounds. The doctors didn't know what was wrong. My mother and father hovered over me. My siblings watched me grow pale and weak; the bones on my hips jutted out, and the bags under my eyes took permanent residence.

Was I making myself sick? Looking for fundamental changes in my life? I loved the children, and I was happy to take care of them after school. All this time, I had been feeling like I was pushing against my skin: was it possible that I was pushing against my very own heart? The idea was a little preposterous. I didn't really believe it, but it nudged at me. But if indeed my heart did need changing, then what part of it? There was a clear division: the Hmong heart (the part that held the hands of my mom and dad and grandma protectively every time we encountered the outside world, the part that cried because Hmong people didn't have a home, the part that listened to Hmong songs and fluttered about looking for clean air and crisp mountains in flat St. Paul, the part that quickly and effectively forgot all my school friends in the heat of summer) or the American heart (the part that was lonely for the outside world, that stood by and watched the fluency of other parents with their boys and girls—children who lingered in the clubs and sports teams after school waiting to be picked up later by parents who could—the part that wondered if forgetting my best friends to life was normal and necessary). My body was surely whole. The doctors said so. What was broken in me must be something doctors couldn't see. I worried. The more I thought about it, the sicker I became: how does one change what one is becoming?

My grandma worried over me. She tried calling my spirit home. My rebellious, independent spirit hated the moldy house and refused to return. She tried her healing herbs. Their smell and taste took my soul far away to Thailand, to other times and places, but could not locate me in the present. Grandma grew despondent.

Something was wrong inside me, and its location was murky, like the origins of the Hmong home long, long ago and far, far away.

One day, I lay on the sofa—another day absent from school (my grades were dropping slowly)—looking up at the wall. Grandma and Dawb had gone shopping. My mother was in the kitchen preparing rice porridge for me. I heard the key in the lock. I heard them come in. I turned and saw that my grandmother had a gift for me.

There was something glittery in her hands. Her uneven gait came closer. She presented a thin silver bracelet made of elephants, bigger mother ones and smaller baby ones, circling together, tusks entwined. It was the most beautiful gift anyone had ever gotten me. She told me that the man at the store had taken off a few of the elephants to fit my small wrist. Grandma put the bracelet on me and said, "Elephants protect their babies by forming a circle around them. You are sick, and I cannot protect you. I bought this for you so that the power of the elephants will protect you and make you well again."

I wore the bracelet every day. I started to eat a little bit of food and took the medicines the doctors gave me (after all of the tests and retests, the doctors said that baby lupus would explain my symptoms). I wore the bracelet and grew stronger in its hold. The idea of a divided heart slowly lost merit: if there was no resolution that I could willingly and happily pick, then why not just live with it? Isn't this how all of life happens anyway? I looked at the glittering bracelet on my wrist and decided that a divided heart can be a good thing. One side can help the other. Why couldn't my chest expand to hold my heart? My father was always telling me that I needed to stiffen the walls of my heart, so it would not waver after the passage of people and places in my life. Maybe the softness of my heart, which I thought would cushion whatever may come, had been my biggest weakness. I had the help of elephants. I wore the bracelet every day and felt better.

One day, the tusks of two elephants lost their hold on each other. I placed the bracelet in a small bag, and I promised myself that I would eventually put the tusks back together again. Or, if that was impossible, I would have another one made, just like it.

I grew well again, but I understood that my body, like every other body in the world, could die. It could be healthy or not. If it carried life, then it could lose it. I was a child of war, and I should have known that we have no choice about when and where we die. When we do, we simply comply as bravely as we can. Getting up in the morning became harder than it had been. But each day, I did get up. That was the point. That had always been the point in the Hmong life, and even the American one. I grew satisfied with myself. Slowly, the sickness eased away.

All around our neighborhood Hmong people were buying the old houses. They were working in factories and coming home to small gardens in their yards. Hmong music could be heard from the open windows of our small, moldy house. When my mother and father were at work, Dawb and I drove Grandma and the children past the big mansions on Summit Avenue. We listened to Enrique Iglesias's "Only You" and admired the quiet tree-lined streets. We knew we didn't belong in the grand houses before us. A certain pride was born in who we were, where we came from, and where we were going. Anywhere at all was o.k. because we were together, healthy, and happy.

Fall came slowly that year. The green grass of our small lawn kept its color late into the season. The leaves in the big tree in the front yard held strong against the cooling winds. The descending sun lingered slowly over the horizon, and night rested gently over the brick Laundromat at the corner and the lines of two-story homes, old and falling apart.

I wanted things to stay the same, for my bracelet to hold its shine for all of time. I noticed the gray in Grandma's hair turning white. I thought about my bout with lupus, such a scary time. I thought about the scariest time in Grandma's life, when she was chased by a tiger in the mountains of Laos. The story, which she told me so long ago, of her broken earlobe. She was in the jungle:

The leaves of the trees shimmered high above her. Deep in a bamboo thicket, she stood working busily with her hands, reaching down for the bamboo shoots, pulling them out of the ground. The child on her back began whimpering. She didn't know why, so she rocked from one foot to the other, hands still searching through the long thin leaves. The bamboo shoots were young and fresh, and she imagined them sizzling, dipped in a mixture of salt and hot pepper flakes, coming together in her mouth with the fluff of newly steamed rice. The trees overhead and their loaded leaves formed a broken umbrella against the sunlight; the droplets of light dancing across the skin of her arms were a poor measure of the passage of the day. The dying leaves on the jungle floor carpeted her movements, softened the swaying of her body. The bag at her side was weighed down with the pale flesh of young bamboo shoots. Such a big harvest; perhaps she could boil the surplus after the meal, crush in chili peppers, add salt, and pickle the shoots in a big clay jar. She hurried her motions, shuffling the leaves aside, tugging with more strength on the shoots she found. When the child did not stop crying, she became quiet, stilled, and straightened to listen to the jungle. She thought to herself: why has it grown so silent?

There was nothing but the quiet shiver of bamboo leaves and the crying child around her. How deep had she entered the bamboo grove, all this foliage between her and the path home? Then she heard the growl. Her mother and father had told her stories of lone girls getting mauled by tigers in the jungle. Taken away aboard their striped backs to caves high up in the mountains, turned wild far away from human care—the beautiful ones turned into tiger brides, the less beautiful ones turned into tiger meals. She started trembling, and her feet, on their own accord, began running—heedlessly and fearfully—in search of a way to safety.

Her chest heaved and hurt as if someone were squeezing her heart between strong fingers. She couldn't avoid the branches or the tall bamboo trunks in her way. She felt them as they tangled with her heavy silver earrings, with the handwoven fabric of her black clothes, with the surface of her skin. She shook her head in agitation. The motion of her flight sent the bamboo shoots to the ground, the nearly empty bag still clasped tightly in one hand. The cries of the child accompanied the air from her expiring lungs. She raised her feet high as she ran against the green that rushed in at her. The labored flight became a long, endless leap into the air, a frozen moment: the jungle vegetation rose into the air chasing her wide feet, jungle bushes holding her back, tree limbs pulling her in, gravity pushing her down.

When the ground beneath her feet changed from the orange and brown of fallen leaves to the hard smoothness of black dirt, the light from the late afternoon sun blinded her. Her thin legs shook, and she had to stop. She looked behind her to see a jungle wall of darkened shadows, no gleaming eyes peeking out. The birds chirped and the bugs flew. It was a welcome relief when she heard the fluttering of wings and felt the wind against her heated skin. She wiped her hands on the red sash at her waist and felt pain. She raised her hand up and saw that it was wet with hot sweat and blood. There were scratches on her hands and feet, her arms and legs. Blood merged with rivulets of sweat down the sides of her swollen face. Her hand traced the flow of blood to her right ear. A branch had caught her earring, a heavy silver loop, and torn the lobe of her right ear in two.

Grandma would never wear earrings again, though only one ear was torn. All her life, Grandma wore the mark of that flight in the absence of decoration.

I put my hands to the broken lobe, and I held the pieces together.

"Grow beautiful in America," she said.

My grandma had outrun a tiger to live in this country. I wondered if a person could run forever.

I relished the fall: the grass turning brown, the leaves falling, the cold air against my hot skin. Fog before my face, air came from deep inside me to gain visibility and presence in the world. A young woman emerged from the moldy house, a young woman who wanted to be a writer and tell the stories of a people trying at life, to look for all the reasons that called life from the clouds. That winter there were heavy blizzards. The snow blotted out the features of our home. Inside, the mold grew in patterns like the dripping of tears.

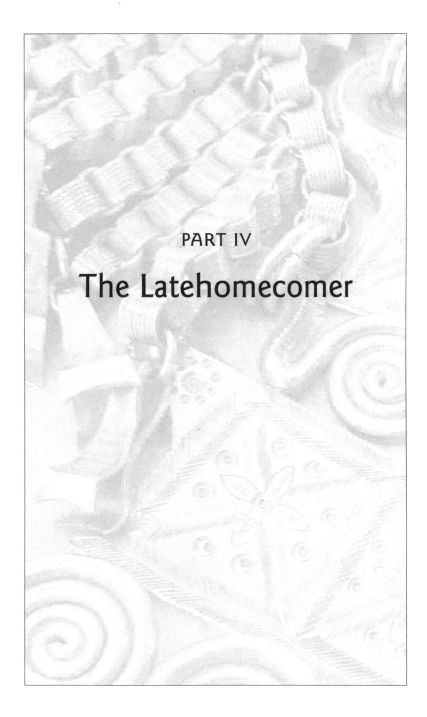

PART IV

The Latehomecomer

CHAPTER 12

WHEN THE TIGER COMES

 In 1999, I graduated from high school. I was still quiet unless spoken directly to. I had a best friend, and then two. The children grew, full of laughter and full of zest for everything new and everything that surrounded them. Our poverty was all they'd known. Life in America was all they knew. It felt like they were much more American than Dawb or me, and we were becoming more so than our parents—who told us so. They said it as fact, not with misgivings or regret. And so we became Hmong American in the eyes of those who loved us.

It seems like a closing of the eyes. Dawb, in her usual hurry to succeed, had enrolled in the post-secondary program at Hamline University: the parking situation was more affordable than the University of Minnesota. We didn't talk about our dreams of the University. The choice became as simple as easier parking. When my turn came to go to college, the University of Minnesota beckoned only a little. Most of my friends were going there. But because it had never been a definite in my eyes, it was merely an option. Many of my older cousins had gone there and to other colleges in the state. A friend mentioned Carleton College casually. It was where her older sister went. It was a small college in Northfield, only an hour south of St. Paul, and it was one of the best in the nation. I applied with nothing to lose. To my surprise, I got in. The departure was hard. That first September I stood in front of Musser Hall and watched family drive away, and if it wouldn't have looked ridiculous, I would have cried out for them to stop. As their car left Northfield, I realized how much I missed them already, my family, the children, their small hands waving from the window.

My life from this point on becomes a series of visits home. There was so much I had never been exposed to: the technology of e-mail, the protocol for choosing among forks at a multicourse meal, and the rigors of an academic program that tried to teach the merits of debate (arguing issues as a way of meeting them in the world was so foreign to me, so unlikable, so false), and time to simply be by myself. At first, the silence got to me, but I quickly learned to love it, to savor and cherish it, to use it to explore. I explored the world via the internet. I explored people's thoughts in chat rooms and in whimsical conversations late at night, staring at the moon, listening to the rush of the Cannon River. I explored the trees in the arboretum. I explored the campus. I explored myself as a cultural identity and as a Hmong person on a college campus without many. I explored how it was to be first generation, financially challenged, and living within the American immigration experience.

I could not translate all the things I was discovering at college to my mom and dad, to my home. But I could not help but apply them. This was when I started collecting my grandma's stories. I began to realize how our lives in America would be *our* stories. I started to understand one of the many truths that governed life: by documenting our deaths, we were documenting our lives. The Hmong had died too many times, and each time, their deaths had gone unwritten. There were no testimonies. The witnesses grew old, and they died, and life continued, as if they had never lived. I didn't want this happen to my grandma, to this woman I adored, whom I could not imagine not loving forever. I wanted the world to know how it was to be Hmong long ago, how it was to be Hmong in America, and how it was to die Hmong in America— because I knew our lives would not happen again.

On my return trips home, I grew attentive. The sunlight trickled in through the glass. I sat on the beige carpet, Grandma's wide feet in my lap. Together, Grandma and I watched the dust flittering to life. Outside it was terribly cold. Outside it was terribly hot. Inside, I was home with my grandma. It was the weekend. It was Christmas vacation. It was summer break. I was home, and Grandma had come to share our moldy house, to spend time with us. She slept on the used queen-sized bed in the little bedroom without a closet, her assortment of bags stacked against one wall. In one bag was a coffee machine— a gift from one of her grandchildren. In another there was a Polaroid camera, another gift. The remaining bags were an odd assortment: a heavy one with flower patterns the color of blood, a gray one that used to be black and had zippers around the sides that could make it big or small, and still more bags from her children and grandchildren, as well as the occasional suitcase she bought for herself. She carried everything with her, unable to trust the safety of place.

No matter whose house she was at, Grandma spent the daylight hours, sitting by the window. A figure in the weak light of the sun, in the gray of a cloudy day, she sat on one of her stools, a round bamboo frame held together and made comfortable by interwoven red, green, blue, and purple plastic strips. The sun gleamed on the silver edge of her old reading glasses when she looked up to check the passing of the day.

Grandma liked to work by the window in the natural light. Sometimes she mended her skirts, the ones she made cuts into so she could sew them up again. She would cut into the spandex waistbands to see what was inside or cut the hems of the skirts to make them a centimeter shorter or longer. Sometimes she used her scissors with the orange handles to cut plastic bags from Rainbow Foods, from Sears, from Kmart, from Wal-Mart, from Cub Foods, the white "Thank You" bags from the Asian grocery stores, into long strips of light brown, mostly white, sometimes red and green. In the last years of her life, she would spend hours before the window twisting the plastic strips into ropes, carefully massaging the lengths of cut plastic into the exposed, unwrinkled skin of her leg. Wearing her thick reading glasses, she spent her days making bags and bags of twisted plastic ropes. She said that there were always uses for ropes in life, things to tie together. My father said that Grandma had never been a lazy woman and didn't know how to keep her hands still. We all watched as she made work for herself.

Grandma's feet were wide and tan, the skin was leathery. The nails of her toes were long and thick, tinged with brown. The soles of her feet showed the cracks of many years of walking in flip-flops or without shoes. The ridged lines were filled with dirt from years before: dirt from California, dirt from Thailand, dirt from Laos. The earth had seeped so deeply into her feet that no matter how hard we scrubbed, it would not come out. With her feet in my lap, I carefully maneuvered the sharp edges of a shiny toe clipper around the strong lengths of her toenails. There were many people willing to cut her toenails—any of the cousins would. I don't remember the first time she approached me with a nail clipper in hand, but it had become our habit. Whenever I came home from college, and she came to our house, Grandma would sit by the window, looking down at the work in her hands, constantly checking outside the window. I would put a smile on my face and walk to her, offer to cut her nails. She never refused.

As I sat at her feet, Grandma would tell me the stories of her life from long ago. I had heard them many times. When I listened to the cadence of her voice, the rhythm of her speech, I stopped hearing the words. Her stories were like music, like the words of a timeless classic, a love ballad played again and again. If I had not thought it disobedient, I could have recited her stories, along with her, in tune with her voice.

According to the Hmong culture, my grandma had been born unlucky. She had learned about death at an early age, felt the distance and despair of being separated from a loved one long before she could have been prepared. Her beautiful older sister was the first member of her family to die. She had fallen prey to the envious greed of a witch in a nearby village, back in Laos. Grandma told me the story this way:

"It was during harvest time. My father and mother were still alive then. They were home with us. I was younger, you see. My older sister, whom you never saw, and whom your father never saw, was a great beauty. She had pale skin and light brown eyes, hair that flowed down her back. Not curly like mine, but straight black hair that the sun and I liked to play with. Everybody knew she was a great beauty, although she could not have been more than sixteen years of age. She went to the next village to join in the New Year's festivities. It was common then. All the young girls walking to the courting fields of nearby villages to toss balls with the young men. The witch was an ugly old woman who lived by herself. She saw my beautiful sister, and she got jealous. She made a brew of tears and other unsavory liquids, letting it boil and boil like her rising anger. It condensed into a single drop that she trickled into her palm. It was a mere toss of her hand in my sister's direction. She saw the old woman, saw the gesture, and in fear, her spirit took flight. When she got home, she was deathly pale, not at all the laughing girl who had run down the path away from our home. She died shortly after."

I interrupted Grandma with questions. Sometimes because I truly didn't know the place and time, the details of the life that she was talking about, and wanted her to paint the pictures more fully. Sometimes because I wanted to keep her talking, make the stories longer, lessen the time she looked out the window.

"All the young people would get to go and court each other in an open field with their fine clothes on—what about the dust?" I asked.

She tried to read the look on my face: was I trying to make fun? She always took the straight route, a simple answer.

She said, "It was the way things were done back then by the old people."

"Were there real witches, Grandma?" I wanted to know.

She would look down at me and away again, a little put off by how little I knew. Solemnly and seriously she would say, "Of course there were witches back in Laos. There were more than witches."

That was how we got from one story to the next.

"You always hear old people talk of people who turned into tigers in Laos. When I was a little girl, I saw one such person. She was an old woman who lived in a house on the outskirts of the village, near the jungle. The villages then were small collections of houses, maybe ten or twenty. It was only in the bigger villages and towns that one saw over fifty houses. Ours was a small village of no more than twenty or so houses. They were all closely spaced. Our house was close to hers, easy walking distance for a child. My parents would go to the garden every day, like your mother and father go to work. I couldn't make the trek with my family; my feet were too young to travel the mountain paths. They would leave me in the village with the rest of the younger children. There were several grandmothers and grandfathers who looked after us. Those days, there were no thieves, no robbers, no one to hurt or take children away from their homes but evil spirits. We could wander around the village as much as we liked.

"This old woman had no grandchildren to watch out for. She must have been lonely. But we were children, so we didn't understand how one person, especially an old one, could be lonely. There was a rumor that she was turning wild staying home by herself all day long while her children went to the gardens. Knowing this, the village children went often to spy on her. The houses in Laos are not like the ones in America. They were just made of split bamboo. Only the wealthier homes were made of wood. We lived in a split-bamboo village. All a child had to do was step close to the wall, find a hole big enough to look through, and the insides of a house opened up. Along with the rest of the children, I went to spy on this old woman.

"We saw her lining up wooden stools around the dirt floor. We watched as she practiced leaping from one stool to the next. She was preparing to leave the house for the jungle, learning how to move like a tiger. We didn't know this. She would hear us giggle during the big leaps and invite us to come into the house.

"'Whose little children are you? Come inside and watch me,' she called out in a voice full of power.

"And we, being children, would enter and sit with her, our stomachs light with fear and fun. She would show us her hands. I have never seen hands like that since. There were fingernails, and then at the knuckles, there were new nails forming, tough nails that touched. When she curled her fingers in, it was just like a tiger's paw. It used to make me laugh with delight."

My grandmother looked out the window, away from me, when she said the last lines of the story. Her voice, deep for a woman's, lost its usual strength and the words reached me from a place further than the distance between us. "One day, I heard that she had disappeared. The adults said that she had left her old life behind and started a new one. She really turned into a tiger—almost before my eyes."

The story of how the lonely old woman turned into a tiger was a particular favorite of my grandmother's. She loved to talk and tell stories, and the ones she liked she told often. Then there were those that she didn't tell often at all. I knew that Grandma had been an orphan in Laos. Once, she had had a mother, a father, an older sister, an older brother, and younger siblings. She said that when she was a little girl, people loved her just as everybody had loved me when I was a little girl. But her life as a little girl was short, and she doesn't remember much.

She never told me or her own children the specific ways her older brother, father, and mother had died. Maybe she chose not to remember; maybe their deaths, unlike the death of her beautiful older sister, carried no magic, had no witch's involvement. Perhaps the pain of the deaths was too sharp, was too sad to speak of, even nearly seventy-five years later. But I think she never told us how they died because in her old age, she was more concerned that we knew how she had lived, more than how her family had died. Whatever her reasons, my grandma only told us that her mother had died of an illness, and her father had followed that same year due to the same illness. She had told me, "He had no spirit for life without Mother."

I know that shortly after her father passed away, her eldest brother had an accident by a river. Was it a dragon? My curiosity never equaled my concern for her pain. It was enough to know that she had become the oldest member of her family, that she was made an orphan and had to take care of a toddler boy and a baby sister who was still breast-feeding. My grandma was only thirteen years old when she left childhood behind, not for her teenage years, but for her entire life.

"The baby was always hungry. My mother had breast-fed her before she died. Before my father died, I had seen how he would grind the rice grains in his mouth and then slowly trickle the liquid into hers, like the birds. After he died, that is what I did. I would put in the rice grains and chew and chew until it was nothing more than soft fluid on my tongue, and then I would give it to her. I don't know how a child manages to grow like that, but she did. She too grew to be a great beauty. I am the ugliest one in my family, my face so broad and my nose so small. My little brother was not much older, but at least he could eat soft rice and pieces of meat that I tore apart with my fingers."

I couldn't imagine myself feeding a baby without a bottle. The idea of grinding grains of rice in my mouth and then trickling them into the mouth of a crying baby did not have a place in my world of responsibilities. The image rested, like the metaphor she offered me, in nature, in hungry baby birds and their parents— their orphaned sisters.

All the stories I had heard about orphans in Laos had been filled with sadness. Aunt Chue had once told me a story about her father and how he had been an orphan. She recalled how each New Year, when all the other kids in the village got new clothes to wear to the festivals, her father would take off his old clothes, yellowed by wear, and dye them with dirt and tree bark.

Even the stories that my father and mother told me as a child, legends from when Laos was still hovering in magic mist, told of orphans with grimy fingers and dirty faces, stomachs bulging in hunger, eyes soaked with tears. I understood that Laos was a country without Rainbow or Cub Foods, without government money or paychecks. In the Laos that the people in my family knew, a person had to grow what her family needed to eat. There was no such thing as extra rice. And so when I learned that my grandmother had been an orphan girl, I asked her if she ever went hungry.

Grandma looked at me and sighed a little under her breath, and then she said, "You do not think so much about hunger if you have never been full."

I felt her words sink into my stomach. I understood that she didn't want to talk about it. Grandma did not like to make me sad.

Grandma had told my mother about how Grandma's baby sister used to cry at night from hunger because the rice liquid was not enough to sustain her growing body. She was scared that the crying baby would wake up her cousin and his family—the children couldn't live by themselves, and since he was their closest relative, they had moved in with him. At night, when everybody else was asleep, Grandma would carry the crying baby in the old child-carrying cloth that her mother had sewn. With the baby on her back, she would walk back and forth, back and forth, around the light of a dim fire. She would hum to the baby. It didn't work; her voice was not the same as her mother's. The baby's crying eventually made Grandma cry, too. Night after night, she would cry quietly with the hungry baby until exhaustion fought the baby into a restless sleep. It was only then that Grandma would tiptoe to the bamboo platform that they used for a bed and slowly crawl up beside her sleeping brother. Worried that the baby would wake up if she took the child-carrying cloth off, she would not untie the child from her back. I imagine a thirteen-year-old girl with a wide, serious face and curly hair tied back in a small ponytail with a piece of old string, sleeping carefully on her side, quiet in the dawn, the trails of dried tears on her face.

In her cousin's house, my grandmother grew to womanhood.

I often asked, "Did he love you enough?"

Her answers were always spoken softly; she would say, "What is enough? He loved me as well as a cousin could have loved his deceased uncle's three dirty children. He loved me better than any stranger could have."

Grandma never became the beauty that she saw in her sisters. Her beauty became such that one had to know her, love her, hear her, and hold her to see. She had a deeper sort of beauty, the kind that took years of looking and thinking to understand. Her face was considered broad, handsome but not pretty. Her lips were soft and pink; they did not curve up or down at the corners; she had a resolute expression, fierce eyebrows, angled and thick. She had a small ball nose that my father inherited and that I see traces of in the faces of my brothers and sisters, my cousins, and myself. She had two dimples, one on each side of her face—like me. She was a short person with a slow walk, a woman of girth and substance. She never depended on her looks for anything, not even for my grandfather's attraction to her.

"Your grandfather wanted to marry me because his brothers thought that I could give him strong sons. He was a widower, old and already addicted to opium by the time he entered my life. His brothers thought that if he married me and I gave him strong sons, he might again feel life beat in his veins. I was the orphaned girl in the village; I worked hard and I was not lazy. They knew this. So they came with bars of silver, horses, and pigs. My younger brother and sister could not take care of themselves. They were still just children, so I did not want to marry. Your grandfather was old. I cried at the ground when my cousin agreed to the marriage. There was nothing I could do. I had to marry him. Later, years later, your grandfather's brother told me how he and all the men who came to arrange the marriage felt sorry for me. He spoke of how he kept on thinking that if I had had parents or an older brother, if they would have heard me cry, I would never have been forced to marry your grandfather. I cried so hard that the whole village came to watch my pain. How can I describe the cries to you? I looked at the sky, and it was gray and blue, and I looked at my younger brother and sister and knew how hard their lives would be without me, and I looked at your grandfather and I could only think . . . if my father and mother were alive . . . but they were not, so all I saw was the gulf in the sky."

My grandfather was not a bad man, as my grandmother grew to know and love him. He was only a man who had also had a difficult life. His first wife, whom he had loved well and had made a life with, was not able to give him children. When she died, he lived all alone in his silent house; he let the fields grow wild. He was thirty-two years older than my grandmother when they were married: fifty-two to her twenty. Their village was small, and wealth was measured by the size of a harvest or the contents of the animal pens. My grandfather's pens were full of pigs and horses. He was famous for giving chicken eggs, valuable gifts, to orphans. His reputation for kindness was well known, even before my grandmother married him, and she had heard of his soft words and gentle actions. My grandfather and my grandmother's cousin, the one she lived with, were best friends. There was no way she could have refused the marriage, but it would turn out to be not such a bad marriage after all.

"When I came to live with your grandfather, he still had livestock," she told me. "He was not a lazy man. There were horses, chickens, pigs, and buffalo. After my initial sadness, I noticed this. Because your grandfather was a silent man who had already built a life, he was not inclined to help me work out a different one. I had everything to myself. I had never had anything, and then I found myself with a whole life to move in. I went to the garden, and your grandfather would go with me. I fed the animals and our many dogs. It was all just me. I didn't mind. He was still a shaman then, and he would go and perform ceremonies and then come home. He was well respected. Everybody thought he had a good heart, and to me he was kind. Even to my brother and sister he was good. He understood the things that were missing when there were no parents.

"When your grandfather's brother died, his son came to live with us. I raised him as if he were one of my sons, and when he grew older, he helped me raise all of them. He was a smart man, much as his father had been. You know? I married the brother who had a good heart but who was not so smart. He taught me that kindness was more beautiful than intelligence."

My grandmother was an intelligent woman. She looked at the pieces of her life carefully, got up slowly, and tried to fit the jagged edges together, no matter how crudely, so that her life was never completely empty. She took her little sister to live with her in the house she shared with my grandfather. There the little girl grew up and married a Hmong man who lived on the border of Vietnam and Laos. When she left, it was the last time my grandmother saw her. At first there were the demands of distance and growing families to contend with, separate lives lived far away, and then later there was the Vietnam War, the departure of the Americans, and the deaths of the Hmong. My grandmother spoke of her sister as a young girl all throughout her life.

The life that my grandparents shared was not long. They were married for close to thirty years. She would say, "Thirty years sounds like a long time, but when I remember my life, he was only a part of the middle years. In the beginning, I was alone, and in the end, I stood by myself as well. My life with your grandfather was like a moment when I could lean on someone, a small period of building a life."

Although Grandfather was worried that he was too old and that he would not be able to raise all of his children, they both yearned for family; it was something neither of them had. Grandma believed that the only way to keep a family together was to have many sons, many people, so that there were many different points holding on. It was easy to tear apart two hands, no matter how strongly they held, but if they had many hands, coming from all different directions, the grip would always hold, at some point, no matter what tried to sever the bond. At the very least, a tearing apart would take longer. She believed that a big family could buy time. She also wanted sons because she had been born a woman, and in her marriage to my grandfather, she had been torn from a family she was not ready to let go of, and she felt that sons would always stay inside a family. Sons could and would stay together, be ties to the earth itself.

They had ten children together: seven boys and three girls. Nine of them survived. I never met Grandma's first daughter, whom Grandma remembered as her "most beautiful baby girl." She died when she was just a baby. My father and my uncles tell me that it is likely she died from a stroke, some form of immediate sickness that caused her little body too much pain, and because she could not bear it, she died. My grandmother said that the baby was not sick. Grandma told me that the little baby was taken away by bad spirits who saw the good baby girl and wanted her soul for themselves. She said that neither my father nor my uncles could know as well as she herself, the mother. For one thing, many of them were not even born yet. She only had three boys then.

My grandmother, looking out the window of our house in Minnesota, her sewing in her lap or her plastic ropes in her hands, spoke of the day her baby girl died.

"She was maybe a month old only, beautiful with clear skin and dark hair. She was young, but I had to go tend the garden. The weeds would not wait. Your grandfather was away. He had been called to another village to heal a sick girl's spirit. I had your three older uncles with me. We went to the garden because we could not afford a bad harvest. I remember the fierce morning heat from the sun that day. Such a thing to remember on the day your first daughter dies.

"It was hot. We got to the garden after a long walk, waving away the busy flies with our hands. Underneath the shade of a tall tree by the side of the garden, I left the baby sleeping. She was such a good baby, always sleeping quietly and never fidgeting like all my other children. I told the boys to look after her. 'Nhia, Chue, and Sai, look after your baby sister. If she cries, come and get me. Play close to her.' I went downhill to tend to the weeds. I was thinking I would start low, from the back of the garden, and climb up the slope to my children. All morning long I was down there, sitting low to the tilted ground, heels planted into the dirt. My hands were busy pulling out the weeds and beating at the flies. The sun was high in the sky when I heard the boys calling me. Three voices, all frantic. I dropped my hoe on the ground. I ran back as fast as I could. The boys were screaming. I rushed under the shade of the tree. And there underneath the tree was a pig, blue and purple, pretending to be my baby. You see—the evil spirits had taken my beautiful daughter away when she was sleeping. In her place, they had set an ugly thing. She was breathing, fighting to breathe.

"Even though I knew my baby was gone, I picked up the thing that looked like her, and we ran as fast as we could home, the boys running beside me. I held her to my chest and pressed her head against me. We were halfway there when there was no breath. Your baby aunt died like that. My most beautiful daughter. Her body had grown cold by the time we reached the village. There was nothing to do. Your grandfather and I buried her along the path to the garden.

"Many days after she died, we would walk past the place where we had hidden her small body into the hard earth and I would cry to her. One day I was crying out, 'My daughter, are you hungry? Your mother misses you. My breast still carries the milk meant for you,' when I heard it. A shrill, angry cry that sounded like my daughter's from the side of the road. She did not want me to cry out for her. I never did again."

After the baby died, Grandma promised herself that she would never let another one of her children die in her arms. My grandma had a fear of death, of dying, of all the ways in which human beings have to say good-bye to one another. Maybe it was this fear that drove Grandma to learn the ways of herbal healing and then to strengthen her armor more by becoming a shaman. But a person did not just become a shaman; their spirit had to be called.

My grandfather had had no choice. When he was still married to his first wife, he became very sick. One day, as he was about to get out of bed, he felt a sickness in his body that would not let him up. He had been healthy the day before and this sudden illness was a mystery to everyone. He had an unbearable toothache, and his body was wracked by high fever. His wife went to the village medicine woman and then to the head shaman. No herbal concoction could ease the pain or lessen the fever. The days passed and he got weaker and weaker. Finally, as a last recourse, he was given opium as a sedative to help ease him into sleep. The head shaman was called again. He tried to find out what was wrong with Grandpa's spirit; animals were sacrificed and the gongs were beaten. More and more opium was administered. How my grandfather became a shaman is also the story of how he became addicted to opium—a habit that he was never able to break.

In desperation, his wife finally consulted a famous shaman who was believed to have great powers. He saw my grandfather and said calmly that the pain was Grandpa's spirit yearning to become a shaman. The fevers and toothache would go away once he started training. The famous shaman agreed to become my grandfather's master, to show him the ways to the spirit world. To my grandfather's astonishment, after the words of the famous shaman were spoken and my grandfather had agreed, the pain miraculously disappeared.

My grandmother's spirit, which carried the fear in her heart after her baby girl died, became sick. She lost her appetite and grew weak. She tried to regain her strength for her children, but felt her body was too heavy, and no matter how she willed her heart, she could not get up. She tried to heal herself with her herbs, but that didn't work. Finally, a shaman was called. When the diagnosis came, Grandma did not fight the path before her. She knew that the role of a shaman was for the entire community. She walked the path to the spirit land with conviction, underneath the wings of her red cloth, driven by a power, perhaps a fear, inside of her to keep her children safe.

However Grandma tried to keep those she loved safe, she could not keep old age from coming to my grandfather. He had been a healthy, strong man in his prime. Even after he started using opium, he was hearty. After his seventieth year, during the heavy monsoons, in the days of endless rain, he became sick. He lost his appetite. His youngest child, my father, was only two years old when Grandpa lost his hold on life. During his final moments, he reached out to his two youngest children, whispered his last words, words that my father does not remember but knows from the voices of his older brothers.

My grandfather said to my oldest uncles, "I have lived this life like a young man, even when age came to me. I have two baby boys that I am leaving behind. They are mine, but I cannot take them with me. They cannot care for themselves. I have nothing left to leave them except for the two small colts in the pen. Please raise my youngest sons for me. One day, if they become intelligent men, then maybe they can love you in return. Raise them because I have raised you."

According to my uncles, when my grandfather closed his eyes and his breath stopped, his body relaxed into itself, like the weight of age and sickness had disappeared from his body. My grandmother pulled her hair for days to ease the pain in her heart.

She said she sat down on the ground and tried to call him back, "If you are so kind, how can you leave me with all these children?"

Grandfather died in 1960, when the inner turmoil of the country had not yet penetrated the routines of their lives. My uncles buried him on the slope of a tall mountain that overlooked their village. Grandma called out to him long after he was buried. He didn't answer, so she beat the earth with her hands.

"Your father, my baby son, has no memories of his father," Grandma said to me. "If his father walked right beside him, he wouldn't know to reach out his hand. All he can remember of his father is a man sitting by the doorway, twisting dry grass into rope. Your father wondered if the old man was making rope for him to tie around the chickens. Your father has always loved chickens; your grandfather did, too. My children were poor. How could they not be with only a mother to care for them? But each New Year's, when other families ate pig, we ate chicken. If they ate cow, we ate pig. I never allowed my children to go hungry."

The sunlight was suspended in the small living room. I held Grandma's feet in my lap, cutting her nails slowly so that the words would not cease. Her hands were light on my head; they brushed the hair back from my face. Her fingers traced the curve of an ear, along an untorn lobe.

Her words mirrored the tenderness of her actions, "You know, your face is much narrower than mine, and the bridge of your nose is higher. You are small, but your skin is smooth, and your hair is straight. If you grew it out and tied it back from your face, like so, you would be beautiful. But you insist on cutting it short, like a man's. This is because you live in America now, far away from Laos, far away from the life your grandmother had."

She shook her head as she said the words. In front of the window with her feet in my lap, she told me the stories of her life in

Laos. It was a life that I didn't know but held close, imagined I saw, wanted to cherish. In my head, the colors of the trees were dark green. The beauty of the hills, the low-lying clouds, the sound of the birds flying and chirping from trees, the buzz of insect wings, her little-girl house, golden like hay in the afternoon sunlight, the winding paths that her wide feet would take, came alive inside of me.

In the floating dust, I made out the beauty of little rainbows born in the circles of light, and I imagined how it would be to walk with Grandma on the narrow dirt paths, my hand held securely in hers. She would point to this plant and the other, this bird, this place where this thing had happened, and in the midst of my daydream, the tigers would intrude. Were they hiding in the jungle waiting, even after all these years, for us to return?

My grandmother's death was the first natural death in our family since 1975. It was the outcome we had been struggling so long for: a chance to die naturally, of old age, after a full life. The funeral would take us back to before the war, before the refugee camps of Thailand, before the life in America—all the way up to the clouds again.

CHAPTER 13

PREPARATIONS

I had been preparing for my grandma's death for a long time. I had never lost anyone I truly loved before. I didn't know what it would mean. For me, death had always been something scary. From my memories of Ban Vinai Refugee Camp, I can still hear grieving people cry out for the return of their loved ones, haunting melodies of loss caught between the world I could see and feel and another, deeper, further place I wished never to know. There was the old dead woman in Phanat Nikhom Transition Camp to America who had waited for my soul in the dark. In America, we were so busy at life that I thought death would come slowly. I believed that I could make it stay away. My grandma had always said that her biggest fear was dying in America. She was scared that she would not be able to find her long way back to the land of her mother and father, to Laos, to the small village where she had been born, to the bamboo platform where she had fallen from the sky to enter the world, the place where life had called her from the clouds. I worried with her.

I couldn't tell anyone about the nights, on various weekends home from college, when I listened to her breathe in the dark. I slept on the couch in the small living room, and she slept in the queen-sized bed in the next room. With her assortment of bags stacked near one wall, she slept on mounds of pillows, her heavy blanket pulled up close to her chin.

The moonlight entered through the space between the two beige curtains at the wide window. It was the same window Grandma sat by to twist her bags, to sew up the unnecessary cuts she had made into her clothes, to tell us stories. It looked empty in the shadows without her there. I heard the ticking away of time, our clock on the wall: a square gilt frame of gold, a thick piece of glass, and inside a space that contained two butterflies, one bigger and yellow, the other smaller and a shade of musky blue, ticking away time beside three plastic red roses in full bloom. It was an old clock, one of our original possessions, given to us when we first arrived in America by some goodwill organization. My mother liked it because it was dependable, never wrong. We had owned it for sixteen years and changed the batteries only a handful of times. In the dark, I imagined the butterflies twirling around slowly on sharp metal needles that pierced their dried bodies. Surely in their world, free of dust, free of age, free of worry, moving, but without life there was no such thing as death.

My own world was not so constant. I had dark thoughts. Was Grandma o.k.? Was she asleep? Were her dreams taking her far away, to places where I could never reach her? I felt a need to hear her breathe. It was always a slow process. I knew that I did not want to hear her without breath. It would never be the same—the person I loved was the one whose forehead warmed to my kiss; whose wrinkled skin, dry and leathery, shifted to accommodate the shapes of my lips; whose smell of menthol oil and herbs I knew with my eyes closed. But then I would tell myself, *You are not a coward. You love her so go make sure she is o.k.* I questioned myself. *What are you afraid of, Kao Kalia Yang? This is the woman who gave you your name, this name that you like so much.* I would take a deep breath then get up quietly from my makeshift bed.

I twisted the doorknob slowly. There was a small click. I opened the door, not a squeak. The one window in the room, covered with light-blue blinds and a thin flowery blue curtain that blocked out the moonlight. When my eyes adjusted to the dark, I made out the mound of pillows, but I couldn't see her form on the bed. When I was a child, Grandma used to snore, but by her ninety-third year, if that was indeed how old she was, she had stopped snoring. She only expelled deep breaths that came in irregular intervals; her chest would rise high and then fall low in a tired, silent way.

I tried to hear her breath, but all I heard was the ticking of the butterfly clock from the living room. I couldn't tell if the ticking was in my heart or my ear. I inched closer and closer to the bed. I reached out my hand for her comforter, a furry one that she had brought from California. I walked slowly up the length of the bed. I sank to my knees beside it. I knew she was under the covers. I wanted to put my hand near her nose, so I could feel for air, but I was afraid it would wake her up. By the side of her bed, I knelt, with my hands cradling my head, staring into the dark, waiting for her to move. I breathed in her scent. I tried to hold it in my chest until the call for oxygen became too strong. A small shifting of the blanket would take me back to the night, and I would hear air expel in a gust, from her chest and my own, air that had been held in for too long. We were both alive.

It was my senior year at Carleton, and I had begun to hope that my grandma would come to my graduation in early June. She would be proud. She would walk slowly around the green campus, her hands held behind her back, through the carefully designed sidewalk, among the green grass and the trees. She would get tired and be impatient for the ceremony to be over. When it finished, I would walk to her and give her a big hug and she would say, "*Me naib*, Grandma is very happy today. You will make your father proud."

I would tease Grandma and tell her, "Aren't *you* proud?" and she would remind me that in America a woman can do anything, be more powerful than a man; she would say it was my job to take care of my father, and that yes, she was proud because I was one step closer. I woke up from my dreams wanting to ask, "How many steps does it take?"

I knew that she was getting weak. She had stopped eating. Even her favorite snack, a piece of toast with peanut butter spread on one half and the other spread with mayonnaise, she would pick at. Each morning we shared together, I made her morning coffee exactly the way she liked it—four teaspoons of sugar, one of sweetened condensed milk, one of Ovaltine, one of hot chocolate, and one of instant coffee—and she would take only a few sips, saying that it was good. She would cover the cup with tin foil and put it in the cupboard. She said she would drink it later, but she never did.

The skin on her hands, which I had always felt was dry and thin, grew lighter in a way that caused me to tighten my hold, hold her hand more securely. My wish to make her proud at my college graduation was only a pleading for more time, a way of envisioning the way the future could be.

In her own way, Grandma tried to prepare us for her death. She would talk to us about how tired she felt and how everyone who loved her was already dead, how she had had a bad dream, and how fighting to surface from the hold of sleep took more and more out of her. We would be watching a late-afternoon show, and Grandma would get up from her place by the window and come and sit between Dawb and me.

She would say, "Grandma had a dream last night. She does not feel good."

Dawb and I would feign interest in the show, look at her reassuringly, and say, voices in unison, "It's only a bad dream, Grandma. There's nothing to be afraid of. We are here."

We didn't ask for her to elaborate; we knew that she would.

She knew we didn't want to hear, but she started to talk anyway.

"Grandma is getting old. She will not be here forever. When she goes, please do not get her anything. I want to tell your father and your uncles, but I can't because they won't listen."

In my chest a small weight grew that made me more aware of each breath.

"When I die, I do not want anything," she would repeat, looking at her hands. "All I want is a good bed to sleep in. You tell your father and your uncles. I know my sons are poor. I do not want many animal sacrifices or a big funeral. I just want a good bed to sleep in. I have never had a good bed to sleep in. In Laos, when I was a child, we only had hard bamboo platforms to sleep on. When we were in the jungle, we slept on the cold jungle floor. In Thailand there were mats and then more bamboo platforms. Here in America, I sleep on old beds from used furniture stores. When I die, tell your father and uncles to get me a good bed to sleep in. My heart wonders how a soft bed would feel underneath my tired body. Tell them that all Grandma wants is for her last bed to be a good one."

I wanted to buy her a good bed, but I had no money. Dawb didn't have any money, either. We were only students. My parents worked every day, and that was only enough money for the bills and the rent; we all slept on old mattresses. But we were not old and we still had the future and we still could get good beds to sleep on, and in my heart, I knew she was not talking about a real bed. I wanted to tell her not to talk like this. I wanted to return to when I was a little girl and how I would cry and make all the grown-ups around me promise me they would never die and leave me. I couldn't cry for her to stay because she was sitting right by my side, so I cried for her bed. Dawb cried, too. We tried to hide our tears from her.

We both knew Grandma was scared of death. Death had taken everyone who had loved her long ago, her mother and father, her brothers and sisters, my grandfather, her most beautiful baby girl, and many others whom she knew and cared for. Many of the dreams that she told us about were the same.

"I had a dream last night. In the dream, I was living in the past again, in Laos. It was early morning, and I could see the dawn flooding in through the split-bamboo walls, and I felt I should get up and go outside to get water from the river so that I could prepare breakfast for my children. I saw that the door was unhinged, and I found myself standing before an open doorway. At the rickety gate into the yard, a man was standing, in traditional Hmong clothes, all black, wide-legged trousers and a shirt secured in front with a large safety pin. In the dream, I knew that your grandfather was dead, but I was not afraid. I ran my eyes over his features, the head of thick gray hair, the small angular face, the strong neck. He was as he had been when I first married him, not the thin, dying man I had last seen.

"'Why are you here?' I asked him.

"'I came to wait for you. It is morning now. Time for us to go,' he answered.

"I thought about my sons, although they were not in the dream, and I said, 'I cannot go with you. I still have to take care of our sons.'

"He looked at me sadly, like he would when he was still alive and I said careless things.

"I urged, 'You go ahead. When I am ready, you can come back, or I can follow.'

"Your grandfather was silent for a long time, and then he looked down at the fence between us. I knew what his heart wanted me to say, but my heart would not let me say it.

"I said, 'My sons are grown men now, but I still worry about them.'"

When she told us her dreams, we would only answer in the way she had answered our nightmares as little girls: "It is only the scaring away of the bad things in your life. You should go spit in the toilet and say you don't want the dream. Tell the whirling water to wash it away."

We said this because we had believed it when she said it to us. And then in our different voices, mine higher and softer, Dawb's slightly deeper and steadier, "We love you, Grandma."

"Yes, you do," was always her response to our love.

When I was a little girl, Grandma would say to me, after a nightmare, "Put your worries aside. Grandma is here. She will protect you."

I wish I could have said the same to her. "Put your worries aside, Grandma. I am here. I will protect you."

CHAPTER 14

GOOD-BYE TO GRANDMA

It was nearing the end of my winter break, early January 2003, when Grandma fell at Uncle Sai's house. My parents and I, along with the rest of the aunts and uncles, went to see her. She was lying on Uncle Sai's gray sofa in the living room, her faced turned toward the window, her body a heavy weight in the soft pillows. She said she was in pain. She did not look like she was feeling very much at all, only thinking very hard. I wrapped my arms around her and held her close. She combed my short hair back from my face. I kissed her on the side of the forehead where I could feel the blood thrum underneath the warm, dry skin. It was time for me to return to college for the winter trimester. I told her that I would call.

I was busy at school trying to get into my graduation thesis when my cousin Lei called me and said that Grandma was not feeling well. Was it serious? She wasn't sure. I called my parents immediately. They told me that Grandma was at Uncle Eng's house and that she was not eating well, but for me not to worry. I should work hard on graduating on time. They promised they would pick me up the weekend after next. I called Uncle Eng's house, and I asked to talk to my grandmother. She couldn't talk to me—she was sleeping.

Lei called a week later to tell me that Grandma was now unconscious and that she would pick me up. It was February 10, 2003. The drive from Northfield to Brooklyn Park took an hour. In the car, we were silent. Grandma was no longer able to eat or drink. I looked out the window at the parking lots along the highway, and a tall hill where a few finger-sized people skied down the white distance. We were full of worry. I was beginning to miss my grandma already.

I entered Uncle Eng's house and wiped my feet on the rug, looked up and saw my grandmother in a hospital bed beside their east wall. She looked like she was sleeping. I took off my shoes and approached the bed slowly. Aunt Chue was sitting by the side of the bed on a chair. A few relatives were on the sofa by the window, talking quietly. When I saw that Grandma was not sleeping but struggling for breath, her hair matted with sweat, her lips opening and closing in desperation, her one tooth showing, the image became blurry. I got as close as I could to her. I felt the resistance of the bedrail against my thigh. I put my head on her chest.

I said, "Grandma, I am here."

I said, "Grandma, are you O.K.?"

I said, "Grandma, I love you."

I said, "Grandma, don't leave me."

I said, "Grandma, Kalia is here."

I said, "Grandma, are you O.K.?"

I said, "Grandma, I am here."

I said the same things over and over, and my heart was heavy in my chest, and every breath became harder. I made a lot of noise.

She raised a tired hand to my head, and she said, "Grandma knows."

I said, "I love you, Grandma."

And she said, "Don't cry, *me naib*. Grandma knows."

She tried to say more things to me, and I tried not to cry, but neither of us could do what we wanted. In all the languages of the earth, in all the richness of words, there is no word, no comparison, no equivalent, for my grandmother trying to be strong for me, her one *me naib*.

More people came to Uncle Eng's house. My grandmother had nearly three hundred direct descendants from her seven sons and two daughters. There were great-great-grandchildren even. Family and kind friends crowded into the house, leaving wet streaks of melting snow at the entranceway.

The next three days, the house swelled with people. The gas stove in the kitchen died because of the heavy Hmong pots that we needed in order to make enough food to feed everyone. My father and uncles turned the small porch into a large kitchen; they put up a thick blue tarp on metal poles. Propane stoves were brought in. No one wanted to go home at night; the three bedrooms were crowded with sleeping children, the smallest babies on the bed, the bigger ones on sheets on the floor. The men sat in the basement talking about the life we'd built in America, the success of Grandma's grandchildren: a chiropractor, a medical student, two law students, a master of social work, and the young ones in college. Upstairs, Grandma's grandchildren sat around holding her hands, her legs, witnessing her struggle to stay with us.

The doctors said that her body was shutting down. There was nothing we could do: it's what happens to the human body after a long life. What could we do to keep Grandma longer? What could we do to keep death away? The doctors said that if we wanted to, we could try to feed her Ensure through a syringe every few hours, if it made us feel better. We tried, but the liquid went into her lungs, and her body tried to expel it. She was too weak and faraway for food, so we had to stop. There were two bottles of medicine that we could give her every few hours. It wouldn't do much for her body but it would help ease our hearts.

On schedule, Dawb and the medical school cousin tried to give her medicine. When she still could, Grandma shook her head weakly. Dawb licked a little of the medicine and said that it was bitter. She whispered in Grandma's ear, "Please open your mouth, please try to swallow a little bit, please try for me. I know it tastes bad, Grandma, but it will help you feel better. Please please please try a little for me."

Grandma heard Dawb's voice asking, and she opened her mouth a little for the medicine to go in.

By February 13, Grandma's body temperature had dropped significantly. She was no longer responding to words, movements, the life we wove around her. Cold sweat seeped from her pores. She stopped smelling like menthol and herbs. I washed her with a wet towel and put baby powder underneath her neck to keep her dry. An aunt told me to stop, but I didn't want my grandma to smell bad. Another aunt said for me to keep wiping away her sweat and putting baby powder on her if I wanted to. My hands shook, and I spilled the baby powder onto her shirt, so I stopped. Near midnight, we couldn't watch her suffer anymore—trying to live without food and water—trying to live only because we could not let her go. We called 9-1-1.

The ambulance came, and she was taken to United Hospital in St. Paul. My mother and father wanted Dawb and me to take the younger children back to our house to bathe and get some sleep. We were too exhausted to protest, so we took the kids and drove home. We all pulled our mattresses onto the floor of the living room and slept in our moldy house. The next morning, my parents woke us up and said that Grandma was conscious. She was getting better; the i.v. at the hospital had revived her. They said we could see her for ourselves. It was February 14, Valentine's Day.

We stopped by a floral shop and Dawb picked out a yellow bouquet of Grandma's favorite flowers, lilies. We drove to the hospital.

We walked into the room, and it was like magic: Grandma was sitting up in the bed, an i.v. in her arm.

She saw us and said, "My girls are here."

We ran to her and hugged her and said we loved her. She was a little disoriented; she didn't know a few of the other cousins, but she knew us. An aunt asked her where she had been, and my grandma said that she had been following strangers who took her on a long journey, and then the night before they told her to stop following them. She was scared that she would be lost without them, so she did not want to stay in place, but they hurried on without her. She opened her eyes, and it was early dawn, and she was going to cry out, but she saw my cousins Sue and Pao sitting in the room with her.

The doctors told us that they had revived her with the i.v., but there was nothing more they could do and that she could not stay in the hospital. We pleaded with them to let her stay. We wanted to go and buy her food, get her to eat something more before we took her home. They said they understood our feelings, but Grandma was too old, and her body would give up anyway, regardless, and it would be best if she could say good-bye in the security of a home she knew. My father was upset. He felt that it was because he and my uncles were uneducated men without money—that their mother, whose life could be extended with an i.v., would have to return home to starve to death. But he had learned that feelings were not persuasive arguments. He was quiet before the American doctors.

"What do you want to eat, Grandma?" All her grandchildren asked.

She answered that she wanted to eat *fawm kauv*, rice-paper rolls with pork and mushroom and spring onions inside. Lei and I would buy them from the best Hmong restaurant we knew on University Avenue. Dawb and another cousin would buy chickens from a local Hmong butchering house to call Grandma's sick spirit in from the cold. We knew where to get what we needed. Grandma would be patient and wait.

It was a Sunday and none of the stores on University Avenue had fresh *fawm kauv*. Our favorite store was closed. Everywhere we went, we could only find dry ones. We couldn't return home empty-handed. We decided that Lei would steam the dry *fawm kauv* at Uncle Eng's house and that they would be o.k. We bought a package of soft rice cakes and California-style Sunny Delight, my grandma's favorite bottled beverage. We went back to Uncle Eng's house and steamed up the *fawm kauv*, and Grandma took little bites. I tried to feed her, but she said they were too sticky in her throat. She drank a few sips of Sunny Delight. We all grew happy at the sight of her with food.

It was dusk by the time Dawb and the cousin returned home with the chickens. The butchering house had been closing for the day, and all they had had left were a few weak chickens, leftovers from the busy weekend; many families must have been celebrating births, birthdays, weddings, maybe a few funerals. Dawb was scared the chickens would die in the cold, so she carried them home in her backpack. In addition, she had brought home a surprise: two big sheet cakes from Sam's Club. She knew that Grandma loved birthdays. We would all celebrate her birthday on Valentine's Day. The children ran around in circles singing, "Happy Birthday to Grandma!"—cheerful voices after the long days of worry.

Lots of candles were placed on the cakes, more than the ninety-three years recorded on her papers. With camcorders we recorded Grandma's words for us to all be healthy and well and live to be old like her and to be, above everything else on earth, good people. She said she wanted us to always remember where and who we came from. She was getting tired and could only manage so many words. The little children helped her blow out all the candles. The black smoke trails from the dying candles vanished slowly into the air.

Grandma's eyes were slowly closing, and I felt scared again. She hadn't eaten very much. I sat by her side, held her hands, and talked all the words out of me.

"Grandma, don't go to sleep. Talk to me. I want you to talk to me. I want to marry a Thai actor someday. You have seen his picture. He is a very handsome man, Grandma. He doesn't know I am alive, but it's o.k. because I am the woman whom he will spend his life with, whose name he'll never ever forget. Your silly granddaughter? Nope. Not me. You must be confusing me with . . ."

She laughed weakly and said, "Keep talking. I want to hear you talk. I do not want to fall asleep again."

I talked until her eyes closed and her mouth stopped moving. An aunt suggested that I let Grandma sleep—she was clearly very tired. She gently reminded me that I could still talk to Grandma tomorrow. There was always tomorrow. Wasn't there?

I held Grandma's hands in mine and whispered into her palms.

At some point, I dozed off. I know that Dawb and a few other cousins stayed up all night by Grandma's side. When I woke up, it was Monday morning. Grandma was unconscious again. My mother and my aunts were busy cooking steaming pots of rice, pots of beef stew with hay leaf and ginger, pots of chicken curry with mushroom and bamboo shoots. The house was full of steam. The littlest of the children were still asleep. I could hear the voices of the men mumbling from the basement living room. My back hurt from the chair.

That day, I comforted myself with the thought that we were living Grandma's dream; all of her children and grandchildren, all of her descendants were under one roof, no matter that the roof wasn't holding and that the heat had died in the house and that everybody was getting sick with the flu from going in and out of the cold patio transferring pots of food.

Later that afternoon, my father called me into Aunt and Uncle Eng's room. He said, "You have to go back to school."

I shook my head. If my grandma was going to leave, I wanted to say good-bye.

"No one knows how long this is going to last. Your grandmother could get well tomorrow or be like this for a long time. Your sister and your cousins go to school in St. Paul. They can go to school and come here after. You go to school far away. You need to go and do your work. I will have Lei drive you back."

I had never knelt before anyone. I had seen it in the movies. I always thought it belonged to a different place and time, to a desperation I would never know. I was my father's obedient daughter, but I could not leave yet. I knelt before him on the carpet, on my knees.

"Daddy, please don't make me go. Please let me stay."

I did not want to say that I wanted to see my grandma off. I did not want to put words to the fear of her leaving.

He lost his temper.

He got up and in a voice he had never used with me before said, "Are you going to make this harder for me?" His voice broke at the end of that question, his eyes glistening.

A cousin went to get my mother. She came into the room with an apron on, her hand over her mouth, coughing. I felt my mother's arms around me, like when I was a child and my vision was blurry with tears.

"Please do what your father says," she said, then started crying with me.

She brushed my hair away from my face. My father stood with his back to the room, his eyes on the wall. When he shouted for Lei to drop me off at school, he didn't look at me at all, didn't turn from the wall. I think he was crying. I walked out of the room. My feet led me to my grandma.

I leaned my head onto her blanket. I was tired, too. I didn't want to get up. Outside, it was getting dark, and the wind was picking up. I didn't want Lei to be caught in a storm after dropping me off. A friend of hers would go with us to make sure that she didn't fall asleep. Grandma was barely breathing. Her body was wet with sweat, and it was cold to the touch. I kissed her temple. I kissed her temple again. I kissed her temple again. I kissed her temple again. A place I had kissed a thousand times before. I felt the warmth of my lips on her cool skin. All my other kisses had landed on dry, warm, wrinkles. This last time, the skin was moist to my lips.

I said, "Grandma, we'll meet again. Grandma, I want to be your granddaughter again in another life."

They dropped me off at school late Monday night.

On Tuesday I called home, and Grandma was still unconscious.

On Wednesday I called home, and Grandma was still unconscious.

It was a Thursday afternoon. I had just climbed up four flights of stairs to my room in the eaves of Nourse Hall. I had just finished my last class of the week. I would go home the next day. I would see Grandma.

The sun came in through the windows, and sunbeams danced on my desk. My cell phone rang. I sat on the desk, and I looked at the name on my screen: a cousin who rarely calls.

"Hello."

"How are you?"

"I'm fine. I'm coming home tomorrow."

"I called because I was worried."

"About Grandma?"

"About you."

"Huh?"

"I was worried about you."

"I'm fine. How's Grandma doing?"

Silence.

And I knew. My grandmother had died. I had no more words, just a silence inside of me.

"You didn't know."

"No, I didn't."

"I'm so sorry."

I nodded as if he could see me.

He said, "Talk to me?"

"I have no words."

Maybe he nodded his head too, and I couldn't see it. The line was quiet.

After I hung up, I took off my clothes. I slipped into my Thai sarong and my shower flip-flops and went to the bathroom. I didn't cry. I went through the motions of washing. The water was too hot, but I noticed only when the white walls of the bathroom started crying, drops of moisture slipping down the tiles.

My grandmother died on February 18, 2003, in the evening, in Brooklyn Park, Minnesota: a country, an ocean, and continents away from the mountains of Xieng Khoung, Laos, where she had been born. She passed away on a metal hospital bed that she hated, in a thinly constructed house made of wood, of steel, of cement, of plaster, of materials she couldn't see through. She had been born on a bamboo platform, in a house made of split-bamboo walls, with dry grass for a roof; sunlight and wind had filtered about the floors. Nobody knows when Grandma was born, exactly. We think it may have been sometime in 1910, but she spoke of how life felt to one who was over a hundred years old. She was on her long journey home to the mountains and the hills.

CHAPTER 15

WALKING BACK ALONE

Metro Funeral Home was designed like a box cut in half, with the kitchens, dining area and refreshment counter in one area, and one big viewing room with space in front for the coffin and rituals in the other. Chairs were lined up along the walls, and like the pictures of American weddings, in rows across the room. I entered the building, and I saw the long dining-room tables and the refreshment counter. In the viewing room, I saw lines of chairs on the carpet, the orbs of silver and gold joss paper in the background, the ornate flower displays in hearts of pink and white, and unlit candles. Words on the high ceiling declared, "We Love You," in bold letters made from joss-paper boats. There were three photographs of Grandma hanging across the front of the room. Her body was on a white cotton blanket on the floor, underneath the big drum of the dead. The coffin, her horse to the other world, would come at noon, after the special guide of the dead had given her directions home. When I saw her body, I became nervous, shy, as if I were approaching a stranger.

Her body was pale blue after a month in the cold storage. Her wide face carried no wrinkles, just tight skin over bones. It was a version of my grandmother I had never seen before. She was dressed in traditional Hmong clothes: the hair turban, deep purple, wrapped carefully over her hair; the collared white shirt, buttoned way up; and then the dark outer garments, red and green sashes that tied at the waist, layers and layers of clothing from Laos. There were two pieces that I had never seen before. She had on a long black jacket with a collar that spread about her head piece, a little like Dracula's cape. Her feet were clad in the shoes of the dead, with pointed toes that curled up and in a spiral, black with red and white seams of connected triangles. It scared me, this woman with no wrinkles in clothes that I had never seen before. I approached slowly with the rest of the cousins to pay my respects. I sat near her head. I tried to convince myself that the body on the floor of the funeral home was the body of my grandma from a long time ago, before the wrinkles, before the sun spots, before me. The only part of her that looked like what I knew and loved were the bones of her fingers, straight and strong.

It had been a long time since my family had been in position to say good-bye to those we loved in such a formal way. There had been no funerals in the jungle. In the camps, I'm sure they attended funerals, but those were small imitations of what had been before. In America, after all these years, we had the work of a Hmong funeral before us. We followed the words of men who had memorized our traditions from before the war, men who held the responsibility of holding on to Hmong culture. These men told my father and my uncles what to do, how to prepare themselves, their wives, and their children to say good-bye.

Hmong funerals are food ceremonies. There are three meals a day, and everybody is welcome. No invitations are needed or even issued—it doesn't matter what clan you are. Nine cows and three hundred chickens were killed for Grandma's funeral; a supply of fresh meat, including pigs and chickens, slaughtered by the young men each morning for the given day's meals. Hmong widows agreed to make rice for each of the meals, and the women in my family worked hard to serve delicious hot dishes.

Ingredients were purchased from Sam's Club and Cub Foods, Cambodian stores and Hmong stores. We would make stir-fry: let crushed garlic sizzle in vegetable oil; add thinly sliced beef; include colorful assortments of red, green, orange, and yellow bell peppers, broccoli, celery, and carrots; use salt, sugar, MSG, and oyster sauce to pull the flavors of the meat and vegetables together. We would make different dishes of curries; cuts of beef, chicken, and pork stewed with baby mushrooms and corn; thinly sliced bamboo shoots seasoned with galanga root, lime leaves, lemongrass, dried chili peppers, coconut cream, and spicy curry paste. We would make dishes of fried tilapia topped with a special red coconut sauce that was a little sweet but mostly sour and spicy. In addition to these, we would keep a snack counter overflowing with constant supplies of fresh oranges, cookies and wafers (including Grandma's favorite, strawberry), an assortment of beverages, steaming hot coffee, tall bottles of beer, and ice-cold soft drinks.

Twenty-four hours a day, the food would flow. People would cry. Rituals and ceremonies would be performed. All for Grandma, and for us.

I wanted to reach my hands out to hold Grandma's, but I didn't. Instead, I helped at the snack counter in the back room: pouring ice cubes into cups, filling the cups with Mountain Dew, Sunkist, Sierra Mist, ginger ale, Coke, Pepsi, and water. I made sure that the snacks were plentiful in their respective bowls and that the napkins were on the table for guests. I kept thinking about Grandma's tightly closed lips. Had the funeral home people glued them together to hold in her single tooth? Where was the color? Isn't there a lip gloss that would make her lips as they were, soft and pink without shine or shimmer? Was she wearing makeup? I didn't want to return to the body. Already it was beginning to intrude on the memory I carried of her wrinkled skin and deep dimples. I decided that if I went back, I would concentrate on the deep purple of the hair wrap. A distant relative approached me and offered to work in my stead, give me time to go and sit by Grandma. The soda bubbled in its cups waiting to be drunk; no one was thirsty for pop. It was too early in the morning.

I went back to the body, took my seat on the carpet. My little sisters sat near her feet, looking young, looking like they were trying to remember what Grandma looked like originally, or as if they were trying to remember the still, silent body before them. A cousin passed a stick of incense to me. I held it clasped in between my palms and bowed my head. With my posture, I showed Grandma the honor of the place she had held in my life. She was the woman who had cushioned my entry into the world with her strong hands. Along with my cousins, I bowed down low, with the incense in my hands, at indicated intervals. Together, we sought the good fortune of the old, the deceased, our grandmother. I felt cold, and I thought the cold air was coming from the back room, the imagined human refrigerator. I tried to concentrate on the purple head wrap but I couldn't, my gaze wandering over her face.

My father and my uncles, Hmong sons, had asked for a man who was well taught in Hmong traditions to preside over the funeral. He had brought with him a selection of men, each specializing in a different part of the ceremony: the dressing of the body; the guiding of the soul to the next life; the beating of the drum of the dead; the playing of the *qeej*, a huge bamboo instrument played by men that carried the heart's wishes for happy weddings, bountiful new years, and words to the dead. The man who would teach Grandma's soul the way back to the place where she was born started chanting. I noticed a dead chicken in a carefully wrapped bag, its feathers still on, tied to the drum. My father had told me that the chicken would accompany Grandma on her long journey home. When Grandma was alive, she had said that we should listen to her stories so that one day, when the time came, we would know the places of her life. I now realized why.

The man chanted in easy rhythm, "Grandfather Nao Lao's wife, you are dead now. You are walking the path to the other land. You have come to America; here are your papers." He placed copies of her Social Security card and her Alien card (she couldn't become a citizen because she couldn't pass the citizenship exam; the only English words she knew were "no" and "hello") into her right hand. He told her she had died in Minnesota, faraway from home, and that her journey back would be a long one. I didn't want to hold my grandmother in place; it was her time to go, and I would wish her a fine journey. But I felt her leaving in the air I swallowed, big gulps, hopeless attempts to fill the empty space.

The guide told Grandma to go back to California on an airplane. She had lived nearly ten years in California with Uncle Hue, Uncle Sai, and Uncle Eng before they all moved to join us in Minnesota. There, in Fresno, he directed her to go to the houses where she had lived, each one in turn. My grandmother had a good memory for homes. Still, I worried, and hoped she would remember. He told her to prepare to leave America behind, to walk through the different houses and touch the walls with her hands. He guided her, with his patient words, to San Francisco International Airport—the same airport where she had fallen down the escalator when they had first arrived in America in 1987. It was 2003 now, but I knew she would still opt for the stairs. She was going to have to board a plane for Thailand by herself, very different from that first flight when Uncle Hue and his family were there with her. Before she left America, the man reminded her to give the authorities her cards of entrance. Her Alien card and her Social Security card would hold no more meaning where she was going. He told her that she would be returning to Bangkok.

I had left Thailand when I was only a child, but I still remember the long flight. I knew that my grandmother would be uncomfortable in the narrow seats. I hoped she would sit near the emergency aisle so that she'd have more room to stretch when parts of her body ached. I hoped that she didn't feel pain any longer in her muscles and bones.

The guide told her that once the air warmed up, maybe things would look and feel more familiar to her. From Bangkok International Airport, she was to take a bus to Phanat Nikhom Transition Camp to America, the place where we had spent those sad six months looking at mountains from inside the barbed wire fence. The bus would be orange and white, just like the one that had taken us away from the guard with the gun in his high tower. The guide told her to take another bus from Panat Nikhom to Ban Vinai Refugee Camp, where she had lived with all her children. He warned her that there would be no one there now. The camp was only a rubber plantation, trees grown to make plastic, he explained. He thought she might be lonely going so far by herself, so he told her there was a chicken to be her friend. If it rains, she should hide underneath the wings of the chicken and walk only in the sunshine. He said that from Ban Vinai, she should start walking, by herself, to Nong Khai in northern Thailand, to the place where they had crossed the Mekong River.

He did not say anything to her about going back to the UN place where they had registered to become refugees of war, or the first place, So Kow Toe, where they had been fenced in like frightened animals. He stopped chanting and asked Uncle Nhia if Grandma could swim. My uncle shook his head. I had been told it was not good to let tears fall near my grandma's body; the sorrow would make her spirit unsure of the journey ahead. I tried to be careful. I held the napkin over my eyes, and I cried into my hands.

The guide said that it has been many years now and the world has changed. He told Grandma that she would not have to walk into the river and try to swim. There was no one to pull her through the heavy currents. Yes, the rains had begun and the river was rising—not so high yet as it had been when they had crossed that long-ago May—but it was not safe nonetheless. He told her how to get to the Friendship Bridge connecting the two countries, Thailand and Laos. His voice gentled, and he assured her that there was no need to be afraid: the authorities would understand that she was only going home, an old woman, alone. The soldiers would not do anything to her.

I was as helpless on my grandma's journey home as I had been flying with the clouds when my family was struggling to flee their homes.

The guide apologized at this point for no longer being able to take Grandma directly to each place where they had been during the five years in the jungle. He explained that after all, it had been a war, and they had been running for their lives, and their homes had been only made of banana leaves, stacked on top of small tree limbs. There would be no markers left. There was no way anyone could remember the many places they had hidden, one mountain cave or the next. He only wanted her to do her best. He said maybe there were roads in the jungle now, and that it might be confusing. Uncle Nhia provided the names of the places that he could remember, outskirts of small villages, the valleys of certain hills, and one place where there was a cool stream, and the water tasted uncommonly good. The guide suggested that my grandmother stop by this stream for a taste of the water before she continued.

I was thankful that the guide was such a patient man. When his voice grew tired, he found enough breath to continue. He led my grandma back to the last village she called home. He directed her to the place where my father had been born, and there he told her to rest awhile if she liked, as she still had far to go. He led her across rivers and mountain streams, over hills and down valleys, to the home of her uncle who had sold her to my grandfather, and then to the house where her sister died, where her father moved them after her mother died, and near the end, he placed her on the edge of the bamboo platform where she had been born. He told her that her placenta, the shirt she had traveled to this world in, was buried underneath the platform in accordance with tradition. She would not have to travel without armor, he said, and I was glad.

My grandma walked slowly. I imagined her treading alone at night and in storms, in the sun, and underneath tall tropical trees. I saw her walking in flip-flops, not the shoes of the dead. I thought that she might rest often, because maybe her money belt was heavy. My Uncle Eng had asked a friend of his, a computer technician, to find an image from a movie of Laos, of the hills where Grandfather had been buried, and to juxtapose a picture of my grandmother onto the hills. The sky was wide and blue, and the hills were a dark green. Everything was too small for details, but in this image, my grandmother stood at the intersection of two hills.

She looked lonely in the photograph, out of place and uncertain. Remembering how much she loved conversation, I urged her to speak to the birds and the bees. They would carry her messages to us. And even if they didn't, at least they would listen to her fears. Would her legs get tired from climbing the tall mountains? I hoped she had a knife with her to cut away the tree branches that might swing into her face as she walked through the heavy jungle. How long would this solitary journey take?

Maybe she'll hear the sounds of the birds and the bees humming, the sounds of crickets chirping that she loved so well, and maybe the wind will blow only warm breezes for her, and the leaves rustle gently, and she won't get scared. I hoped that my grandfather was there, making sure that she didn't lose her way and that her feet would not bleed, the dirt in the cracks of her feet coming undone. I prayed that he would befriend her again, maybe with his first wife, too, and they could all go together.

I imagined how she would open the door to her old thatch-roof house where she had lived as a little girl with her parents and brothers and sisters, and find them all there. They might be eating dinner near their little fire, sitting close to the compact ground, all looking up as she opened the door. They would smile and reach out to her in welcome, her older sister with the pale skin and long hair, and her little sister who had drunk rice juice from my grandmother's mouth. Her parents would ask her where she had been, tell her that they had been so worried, and everybody would say how they had missed her.

The chanting slowed. My legs got numb, and I switched positions, leg first to one side then the other, back straight, my head bent low over my hands. When the words stopped, there was a commotion from the side door: the coffin had arrived. It was a big boxy thing, made of wood from Laos, strong wood that my father said might last thirty years. Wood that would repel all bugs and insects with its strong smell, strong but clean, my uncles added. I had never seen such a thing. At all the other funerals I had attended, there had been American coffins lined with shimmering fabrics. This one was plain, not painted at all, just smooth wood. It was purposely made deep so that there would be room to pad the bottom with the many articles of beloved clothing friends and family had purchased for Grandma's new life, traditional Hmong clothing. The lid of the coffin did not close down; it slid into place from the bottom up. Metal was bad luck, so it had been put together with measured lines and strong glue. It was the best bed that my father and my uncles could afford. I did not stay to watch the men carry my grandmother's body into the coffin, the horse that would take her to a faraway land. I went to the back room to help pour more drinks for dinner.

There were many people who came to see Grandma off. The funeral home was full of strangers' faces and the chatter of people. The buzz of the living accompanied the beating of the drum of the dead. In the back room there was a TV, and some men were watching home videos of visits back to Laos and Thailand, reminiscing about the memories of living there, the names of the great men and women who had died in the war. Little boys and girls sat at the dining tables eating cookies and drinking pop; mothers were busy peeling fruit for their children. All the living in the back room blotted out the death in the front room. Dinner was set, and the guests sat down to food. I remember chewing each mouthful methodically, feeling it with my tongue, trying to impress its flavors into my flesh. I can't recall what I ate, if I ate a lot or a little, or how long it took for me to swallow each bite. Everyone said the food was well prepared; Grandma's funeral was a success.

I spent Friday night with my head against the wall, talking a little to my cousins, mostly thinking about the state of the funeral home. I could walk around and pick up trash or maybe spray flowers with water; some of the more fragile ones had begun drooping. But I didn't. I fell in love with the carnations. Of all the flowers in that space, the carnation's scent seemed the weakest to me, the least overpowering. It was humble beside the layers of blooming roses. As my grandmother had said many times when telling me the stories of loss in her life, it is funny the things we remember on the days that people we love die. Even the days after, we still think only of funny, small things. Like my cousins, I stayed up all night. The funeral home got quiet in the early morning hours, but there were many of us, all three-hundred-something of us, trying to stay up together, whispering. I went home in the morning, showered, changed into another black outfit, and returned to the funeral home.

Saturday was a busy day. The guests came early in the morning to show the respect they had for my grandma and our family. Many of the men and women stopped by the photographic family tree in the front room. We had it placed beside the wall on the way into the viewing room, each family at a time, beginning with Uncle Nhia, Grandma's oldest, and his family, and then ending with my father, her youngest, and his family, us. There were eight of us, two parents and six children, but our family remained the smallest—we had no extensions yet, no in-laws. People talked about the size of our family, the surviving numbers. How often does this happen in the world anymore—that one person could lay claim to so many people? Grandma had always been proud of her many descendants.

She used to say, "They look at me, old and wrinkled and not much. They do not know the reaches of an old tree, the high branches that go up to the sky. Do you know that I have over 250 grandchildren?"

Many of the guests commented on how there was not a bad looking one in our family, and I hoped that my grandmother heard them. I played with the idea of her spirit walking around in her black sweater, the aqua and red print of her shirt showing through her black cotton pants, their wide elastic band secured underneath the money belt; her arms clasped behind her back, her face relaxed and full of wrinkles. She would wander throughout the funeral home, see what was in the pots and pans in the kitchen, walk to me near the wall, smooth her wrinkled hands over my hair, and know how much I wished she were still alive.

Late Saturday afternoon, a microphone was brought up in the viewing room, and Uncle Eng stood up to say Grandma's eulogy. He was a short man with broad shoulders and a shiny brown head, dark from the many years of picking tomatoes and planting cabbages in California, and the leafs of paper shook in his hand. He blew his nose with a handkerchief and called for everybody to gather in the viewing room. We, the grandchildren, were told to sit up in front, on the carpet, with our shoes off.

His dimples were like my grandmother's—I compared his face to the picture of my grandmother hanging above. It was a photo that Dawb had taken during a family picnic, a close-up of her face. Her eyes are cast down in thought and her dimples are show- ing: a happy moment of contemplation.

Uncle Eng cleared his throat, and he began in his deep voice, "My mother was a woman who had many ideas."

He cleared his throat, and he began again, "I am her son, and it would not be well done of me to tell you about how I saw my mother."

"Forgive me," he said. "The only thing that I will say by way of showing you how my mother was good to us is the fact of our survival. We grew up in the old country, in Laos, during the Indochina wars. Everybody knows that the country was ravaged by the long wars. A woman alone, she carried us through with her guidance. Long after our father died, she taught us how to find lives in a world where life was hard to come by. She, a woman, taught us how to be men."

I could see Uncle Eng struggle. The words he had written on the notepad he carried he could no longer speak. He gestured to a television screen on a small table beside him. A cousin crouched down and held the microphone before the small screen and then pressed play. There were hundreds of people, over five hundred, crowded into the room. The static was bad. I was up front, so I was lucky enough to see the images.

I was not ready for the sight of airplanes zooming across the sky, bombs being dropped. Uncle Eng had spliced the images from a French documentary of the Vietnam War in Laos. I was less prepared for the sight of my grandmother, alive on the screen. She is sitting on a big porch swing with my little cousin Peter on one side and Great Aunt Yer on the other. The swing was located in a small park a block away from Uncle Eng's house. My cousins Sabrina and Lisa are pushing the swing. The late afternoon sunshine is in their eyes, and they are all squinting except for Great Aunt Yer who is nearly blind. She looks scared; she's holding on tight to the rail by her side with both hands. My grandmother is not smiling, but she is looking at the camera directly. She has an arm around Peter's small body. He's smiling joyfully. I could tell the footage was recent.

There was no weight on her face—her eyes peeked out from heavy lids, and her dimples were deep in her wrinkled cheeks. She had on her black sweater and her black shoes, the "cool" pair Dawb and I had gotten her during the summer. The footage was taken in August of 2002. Everything swam out of my sight, voices rose around me. The last thing I saw was my grandmother's back moving away from my field of vision. I could tell it was her because the gait was uneven, lopsided. On her back, she carried a makeshift basket. Her flip-flops kicked up dust from the dirt path. I cried from my stomach.

I had not seen Grandma's arrival in America. I had not seen her departure from it.

A few of my cousins, Dawb, and I, sat by Grandma's coffin all Saturday night. We leaned back against our chairs, careful not to crush the flowers on either side. The sliding door of the coffin covered her body up to her chest, and a clear, plastic cover shielded her upper torso and face from any hands. The smell of the chemicals coming from the body mingled with the odor of the flowers and filled my nostrils. They did not belong together; they could not overpower each other, so they struggled heavily against each other, one created by nature, the other by humans. At intervals, I studied her dormant face. Around the eyes, I thought I saw familiarity. In the heat of the lights on the coffin, she was defrosting: her skin seemed to have lost some of its tightness. The cover kept my hand from reaching to touch her. I wasn't sure that I wanted to, but my fingers traced the flat bridge of her nose and drew imaginary wrinkles on the surface of dead skin. Again and again I put my hand against the plastic, and I measured the distance between Grandma's body and my own.

Near dawn, we went home to change. In our house, in the dim light, I sat on the sofa to take off my shoes. I would just take off my shoes and free my toes; I would hurry and return to the funeral home to be with my grandmother. Two hours passed. Dawb woke me up. It was time to shower and get ready and go. I was not supposed to fall asleep; my body was beginning to mirror the exhaustion of my heart. I resolved to let my will lead the way. I got up and showered, wore a conservative black dress that I liked. I was running out of appropriate black clothes.

On Sunday the ceremonies were continuous, and there were more cars in the cement parking lot and around the funeral home, mostly Toyotas and Hondas. People gathered in the two rooms, talking. Food was cooked in great abundance; we did not think about saving money. It felt like the last chance to do something for Grandma. Of course, there was also a small matter of prestige involved. Every little thing felt both public and private at once. The man who worked in the small office of the funeral home had never seen such floral displays, profuse blooms even in winter: circular wreaths of baby's breath among dark green leaves and large vases full of lilies of the valley, ornate arrangements of lilies and white roses, petals unfurled, the puff of carnations in the middle. The guests marveled at the level of the good-bye we were having for Grandma. They said that we could do it because there were so many of us and we could divide up the work and collect money from so many different angles. They were right.

Sunday night is the crucial night in a traditional Hmong funeral in America. It used to be that in Laos the funerals were longer, up to a week, the crucial night being the last night. In this new country, it was three days and three nights, and we were at the hour of saying good-bye: midnight. All of Grandma's descendants, anyone who was a "child" in any way, had to sit the night through on the carpet floor, below her coffin. Two men would chant in songs the words that Grandma wanted us to know. Their job was to tell us her last words, for all our lives ahead. They chanted a combination of memorized poetry and improvised melody and meaning, giving us our last conversation with our grandmother.

With sticks of incense in our hands and boxes of tissues positioned before our knees, we sat on the thin carpet and listened. The three big, framed photographs of my grandmother looked down at us. A fourth smaller one, in a frame of flowers, was positioned at the foot of her coffin amid the flowers. It looked directly at us. Her face carried a smile; her single tooth showed proudly, her dimples deep in either cheek. The younger children were already tired, and we had barely begun. Taylor was already leaning on my mother's arm. All of us were told to pay special attention to the words.

The words of the chanting man entered my consciousness slowly. It took my mind a while to pick up the rhythms of his speech, the lull of the Hmong language, the delicate subtleties of tone. He paced in front of the coffin slowly, the microphone held close to his mouth. The sleeve of his gray suit was a little too long. He looked at the sleeve for a brief moment, and then he was looking deep at the ground.

"Your mother, your grandmother, your great-grandmother, your helper, your friend, is on her way now, walking the path to the land where they do not return. Her pack is heavy, and she is walking alone. Her steps slow, she remembers; she turns around. She sees me, a stranger on this lonely road, and she wanders over. 'Are you returning?' she wants to know. I look at her, the woman you knew and loved, and I say, 'I am only here to send the words back.' She looks ahead on the road; she walks to the side where the short grass grows, and she sits down. Maybe you will see another woman who looks like your mother, but before you approach her, you should remember: your mother is no more. The hands that rocked you as a child, the ones that put you to her breast, are only a memory. She sits on the side of the dirt path and wrings her hands. She loves you, but she cannot come back."

I looked around to see my aunts and uncles with pieces of tissue in their hands. We all knew that the words might or might not be hers: he wasn't in a trance, but we knew they were words that any mother might say on her way to the afterlife, if she had one more chance to say something to her family.

My father sat by me, his head low. His hands, rough from years of working with machines, held on tightly to each other in his lap. He had said many times that he didn't know how to miss his father, except by searching. I wondered if he had begun searching for Grandma already.

Uncle Nhia, Grandma's oldest, sat rocking a little bit. He seemed to have no control over the motion, no awareness of his surroundings. Whatever his thoughts or feelings were, he kept them inside, contained in his rocking body.

Uncle Chue had his glasses off and tissues held to his eyes. He had been her most obedient son, able to count on his hands the number of times she'd been angry with him. She was the first woman in his life to tailor her words to his short temper. He knew he'd never hear her voice again. He cried because she was leaving, and there was nothing to do but obey the laws of nature.

Uncle Sai, Grandma's most disobedient son, whispered in his rusty voice, "My mother, my mother, my mother." He called her back to our world, heedless that she could not return.

Uncle Hue sat with his thin shoulders shifting up and down with each deep breath. He had always been the most silent brother. The words he didn't speak he breathed into the world.

Aunt Ka, Grandma's favorite daughter, sat looking straight at the flowers. She had moved from France to be with her mother. Now, her mother was no more. They had been separated for many years. First to marriage and then to the war and the new countries that welcomed them. She had learned patience, the strength of waiting for time to reunite hearts that hold on tight.

Aunt Yang, Grandma's oldest daughter, sat bowed over. Her face, wide and wrinkled, looked so much like my grandmother's that I had to look away. The physical pain of her posture, her hands beating into the carpet just like Grandma had expressed her pain at Grandpa's death.

My mother sat with one arm around Taylor. All my aunts sat close to their youngest children. All of them had called Grandma "mother" for longer than they'd had the opportunity to call their own mothers. They saw the grieving men, they remembered the strength of Grandma, and they all held strong for their children. My cousins and I looked to those we loved, those that had traveled so far, through so much death, to bring us here. We knew that behind the white-collared shirts of the men and the black sweaters of the women, there were scars from old wounds from the war. Backs hurt and legs shook. Someday, they would all leave us. Life was a fragile, fragile thing.

I looked at my small, crooked hands so unlike my grandmother's larger, straight ones. I looked at the photos on the wall. In the overhead lights, they seemed to be crying, too. That was when it came to me: I would never see my Grandmother's face again. If I wanted snatches of her, I had to look to those around me, had to find it within myself. Grandma would not return to us. This is the way of a long life.

The man said, "She sits on the ground, looking at her feet, and says, 'I cannot return.' She says, 'Tell my children to stay together, to love their wives and husbands and teach their children as I would teach them, as if life could continue and death did not call. Do not steal, do not cheat, do not hurt, and do not take from others.' She says the words that all mothers say to their children. She says her final hope, 'Be safe and stay good. Lead a life that was better, filled with less tears and heartache, more laughter and love, than mine.'"

We went through many boxes of tissue that last night as the man spoke to us, microphone in his hand, his eyes on the carpet. He walked back and forth along Grandma's coffin. I followed his motions in my stillness, and I wished for morning never to come. My legs were cramped, but I wanted to stay with my family in one room, missing my grandmother together, forever. But morning came.

The man saw the coming of dawn through the open door—we had left it open for ventilation—and he said, "The morning light is coming. She must be on her way now. She stands up. Her body is heavy after this long life. You who love her must say good-bye."

The grown-ups got up and made their way on stiff legs to the coffin. They walked for duty and love, as examples, so that we would know how when the day came for us to be strong for our children. In long lines with no order, they waited to say their good-byes.

I waited. I had said my good-byes already, when Grandma could still hear me. I went to stand by the door and looked out at the dawn, at the parking lot and the outline of trees at its edge, the gray sky overhead. The chill seeped through the fabric of my dress. I didn't shiver. Noise was behind me, but the world before me was silent. Not a bird in the sky. No sign of spring in the air.

We drove out to bury Grandma at ten in the morning. The gray had lifted. The wind blew the snow off the ground. The big trees in the cemetery looked invincible in a world gone blurry. My father and my uncles had chosen a two-person plot so the coffin could be laid diagonally, facing downtown St. Paul, a place of prosperity and commerce. It was on a small rise, nothing like the mountains of Laos or the hills of Thailand, but high ground in Minnesota.

The family huddled together to keep warm. Icy wind blew in the spaces between us. Without language, we moved rapidly in a line past the coffin. In just a few minutes, I found myself beside her. I stood on tiptoes to see inside. I reached out my hand to touch her gray forehead. I thought I saw wrinkles near the side of her eyes and traced with my calm fingers the solid lines I imagined I saw. I moved away to make room for Dawb. Like all the other times in our lives, on the day Grandma was buried, she let me stand before her.

When it was time to hide the wooden casket in the frozen earth, we all grabbed handfuls of dirt. In my palms I warmed the dirt of America, blew warm breath to melt its frozen edges. I let it slip from my fingers. I knew my actions urged my grandmother's horse on its long journey to the land of our dreams.

I promised my grandma that we will meet again, that I will be her granddaughter again in another life. I told her that we will not become the birds or the bees. We will become Hmong, and we will build a strong home that we will never leave and can always return to. We will not be lost and looking our whole lives through.

I said I would love her forever even though she is in a new world and I remain in the old one.

I told her to please not be scared. I know that her new life will be a good one. There will be no sickness or death. No fighting and no war. She will have peace and strength in her legs to walk far.

EPILOGUE

Hmong in America

In Duluth, Minnesota: Summer 2007

I know that the last of the crabapple blooms will fall today. The ground underneath them will be petaled with the pink, white, and magenta of the drying, dying flowers. The dahlia bushes, in an orchestration of spring, will hold to their scent and their bloom. The wind blows from the open window, and I am glad that the warmth of summer is visiting Minnesota for a time.

On the long drive to northern Minnesota, my father and I talked about the publication of my first book. Against the lush green of early summer, beneath a blue, moody sky full of clouds, we are happy. The terrain outside the window of our Honda CRV changes in small ways: the deepening growth of pine trees, the light fluorescent shade of the leaves. Spring has already visited St. Paul. A new arrival up here, its hold is pure and powerful—the grass is wet with dew and the sunlight envelops the leaves in gentle welcome.

My family and I had dreamt that the road to writing and publishing a book would be much faster. Like so many others who had no experience in publishing, we had not known. Like so many others who are new to publishing, we are learning. Like so many other dreamers, we hold on to the final dream.

In the four years since I began writing this book, my father has aged. He didn't inherit Grandma's strong blood or her health. He has type 2 diabetes. His blood sugar is high. His eyes have grown blurry. Depleted of the ability to process carbohydrates effectively, his body is starving for energy. My grandma never had these health problems. The Hmong never even knew what diabetes was until America. Four years and the dream of a book is slow in coming.

I think of life and I think of death. Death by guns and bullets like so many Hmong in the Secret War and the genocide of its aftermath. Death by old age, of natural causes, so tragic for the long good-bye, the unwavering hold of longing, like my grandma's departure had been four years ago, or by disease, will carry the same pain for the rest of us in the end: the absence and the cold, the steel gray of skin without blood, of a heart that ceases to beat, the floating of the spirit into the clouds. I think of death, but I am not sad; I know that it is a part of life.

If my grandmother were alive, she would make herbal drinks for my father. She would call his sick spirit home with joss paper and incense sticks and an egg and a chicken. If she were alive, she would be on the drive with us, sitting in the passenger seat. If she were alive, my father would be driving and I would be in the middle of the backseat, leaning in between Grandma and Daddy, chattering away. I would be like a kid, still. But all that is a long time ago. I am driving today. Daddy is tired.

Grandma is no longer here to take care of my father. I do not know how to boil herbs, how to find them, how to prepare them, how to have him drink them, but I look at my father and I see the fragility of love. I see the thinning hair, the heavy movements, the hesitance of approaching time. I miss my grandma today like I missed her yesterday and the day before. I miss that she isn't here to love my father with me.

I close my eyes miles away from my father now, and I see him sitting beside me in the Honda, the miles and miles of open road before us, and I hear him telling me to slow down, to pace the long drive, and to add one more thing to this book I've written.

He says, "It is very important that you tell this part of our story: the Hmong came to America without a homeland. Even in the very beginning, we knew that we were looking for a home. Other people, in moments of sadness and despair, can look to a place in the world: where they might belong. We are not like that. I knew that our chance was here. Our chance to share in a new place and a new home. This is so important to our story. You must think about it, and tell it the way it is."

I must tell it the way it is.

It is over thirty years after the first Hmong families arrived in Minnesota in the winter of 1976. In a documentary of Hmong and their Minnesotan neighbors, the first Hmong man to come to Minnesota talked of how they'd seen the trees without leaves in the depths of a cold winter. The American woman who welcomed them had explained the changing seasons, how trees without leaves will get all dressed up again in the warmth of summer. The group hadn't believed her. They thought it was the chemical rains: the government killing the people all at one time, all over again.

What happened to the Hmong happened before us and will happen again after us. It is one group and then another. We were afraid. Now, we are beyond the fear.

Today will be warm. The earth will heat up, the grass will stay green, and I wonder how many Hmong people will be buried as Americans today.

In the heat of summer, the cool calm of fall, the turgid cold of winter, and then spring at last: the petals on the crabapple trees in glorious bloom, again. The dahlias will outlast the season. Life will continue.

This year we tell the Hmong story the way it is, Father. Hold on, our dreams are coming. We didn't come all the way from the clouds just to go back, without a trace. We, seekers of refuge, will find it: if not in the world, then in each other. If not in life, then surely in books. Our dreams are coming, Grandmother. I am holding on to you as you are holding on to my father and me. Mother, I didn't forget you. My hand is all caught up in yours. Together, we are typing on the keyboards of time. We will pick up the same warm breeze, the winds of summer. Our dreams are coming true, my Hmong brothers and sisters.

ACKNOWLEDGMENTS

For loving me, from the day I came from the clouds: my grandmother Youa Lee, my father Bee Yang, my mother Chue Moua, my older sister, Der Yang, and my extensive family of aunts, uncles, and older cousins. As important are all the younger ones who brought cloud dust with them and made magic possible in our lives, time and again: Xue, Sheelue, Shoually, Taylor, and Maxwell Yang, and my young nieces and nephews and cousins.

For supporting me from before this book began and throughout its process: Stan and Connie Heginbotham, the Turner Trio, Leslie Vanderwood and Helena Kaufman for their encouragements, and Ms. Angela Yoon, my New York City family, and Lucie Passus, my dear friend.

For teaching me, as I struggle slowly time and again to learn a little more, a little better, the many ways there are to do things right: Mrs. Galletin and Mr. B. from Harding High School; Professors Robert Tisdale, Richard Keiser, Diane Nemec-Ignashev, and Monica Torres from Carleton College; and Professors Patty O'Toole, Richard Locke, Lis Harris, and Stephen O'Conner from Columbia University; Professors Gary Yia Lee and Paul Hillmer from Concordia University; and my peers who have shared generously of their perspectives, their time, and their encouragements, three of whom I really owe tremendous debts of gratitude to: Annie Choi, Rhena Tantisunthorn, and Cris Beam—for agreeing to help long after the fact of learning together.

For guiding me along the path to becoming a professional in what I do: Dr. Zha Blong Xiong, Tou Ja-Vue Yang, Dyane Garvey, and Lee Pao Xiong.

For publishing me and helping me edit and think about the book as a contribution to literature: Chris Fischbach and the Coffee House team.

For enriching me and making possible my education and venture into writing: the Paul and Daisy Soros Fellowship for New Americans, Columbia University's Dean Fellowship, and Minnesota's literary arts initiatives.

My efforts would be very little without the personal and individual care of the people who work actively, each in his or her way, to make me a better human being.

READING GUIDE:
DISCUSSION QUESTIONS AND
AN INTERVIEW WITH KAO KALIA YANG

DISCUSSION QUESTIONS

1. The Hmong language is intimately tied to Yang's experience of, and expression of, Hmong culture. Her arrival in the United States means learning English and having to navigate a new culture in that language. How do the languages of our families, communities, and cultures color how we inhabit those spaces? How do they create and sustain those bonds?

2. Yang's grandmother is a powerful figure in *The Latehomecomer*, and her resourcefulness and wisdom in many ways make possible the family's journey from Laos to Minnesota. The attention to her role in their story is one of many ways the author focuses the story on others, making this a "family memoir." How does that choice affect your reading of the book? What does it mean for an author to define "self" in the context of "family"?

3. The United States was populated by colonized Native peoples, voluntary migrants, refugees whose migration was coerced by conditions at home, and slaves. How do the complexity of our origin stories and learning about the conditions under which Hmong families like the Yangs arrived change your understanding of citizenship, Americanness, and home?

4. When the Yangs cross the Mekong, they're forced to leave their family photos behind. How do belongings carry meaning in *The Latehomecomer*? What other objects take on significance beyond their utility in the book?

5. Yang pays close attention to her characters' surroundings—we can see, smell, and hear the mountains of Laos, the refugee camps in Thailand, and the family's first winter in St. Paul. How does evoking the spaces her family inhabits create emotion? How do those contrasts give weight to their journey?

AN INTERVIEW WITH KAO KALIA YANG

1. Families tell themselves their stories all the time—it's one of the ways that we define ourselves as related, as more than demographic units. What inspired you to move from sharing stories within your family to capturing your family's stories on the page?

   Too many people in my community have lived for far too long without understanding on their side. They have not had the language, the time, and many times the opportunity to answer an often-asked and sometimes-acted question, "What are you people doing here?" I want to work on behalf of a deeper understanding of how it is that the Hmong are here in America, spread across the globe; this was a source of great motivation and inspiration for me to write the book, to become a writer.

2. How did you capture the parts of your family's story that happened before you were born? What research went into representing those moments in a way that felt real to the people who lived them? Did you worry about the ways in which their stories and your research might diverge?

   I was born at a time and in a place where stories were the only means by which the Hmong could leave the confines of the refugee camp. I was a vessel for these stories, some hope of some future somewhere. A big part of the work I did in the writing of this book was to piece together the stories inside of me within memories from my family, within the larger framework. I read pretty much all that had been written in English on the Hmong American experience. I took the stories I had been told by my loved ones and wrote them alongside the documented histories; we've been sadly neglected, often misrepresented.

3. Oral storytelling is a big part of Hmong culture, and so many people first experienced *The Latehomecomer* from your presentations and live performances. Does telling your story to communities, schools, and groups alter your relationship to your book? Does it change your relationship to your family's stories?

    I belong to a people who are new to what is written. My father says that when I write, I write on paper, but when I speak, I write on the fabric of the human being. This is what gives me the courage to speak. I am much more comfortable on the page. Living a comfortable life is not one of my goals. Telling these stories out loud has forced me to become a much more public, more influential, perhaps more responsible person.

4. How do the rhythms of oral storytelling shape what's on the page?

    My Uncle Eng once told me that the purpose of a story is to serve as a stop sign on the road of life; its purpose is to make audiences pause, look at both sides, check the trajectory of the horizon. This is a guiding principle for me on the page. I don't stumble over traditional beginnings, middles, and ends; I am interested in making my readers act—which is very much the function of oral storytelling, the form I come from.

5. *The Latehomecomer* is, in many ways, a series of love stories—
   between your parents, between you and your grandmother,
   and between you and your family. How does love animate and
   reshape what is, in purely historical terms, a story of war, loss,
   and trauma?

   *Love, for me, is the reason why we remember our lives in stories,
   with characters and places, vivid and true. It is easy to talk of the
   contents of a book. It is far harder to forget the love one encounters
   between the pages of lives.*

Coffee House Press began as a small letterpress operation in 1972 and has grown into an internationally renowned nonprofit publisher of literary fiction, essay, poetry, and other work that doesn't fit neatly into genre categories.

Coffee House is both a publisher and an arts organization. Through our Books in Action program and publications, we've become interdisciplinary collaborators and incubators for new work and audience experiences. Our vision for the future is one where a publisher is a catalyst and connector.

LITERATURE
is not the same thing as
PUBLISHING

FUNDER ACKNOWLEDGMENTS

Coffee House Press is an internationally renowned independent book publisher and arts nonprofit based in Minneapolis, MN; through its literary publications and Books in Action program, Coffee House acts as a catalyst and connector—between authors and readers, ideas and resources, creativity and community, inspiration and action.

Coffee House Press books are made possible through the generous support of grants and donations from corporations, state and federal grant programs, family foundations, and the many individuals who believe in the transformational power of literature. This activity is made possible by the voters of Minnesota through a Minnesota State Arts Board Operating Support grant, thanks to the legislative appropriation from the arts and cultural heritage fund. Coffee House also receives major operating support from the Amazon Literary Partnership, the Bush Foundation, the Jerome Foundation, The McKnight Foundation, Target Foundation, and the National Endowment for the Arts (NEA). To find out more about how NEA grants impact individuals and communities, visit www.arts.gov.

Coffee House Press receives additional support from the Elmer L. & Eleanor J. Andersen Foundation; the David & Mary Anderson Family Foundation; the Buuck Family Foundation; the Carolyn Foundation; the Dorsey & Whitney Foundation; Dorsey & Whitney LLP; the Knight Foundation; the Rehael Fund of the Minneapolis Foundation; the Matching Grant Program Fund of the Minneapolis Foundation; the Schwab Charitable Fund; Schwegman, Lundberg & Woessner, P.A.; the Scott Family Foundation; the US Bank Foundation; VSA Minnesota for the Metropolitan Regional Arts Council; the Archie D. & Bertha H. Walker Foundation; and the Woessner Freeman Family Foundation in honor of Allan Kornblum.

THE PUBLISHER'S CIRCLE OF COFFEE HOUSE PRESS

Publisher's Circle members make significant contributions to Coffee House Press's annual giving campaign. Understanding that a strong financial base is necessary for the press to meet the challenges and opportunities that arise each year, this group plays a crucial part in the success of Coffee House's mission.

Recent Publisher's Circle members include many anonymous donors, Mr. & Mrs. Rand L. Alexander, Suzanne Allen, Patricia A. Beithon, Bill Berkson & Connie Lewallen, E. Thomas Binger & Rebecca Rand Fund of the Minneapolis Foundation, Robert & Gail Buuck, Claire Casey, Louise Copeland, Jane Dalrymple-Hollo, Ruth Stricker Dayton, Jennifer Kwon Dobbs & Stefan Liess, Mary Ebert & Paul Stembler, Chris Fischbach & Katie Dublinski, Kaywin Feldman & Jim Lutz, Sally French, Jocelyn Hale & Glenn Miller, the Rehael Fund of the Minneapolis Foundation, Roger Hale/Nor Hall, Randy Hartten & Ron Lotz, Jeffrey Hom, Carl & Heidi Horsch, Amy L. Hubbard & Geoffrey J. Kehoe Fund, Kenneth Kahn & Susan Dicker, Stephen & Isabel Keating, Kenneth Koch Literary Estate, Jennifer Komar & Enrique Olivarez, Allan & Cinda Kornblum, Leslie Larson Maheras, Lenfestey Family Foundation, Sarah Lutman & Rob Rudolph, the Carol & Aaron Mack Charitable Fund of the Minneapolis Foundation, George & Olga Mack, Joshua Mack, Gillian McCain, Mary & Malcolm McDermid, Sjur Midness & Briar Andresen, Maureen Millea Smith & Daniel Smith, Peter Nelson & Jennifer Swenson, Marc Porter & James Hennessy, Jeffrey Scherer, Jeffrey Sugerman & Sarah Schultz, Nan G. & Stephen C. Swid, Patricia Tilton, Stu Wilson & Melissa Barker, Warren D. Woessner & Iris C. Freeman, Margaret Wurtele, Joanne Von Blon, and Wayne P. Zink.

For more information about the Publisher's Circle and other ways to support Coffee House Press books, authors, and activities, please visit www.coffeehousepress.org/support or contact us at info@coffee housepress.org.

COLOPHON

The Latehomecomer was designed at Coffee House Press,
in the historic warehouse district of downtown Minneapolis.
Fonts include Caslon and Goudy Sans.